Sophia

Sophia

An intimate biography

by

DONALD ZEC

W. H. ALLEN · LONDON
A division of Howard & Wyndham Ltd
1975

*Printed and bound in Great Britain by
Richard Clay (The Chaucer Press), Ltd,
Bungay, Suffolk
for the Publishers, W. H. Allen & Co. Ltd,
44 Hill Street, London W1X 8LB*

ISBN 0 491 01732 4

For Frances

Contents

Introduction

There's no point in hedging. Sophia Loren is an extraordinary woman who happens to be an actress. This is simply stated, more difficult to explain unless you cut through the diamond to reach the source of the brilliance. She is not what she seems to be, and to embalm her inside that pallid wrapping 'superstar' would be close to committing grievous bodily harm. Even the most celebrated movie stars have tended to be slightly over-blown versions of themselves, and those who imprudently chase after what Hollywood in its dotage calls 'charisma' usually finish up as the sum total of their banalities. Programmed and manipulated, they have a short and not always happy life in some corner of the public eye, finally retiring on alimony or shrewd investments, to read their fading reviews over vodka or 'low-cal' Coke.

Always there is the double image; and the most familiar example is that of the sensual primadonna, all breathy and moon-breasted brazenly performing in public a role which she privately despises. Marilyn Monroe was doomed not because of complexities in her personality—these were remarkably few—but because even the most resilient marionette could not hope to survive the frenzied wire-pulling of that bizarre collection of experts and self-interested parties who formed the *dramatis personae* of her tragedy.

Jean Harlow was similarly manipulated by the entrepreneurs of the trade. In those extravagant days scandal was big business and with Chicago mobsters eager for a piece of the action, Hollywood, and Harlow, were easy set-ups.

The pressure on an actress to be what she is not; to say what she does not believe; to act out the fantasy like some animated dummy for the benefit of foyer gawpers and the gossip columns, is

9

as formidable as the money is big. Few can resist it. And for those with an urge to see their name in print, there is no fever quite like it. They are the victims of the system and of the public craving which helps to sustain it.

Sophia Loren stands some distance from these clockwork dolls. She defies comparison, unassailably, and deliciously, in a category of one. As with Marilyn she is immediately identified across five continents by her Christian name alone.

All her womanly gifts—they were not lost on such contrasting dictators as Marshal Tito of Yugoslavia and Frank Sinatra of whom more later—serve to challenge rather than nourish an image. 'This is what I am,' she proclaims, and what 'this' is, has more to it than merely a luscious grandeur. It has warmth, wit, insight and undoubted class. She is no femme fatale. She disarms rather than devours which explains why women share the male enthusiasm for her.

Artists, photographers and film directors have found her features infuriatingly flawed—short chin, too wide a mouth, the neck and the nose at some odds with the whole ensemble. But when it is all put together, set sensuously in motion, the said experts hastily review their terms of reference.

If she began as an actress of narrow range she has now blossomed into a performer of considerable depth. Some gibe that she is merely playing herself, forgetting that the same point was made about Bogart, Tracy, Cooper and Marilyn Monroe. But even on those terms, when Sophia turns her hips sideways on, giving the camera the full treatment with those hustling eyes, you may settle for the woman and take a rain-check on the performance. Add to this a determination and resourcefulness carved in granite. How else could she have withstood the hysterical accusations, threats of ex-communication, hellfire and all, sparked off by that spectacular scenario, the Loren–Ponti Affair?

There is, of course, no shortage of special pleaders who claim credit for the transformation of this untutored Cinderella into a major screen name; one of the few Continental actresses—Garbo and Bergman preceded her—to achieve international status in motion pictures.

There was for instance, a wet-nurse named Zaranella who for years claimed that as a baby Sophia drew all the necessary sustenance for stardom at the breast. It is an interesting theory, although since the said mother superior suckled others into total obscurity, the claim is more nourishing than convincing. There has also been the odd Svengali, usually a failed producer, who declared that but for him Sophia would never have developed the style, elegance and finesse which help to make her the most stunning heroine of her generation.

The truth is, not even the shrewd Carlo Ponti who discovered her, nor the great Italian director, Vittorio de Sica who fashioned the raw material into a talent of rare versatility, claim more than a marginal share in her triumph.

Born illegitimate in a ward for unmarried mothers in Rome, scavenging around with the rest of the hungry *scugnizzi* in a drab suburb of wartime Naples, Sophia Loren has battled through to acquire a prestige way beyond the embroidery of ordinary stardom. Royal Households and distinguished world figures who have entertained her have done so, not as a routine courtesy, but on the basis of mutual admiration.

There can be few actresses who can say they stood alongside an aproned President Tito at his private villa on the island of Brioni, cooking his spaghetti, inviting the Supreme Commander of the Yugoslav Armed Forces to pronounce upon the sauce. But equally there can be few world statesmen who can command so celebrated a chef to stand over the Presidential stove—and cook.

It is fascinating that Rachele Mussolini, Il Duce's ageing and melancholy widow, should have found solace not from some unrepenting Fascist, but from a film star whose sister happened to marry a Mussolini.

But then if Sophia's shoulder could successfully accommodate the protracted drama of the Taylor and Burton marriage, there was room enough for dejected widows.

Elizabeth Taylor in an inspired moment—she had just bitten Richard Burton—described Sophia as 'a miraculous woman. An Earth Mother.' Burton who is also very good with words sat down during a lull in the production of *The Journey* and wrote a piece in which he described his co-star as: 'a great cwtcher', (Welsh for 'comforter'). Adding, 'she would be an outstanding woman in any age. She is as beautiful as an erotic dream, and as sane as bootlaces.'

All along the undulating route from rags to riches, other men have been similarly lyrical, notably a couple of leading actors who were so hopelessly in love with her they were driven to pleading if not for marriage, at least for mercy. We will meet them.

Certainly her film career, that long haul from playing bosomy caricatures in second rate Italian epics to the Oscar for *Two Women*, is familiar, even to those who don't read the movie magazines. Ex-beauty queens who became film stars after being say, waylaid outside Doney's on Rome's Via Venito, are as numerous as the *paparazzi* who grubbed a living snatching pictures of them.

But few beauty queens have the diligence and will to master a new language, acquiring sufficient skill to swear on even terms with Peter Sellers and speak a passable Cockney in *The Millionairess*.

She was able, twice, to beat Richard Burton (B.A. Oxon) at Scrabble, careful to lard his ego afterwards to soften the blow. Games, particularly those played for money, are very serious matters to Sophia.

Playing poker with Peter O'Toole on the set of *The Man of La Mancha*—(it might have been less costly had they stuck to the card game and dropped the film)—she accused him of cheating. All in good fun of course, but as she rose, thrusting the winnings into her handbag, he grabbed it hollering blue murder, and savagely ripped it to shreds. This was no way to treat a Gucci product, nor Sophia Loren. She promptly sat down, re-started the game, doubled the pot and won the price of a replacement. 'I love that cow!' was Mr O'Toole's rueful salutation, a compliment which may not compare with Burton's eloquence but matches it for affection.

The key to understanding the several textures of Loren's personality and character is no easy one. Like the two million pound Taj Mahal Ponti lovingly created for her beneath the

Albano Hills, she is a fortress to which callers come by invitation, 'screened' right up to the massive front door.

Actors who interpret the offered cheek and the mocking sensuality of her smile as a kind of Neapolitan 'come on' do so at their peril. Marlon Brando and Frank Sinatra—we can discard the shoals of small-fry—swiftly discovered the fact in some ripe exchanges with their mettlesome co-star. Brando, who may have imagined he had some kind of diplomatic immunity when it came to slapping girls' backsides, particularly the more inviting Italian model, playfully did so on an occasion when Sophia's back was turned. She swung round and gave him a swift come-uppance which must have taught him a thing or two about Italians, and Sophia Loren.

Those familiar with the barter system operating between the big names in movies and eager starlets willing to succeed horizontally, might have been tempted to include Sophia Loren in that category. She went into *The Pride and the Passion*, young, nervous as hell, with a parrot's grasp of guide-book English. It was the kind of vulnerability the million-dollar movie stallions of the era found so promising. Most foreign actresses in a similar situation would have gladly played the game, or bitten on the bullet. Sophia Loren had other notions. And Carlo Ponti. When Frank Sinatra made a characteristic, ring-a-ding-ding pitch to the lady she flashed back at him, proving that nobody can put down a Sicilian swifter than a Neapolitan.

Behind those bantering exchanges lies the most powerful of Sophia Loren's driving forces. It is a craving not merely for respectability, but for respect. Part of it derives from her deep-rooted complex at being born of unmarried parents. A *figlia naturale*. Perhaps too, gaining world esteem in some way compensates for her mother, Romilda Villani's bitterness at having two celebrated daughters, but no husband.

Thus when Sophia Loren found herself in the prestigious company of, say, Moravia, Visconti, de Sica, Chaplin and in earlier times Picasso and Pablo Casals, she is not only emphasizing her status. She is thumbing her nose at that slightly incomplete birth certificate.

All is sweetness and light between Brando, Sinatra and Sophia, of course. The actors discovered, as other male stars were to later, that a girl raised midway between an armaments factory and an erupting volcano is about as easy a push-over as a phial of nitroglycerine.

Okay, so some actors I talked to found her so disturbing to work with, that a love scene presented the sort of occupational hazard for which there is no known, or at least acceptable antidote. But then, as President Truman said in a less erotic context, 'if you can't stand the heat get out of the kitchen'. And anyway those who have been shaken by Sophia's insistent beauty have also come right out and declared that she cooks the best Saltimbocca alla Romana that they, and say, Doctor Christiaan Barnard, have ever sampled.

Inevitably, a girl who has made it big from film extra to Oscar, marrying a multi-millionaire on the way up, is a set-up for jealousy and rumour. One July night in Rome, at Angelino's, an outdoor restaurant where reputations are carved up as neatly as the veal, her name was mentioned at the table. It was a large party and the woman on my left whispered, 'I could tell you a thing or two about Sophia Loren', then proceeded to do so with the kind of exquisite malice which makes most analysts cancel the rest of their appointments for the day. Having hinted (with the subtlety of a gravel crusher) at the steamy affairs, she went on to talk of the 'improvements' which, she gleefully alleged, Sophia had made to her face and figure.

If only a fraction of this re-furbishing had taken place, then Sophia Loren is a walking transplant with only the soles of her feet that can reliably be called her own. Fortunately, Sophia, like Carlo Ponti, gives bitchiness and fulsome admiration equal attention—none. And anyway, perhaps one needs rumour to relish the real McCoy.

When all the acrimony of the church, the stage, and the Italian press was turned upon her and Ponti, with 'they should be burned at the stake' among the less felicitous recommendations, they neither flinched nor ran for cover. It is a tribute to Sophia that, unlike Ingrid Bergman whose steamy affair with Rossellini

incensed middle America, she went there, quietly proclaimed her
love, and won the understanding if not the approval of the great
matriarchal battalions of the U.S.A.

Burton, Anthony Quinn, William Holden, Stanley Kramer,
Ustinov, Charlton Heston, Joe Levine, Peter Sellers, Ines her
secretary and a genial Sicilian-born writer named Basilio . . . all
came forward to tell different tales about Sophia, adding some
penetrating variations on the theme. Sophia's Aunt Dora who
still lives in the house at Via Solfatara where the girl born Sofia
Scicolone was raised, fervently clasped my hand and described
her niece as 'La migliore che possa essere' (the best person there
could possibly be.) So the pungent fumes rising from the vinegar
factory immediately beneath Sophia's bedroom in no way diminished the reverence with which she ushered me around
proudly prodding The Mattress Where *She* Lay.

Romilda Villani, Sophia's mother, is no less proud but carries
a chip on her shoulder as big and as fervid as Vesuvius on a bad
day. She sees herself as the 'scorned woman' saying with some
bitterness, 'Every time I think of the past I am destroyed—the
memories are all ugly.' Yet, with her younger daughter Maria
(now parted from Benito Mussolini's son, Romano) acting as
interpreter, she ransacked her memories, concealing nothing.

Vittorio de Sica was a sick man when we talked together in his
apartment though he had no suspicion of the massive lung operation he was to undergo some weeks later. He died 13 November,
1974. When he directed Sophia it was a performance in itself.
Communication was by smile, scowl, an imploring glance or some
folksy insult known only to Neapolitans. It worked well.

And, of course, there is Carlo Ponti, acting out the various roles
of the husband, the lover, the father-figure, the companion, the
sole custodian of the treasures, physical and fiscal, which he
master-minded from the beginning. He has been called 'a pizza
Pygmalion . . . with a managerial cunning close to genius'. The
charge can be refuted on the grounds that Mr Ponti does not eat
pizza, and that Sophia, unlike the legend, required no help from
Aphrodite.

True, Ponti is the one who goes down into the market place,

reads the fine print, extracting the last cent on behalf of his valued client. But what is a husband, lover and father-figure for, if not to act in the best interests of the lady he shares his bed and breakfast with?

Both parties accepted all questions, unlocked all doors including those in the catacombs beneath their villa where other skeletons in cupboards were similarly exposed to view. No need to look through keyholes when the occupants throw open the doors. My own long friendship with Sophia is based on equal rights and the tacit agreement that I approach the subject at ground level, not view it through a stained-glass window.

Those whose success is predicated entirely on having their ears tickled by the press might regard their candour as being incautious to say the least. But Ponti explained it to me quite simply. 'I have had to fight like a dog against the Fascists, the Church, the Establishment, even,' he added with a wry smile, 'the critics. Why should I care?'

Sophia Loren feels the same way, orchestrating her entire existence on the basis of clearly defined priorities. Hers. Once, during some major crisis involving a mere couple of million pounds or so, producers, lawyers and others converged upon the villa for urgent discussions with her. They were told to wait. It was a long wait. As they sat frowning at their watches, around the enormous Roman pool, they naturally assumed the 'queen' was engaged on even more vital business.

She was. She stood some distance away, outside a fumed-oak toilet involved in an intimate dialogue with Cipi, her son.

'Cipi darling, it's Mamma.'

'Yes, Mamma?'

'Have you done good business?'

'Si, Mamma. Very good.'

'Bravo, Cipi. Ciao.'

'Ciao.'

She then strolled into the conference, smiling broadly at the agitated moguls. 'Okay, gentlemen,' she said, 'shall we start?' As good a cue as any with which to open the proceedings.

I

Via Solfatara No. 5

'He saw me in the street and came up behind me. We met again some times, and after three weeks we went to bed together. Then one month and twenty days later I am carrying Sophia. When she is born I do it quickly, easily, like an animal.' Romilda Villani, Marina San Nicola, near Rome, 12 July, 1973.

The town of Pozzuoli, until the Loren connection upgraded it, was content to blush in the reflected sensuality of its Big Sister, Naples, which lies eight miles to the north-east. If it has any complaint at all, it is at being written off as a slum. Magazine writers and newspaper columnists across the world have perpetuated the myth in deference to that rags-to-riches cliché on which Hollywood, at least, was weaned. In fact, neither Pozzuoli, nor the woman who put it on the map, require this kind of ballast. And the travel book which once described it as 'perhaps the most squalid city in Italy' has been quietly told to take its custom somewhere else.

The wide waterfront with its fishing port, whitewashed houses, the shawled women haggling over the day's catch, is as picturesque as any other town on the vast Bay. Moreoever it can boast that it was once the port of Rome; that St Paul landed there in A.D. 61; and that the martyr Gennaro—patron saint of Naples— achieved that distinction after a brave but decidedly unsatisfactory encounter with the lions in Pozzuoli's Roman amphitheatre. The arena still stands in all its gladiatorial malevolence, the cells, lions' dens and craftily linked tunnels recalling an average fun day in the lives of the Romans. It is all visible from what was once Sophia Loren's bedroom. Had she been silhouetted against the window around A.D. 305, the lions might have been sufficiently distracted for St Gennaro to beat the rap. As it is, Naples has its martyr, Pozzuoli its movie star.

It is not the amphitheatre, however, that dominates the Via Solfatara, but the semi-active volcano which gives the street its name. A tourist haunt lying high up behind the town, it dutifully belches sulphurous steam, mud and hot sand from inside its crater at two hundred lire a look. Sometimes girls in bikinis can be seen to tip-toe into one of Solfatara's steamy grottoes for a sauna-on-the-house, leaping out only when the heat begins to liquefy their synthetic bras and panties. This feverish mixture of sex and sulphur suitably prepared tourists for the next stop on the way, Number Five Via Solfatara, the house where Sophia lived.

To the people whose homes were, and still are, on the rim of the crater, Solfatara is more of a minor threat than a major attraction. The town is in earthquake territory—it was twice devastated— once in 1198 again in 1550—and intensive bombing of the area by American and British planes in World War II had everyone praying that the monster up the street would keep his peace. With their menfolk fishermen, working in the town's huge armaments factory, or making 'Pozzuolana' a building cement, formed from the volcanic ash, Pozzuoli's wartime pre-occupations were identical to those of Naples—survival, the Church and the bambini. Especially the children. For them, they stole, begged and bartered, all the while cursing the Germans who grabbed most of the food. They drew on the Neapolitan's flair for crawling out from under; the ability to sift a passable existence from the debris, making ersatz coffee, crude pasta and their special music, the most therapeutic sound in the world. And if, like the shrewd operators in Naples, they were able to show a profit on the unaccountably mislaid hardware of the incoming Allied Forces, well, it was to fill bellies not bank accounts.

The combined British and American air offensive in the spring of 1943 gave Naples and Pozzuoli their most savage experience of the war. Eighteen years later, Sophia Loren was to revive the horror of that attack and its aftermath, in *Two Women*, giving a performance of almost painful authenticity. She portrayed a young mother, desperately striving to protect her adolescent daughter as they flee from the bombing around Rome. At last they find shelter from the terror in the apparent safety of a bombed-out church. But there, both mother and daughter are raped by Moroccan troops of the Allied Forces. Their deliverers.

Much of Sophia's own harrowing experiences as a child must have been basic to the dramatic intensity of her performance. It is a fact that a Moroccan officer was billeted beneath the family home at Via Solfatara Number 5. Sophia dismissed it as a coincidence but concedes that during that time, 'Some girls were raped— I was not.' Her tone was emphatically Neapolitan. Defiance wrapped in a steely smile, reinforced by the long, expressive finger which is the Bofors gun of Italian womanhood.

Those who have been intimidated by it, or all but impaled upon it, may wonder where the source lies. Who, or what, was at the nucleus of this volatile force which de Sica, the great star-maker, described as 'a revelation, a miracle created out of intuition, different from any other woman I have known'? What quality of female drives a man (in his own words) to 'fight like a dog' in ten years of legal battling around the globe; spend millions of dollars acquiring French status and citizenship both for himself and his former wife, all to legitimize a union which Cupid, if not the Catholic Church, had smiled on for years?

The scenario is set in Pozzuoli, and though the characters in order of appearance begin with Sophia's grandfather, Domenico Villani, it is his eldest daughter, Romilda, Sophia's unmarried mother, who plays the leading role. Domenico, a short, thin, but powerful man, had come from his home in the shipbuilding town of San Giovanni A Teduccio, near Naples, to work as an engineer in Pozzuoli. It was there that he met and married Luisa, and they set up house on the Via Solfatara. Luisa gave him four children, Romilda the eldest, another daughter, Dora, and two sons, Guido and Mario. 'A woman's duty,' she preached, 'is to have children.' Complying with that injunction was to have vastly different consequences for Romilda and Sophia.

The balance of power in the neat four-roomed apartment over Capuano's vinegar factory on the Via Solfatara was standard

Italian. Papa worked—in Domenico's case, ferociously—while Luisa was the boss of the household, holding it all together. They were good years and Domenico was sorry his brother Vincenzo, who married Luisa's sister, had emigrated like so many thousands of other Italians, chasing the promised gold on the streets of New York. Unhappily for Vincenzo and his bride, their son, Antonio, born, doctors said, mentally retarded, was detained on Ellis Island. He was finally admitted into the country. Now a quiet, middle-aged stooping figure, he works at bricklaying and other jobs in a monastery at Scranton, New Jersey. He never married. His life is as enclosed and as tranquil as it is for the monks for whom he works.

But he thinks about Sophia and adores her, remembering his first view of her as the pale, almost skeletal child who few thought would survive. The last time he saw her was early in 1959. Sophia recalls the meeting with some sadness.

'I was in America working on a picture, I think it was *That Kind of Woman*. I only remembered Antonio as a young man. He was blond, had blue eyes, very beautiful. It was a three-hour journey by car from New York. I went alone. Sofia Scicolone from Pozzuoli, calling on great Uncle Vincenzo's son, Antonio.

'He embraced me and began to cry. I didn't,' she said, 'I suppose I felt I had to be strong. Anyway he wept enough tears for both of us. For two and a half hours he clung to me. We stood there in the garden and he wouldn't let me go. Finally I had to leave. He stood there by the gate and watched the car take me away. I didn't have the strength to wave goodbye.'

Until Romilda's restlessness had begun to show—and be heard—the Villanis were content to settle for the best that Pozzuoli could offer—work, sufficient food, and the secure, though leaden certainty that one day would be very much the same as any other. When Domenico became foreman, he acquired the status symbols of the street, the Venetian glass chandelier in the living room, a piano in the corner. Later he bought the tall hall-stand with the hand-painted ship in the middle of it, and the large cabinet Marelli wireless set. These are all, like Domenico's and Luisa's large oak bed, solidly and determinedly still there, un-awed by the gallery of film-stills and famous photo studies of Sophia which smile out from every wall, alcove and highly polished surface in the apartment.

Taller than average, Luisa set the ground rules for her daughters Romilda and Dora, insisted that Domenico and the two sons who followed him into the factory, dress immaculately. At the fish stalls and the vegetable markets, she reached out across shawled heads, chose the best, won all arguments.

She made her own dresses and those of her daughters. She cooked, she prayed, she played the guitar and she settled all quarrels in the house with a shrill, awe-inspiring judgment, finally bringing the contestants into the cosy haven of her bosom.

It was village life, Italian style, and Romilda loathed it. If her sister Dora was content with it (as she was and still is), Romilda gave a derisory sniff and said, 'good luck!' At sixteen, she was already a tall, maturely developed redhead, restless and ready to run. She had studied the piano at the Naples Conservatoire, at San Pietro a Maiella and gave concerts in Naples and Pozzuoli. Audiences didn't frighten her. She loved them. Like Sophia, she had, and retains, the physical turbulence that stops men in their tracks and she knew how to use it. But her dreams floated up from the crater dust, through the fumes from the vinegar works, wafted over the rooftops, away from the numbing dreariness of it all. She knew precisely what she wanted. To be a star. A great star. It was happening to others. Why not to her?

If Hollywood represented the one radiant objective in the heavens, Cinecitta, the vast studio complex outside Rome, was clearly the launching pad to it. This ingeniously designed film city, occupying scores of acres a half an hour outside Rome was built by Mussolini. It was intended to be Il Duce's answer to that great concrete citadel in Culver City, California, Metro-Goldwyn-Mayer.

If the ill-fated dictator who was to end ignominiously on a meat hook in Milan hoped his creation would lead to films honouring his memory, it is as well he was spared the truth. In the event, all the agony he inflicted on the Italian people crystallized into such masterpieces as Rossellini's *Open City* and de Sica classics like *Shoeshine* and *Bicycle Thieves*.

But before World War II, Cinecitta turned out home-grown corn, the Italian screen being dominated by American idols of whom Garbo was the most lustrous example. Almost every girl with secret yearnings to be discovered chose this aloof, disdainful beauty as their heroine. And none more fervently than Romilda Villani. She not only looked like Garbo, she was convinced she had some of the same magic which needed only a match to the touch paper to lift her into the firmament.

No self-respecting Destiny could ignore an ambition as fierce as that, particularly as while it remained unsatisfied Romilda was edgy, always close to flash-point. Destiny obliged, in the large, imposing shape of Metro-Goldwyn-Mayer. With Garbo as the biggest, most valuable jewel in the Culver City crown, the studio decided to exploit their investment by organizing with splendid unoriginality, a contest to find 'THE GIRL WHO IS GARBO'S DOUBLE'. The first prize was a trip to Hollywood and a screen test. Unlike some of the fanciful stunts dreamed up by anxious press agents, this contest was genuine, its status confirmed by the arrival of an American film director in Italy to master-mind the proceedings and short-list a handful of the three hundred and fifty entrants.

If the people of Pozzuoli and Naples were highly amused by the bizarre procession of tall, floppy-hatted, limpid-eyed Garbos all flour-white and pencilled eyebrows, Romilda Villani, who had privately seeded herself Numero Uno, failed to appreciate the joke. She had surveyed herself in the mirror on the first floor of the house on the Via Solfatara—and saw Garbo. She pulled on a large hat, slid into some flat-heeled shoes, announced haughtily to Mama that she was going out on urgent business, and took the bus to Naples where the contest was being held.

If Luisa Villani had been rendered speechless by Romilda's transformation the same could be said for all the judges, except one, who was hardly at a loss for words. His name was Pirandello, Italy's revered dramatist, novelist, poet—and on that day, chairman of the panel. (Neither Destiny, nor Metro-Goldwyn-

Mayer believed in half-measures.) The events that followed had all the ingredients required to match the tremulous occasion.

Greta Garbo, at least the Pozzuoli version of her, strode on to the stage, stared loftily at the judges. Though she did not in fact languidly declare 'I want to be alone' everything about her conveyed that legendary message. No need to count points, she had won, and won handsomely. She would sail on a first-class ticket to New York, travel from there to Hollywood. A screen test would follow, and after that? Romilda Villani was too bewitched to think beyond the trip to New York. All that remained were the formalities—and the confrontation with Domenico and Luisa back home on the Via Solfatara.

They reacted strictly according to the codes, taboos and superstitions of that era. Luisa raged at her daughter. 'I will not let you go! It is madness. It is not right for a good girl to be alone amongst all that sin.' When this failed to move Romilda, Luisa and Domenico switched the attack, making ominous references to 'The Black Hand'.

This secret society of Sicilian origin flourished during the early days of the Mafia in the late nineteenth century. It shifted its operations to New York, terrorizing and blackmailing Italian immigrants. Luisa and Domenico were convinced that Rudolph Valentino had not died a natural death but had been poisoned by the 'society' as a reprisal for not paying up. They believed all Italians in the public eye were vulnerable, and warned Romilda: 'Garbo's friends will be angry, they are sure to poison you too.' The notion that Romilda Villani of Pozzuoli might pose so serious a threat to the great Garbo that someone would put a 'contract' out for her would today be considered too hilarious a sub-plot even for Mario Puzo on a bad day. But in those years in Southern Italy, superstitions and fears were embedded deeply. Luisa's warning, and Romilda's own subconscious anxieties of being alone in a new country, finally wore her down. Garbo, Pirandello, Hollywood, The Black Hand—it was all too much for a girl who merely wished to get the crater dust off her shoes and fulfil a dream or two. She caved in, the offer lapsed, the trip was cancelled.

SOPHIA

But if Luisa believed that Romilda would now settle for the snug, self-effacing life of Pozzuoli, she was wrong. The Garbo affair was over, but Romilda had had a foot in the door. She delivered the ultimatum in a tone which even Luisa regarded as final. 'My mother has the ferocity of a lioness,' Sophia says, 'and she fights like one when she is protecting someone or when she knows this is the only way she can get what she wants, for what she believes.'

With a thousand lire in her purse, Romilda Villani, then aged eighteen, took the train to Rome, installed herself in a box-sized room near the Trevi Fountain, and sauntered out into the city.

No healthy, heterosexual Italian male was likely to be indifferent to the sight of Romilda Villani, tall, generously rounded, her red hair flame-bright in the Rome sun. Riccardo Scicolone was no exception. He was six feet tall, powerfully built, the vaguely haughty bearing suggesting a man of strength, if not substance. He too had his ambitions. He had been studying for an engineering degree but family problems forced him to give up the course in his final year, and he took on a series of jobs. If, like Romilda Villani, he felt cheated too, the situation was neatly poised for their urgent duet on a street in Rome.

Mr Scicolone, now a distinguished-looking man in his late sixties, the silver-grey hair neatly combed back from prominent features, has his own version of the affair, as he has of his ensuing relationship with Romilda and with the two daughters she bore him. It is unlikely, however, that he would say, as Romilda Villani did with some anguish: '*Ogni ricordo mi distrugge—i miei ricordi sono tutti brutti*'—'every time I think of the past, I am destroyed—the memories are all ugly'. How much of this was the bitterness of frustrated ambition, or the resentment of a scorned woman (or one who felt she'd been scorned) depends on how you rate the principal witness.

We had met on a couple of occasions before in London and Paris. This time we were to talk at the summer home of her younger daughter, Maria, who would act as interpreter. The location—an unpretentious bungalow at Marina San Nicola on the

24

coast not far from Rome. It is a furnace of an afternoon, the stone
path to the porch is grilling white in the sun. Maria Mussolini—
she is no longer living with her husband, Romano (Il Duce's
son)—leads the way into the living room. She is fuller in the
face than her elder sister Sophia, shorter too, but the family resemblance is unmistakable. She is handsomely built, the work of a
craftsman rather than an artist, more flesh than fine lines.

Signora Villani is dressed for the beach. The red hair is bal-
looned up, beehive style. A heavy gold medallion swings across
her bosom as she walks, her cork heels clacking on the marble
floor. Even with the eye make-up and the pale lipstick, she is still
astonishingly like Garbo. She is an attractive woman with a
luxury apartment in Rome, a large car, servants and is as well-
heeled as any mother could be whose daughter can earn a million
dollars a film; whose son-in-law can parlay a picture like *Doctor
Zhivago* into a world gross of a hundred times that sum. But when
she speaks there's a hint of suppressed fury, softened by the
thought, perhaps, that reflected glory was probably better than
no glory at all. 'Tell him I am going to speak my mind! Tell him
that!' Romilda Villani rips the words out, draws ferociously on a
king-sized cigarette. She pulls a chair to the table treating with
equal suspicion my questions, Maria Mussolini's translations.

'What kind of man is Riccardo Scicolone?'

'I never liked him!' (Maria frowns at her mother in disbelief.)

'That's right—you tell him so. It was pure chance that I met
him. One of those chances in life. There are incredible things that
can happen. And you must tell him so. Tell him, Maria!'

'Okay, I tell him, Mamma.'

'It was just a chance I had two daughters from him. It was the
case of a young girl from the country who finds herself in a big
town. She meets a man. And she makes a mistake. I was a concert
pianist when I came to Rome. Then I meet Riccardo. In the street.
He saw me from far away and ran up behind me and spoke to me.
He said he was in films and as I was such a beautiful girl . . .
(Romilda growls on a laugh) he said he could help me. We met
again some times and after three weeks we went to bed together.
After a month and twenty days I am carrying Sophia.'

SOPHIA

'You must have loved him?'
'I didn't know him! For my part, I wanted work and I thought he could help me. I was not in love with him. He wanted me. For me it was all a mistake.'
'Where did you go when you were seeing Riccardo?'
'In my room. Where do you think, in the street?'
'Was he a handsome man?'
'No.'
'What did he look like when you met him?'
'Very thin, very tall, with a big nose.'
'For all that you stayed with him and had a second child by him?'
'What do you expect? I was hoping he would marry me. It is the mentality of a small village. If you have a baby you marry the father of your child. I'd abandoned myself to the situation. I wanted Riccardo to marry me even though I didn't love him, for my daughter's sake.'
'Why didn't Riccardo marry you?'
Maria submits the question, begins to translate Romilda's sharp response, but traps the words behind her hand.
'I can't say it.'
'Tell him!'
'It's impossible.'
'Tell him.'
'The word she used means, like "sonofabitch".'
'Thank you,' Romilda smiles, satisfied.

Romilda Villani's ungarnished rebuke will not surprise Riccardo Scicolone. He knows that with this formidable, passionate Neapolitan, it is necessary to take the rough if you wish to relish the smooth. But even on that equation he must have felt a fortunate lover when, as a young beauty, barely twenty, she shared her bed with him. She became pregnant and expected Riccardo to marry her. He didn't for personal reasons which convinced him, as they infuriated Romilda. She thought of Luisa and Domenico back home in Pozzuoli. And the neighbours on the Via Solfatara. 'I've always felt deeply for my mother,' Sophia says. 'Coming from a small village before the war, the narrow mentality of the people. She knew that they would regard her, with a baby and no husband, as being indecent, almost a whore.'

Romilda Villani went into the Clinica Regina Margareta, in Rome, and was put in a ward for unmarried mothers. It was for her, in the Italy of the early 'thirties, a humiliation, a disgrace, and she wept. Fortunately she endured none of the child-bearing problems that were so acutely to afflict Sophia. 'I had the baby quickly, easily, like an animal,' she said. The child was born on 20 September, 1934 and registered in the name of 'Sofia Scicolone'. A disc 'No. 19' was tied around her neck.

Unmarried mothers of that time, especially those too poor to clothe and feed their infants, always had 'The Wheel' (La Ruota) as a last resort. Nearly all convents, even those of the closed order, had, some still have, a wheel placed immediately behind a shutter. Supplies would be brought to the convent, a bell rung, the shutter raised and the wheel turned—the goods would then be taken into the convent without the nuns making any contact with persons outside. Unwanted babies were sometimes delivered in the same way. The swaddled infant would be placed on the wheel usually at night, the bell rung, the mother drifting away in the darkness. If Romilda Villani, alone in the ward for unmarried mothers had any such thoughts, they faded with a glance at the pale, painfully thin child she held in her arms. It seemed to be more bones than flesh.

Three months later she herself fell ill. It was time to go back home to the Via Solfatara, face Luisa, Domenico and the people of the street.

Puzzuoli had survived two earthquakes. It would have to take Miss Romilda Villani, and child.

2

Thief's Eyes

Romilda Villani's train journey home from Rome to Pozzuoli had all the tear-streaked pathos of a Victorian melodrama. Her apprehension, shame and resentment of Riccardo Scicolone for not wedding her increased as the long ranks of cypresses and eucalyptus trees on the plains merged into the ugliness of the Naples' suburbs. She might have felt less forlorn if the infant in her arms had displayed all the gurgling indications of being a typical, healthy, pinch-worthy bambino. What she looked down at, however, and wasn't tempted to submit for the lyrical approval of other mothers in the crowded carriage, resembled an emaciated chicken, the long limbs protruding grotesquely from the baby clothes, the skin ashen, the eyes large and expressionless. This child to whom Riccardo Scicolone had consented to grant his surname, was plain, no doubt about that. Ugly in fact. And illegitimate. An unsought souvenir of a year in Rome and a feverish encounter near that haven for wishful thinkers, the Fontana dei Trevi.

Romilda Villani knew what she was about to face. The people on the Via Solfatara would stare, whisper and pretend not to be looking over the top of the sheets billowing in the Mediterranean sun. 'There's Romilda Villani and her "love child". That's what happens when a young girl goes to Rome!' And then there would be the assorted verdicts of the family; Domenico and Luisa reacting with the mandatory outrage of good Catholics with Mario, Guido and Dora privately commiserating, rallying round.

In the event, because a new-born baby defuses all dramas, Romilda Villani walked into the squealing, weeping demonstration of fierce family unity which Neapolitans reserve for prodigal daughters and nosy neighbours. When the wine had been drunk to the everlasting health and happiness of the child, Luisa Villani looked closely at the drawn features of her daughter and diagnosed a fever. The woman who owned the house in which they lived prescribed a powerful drug. It cured Romilda's illness but dried up the milk in her breasts. She turned on the woman, screaming, 'Why did you do this to me? I can no longer feed my baby!' The woman shrugged. 'It is just as well,' she said. 'What kind of life will it be for the child? She is ill, you have no husband, it is better that she dies.'

Fortunately for Sophia Loren and all the preferential shareholders in that desirable property, Italy may have been afflicted by other shortages—but never of mothers' milk. The country is virtually awash in it, and a mother stricken by the loss of her own can turn to a battalion of wet-nurses brimming over with it. Even in wartime when almost all went hungry, food was found for these huge, amiable filling-stations so that the deprived bambini could be hooked on to their emergency pipe-lines.

It was to one of these inexhaustible Amazons that Romilda Villani went in her despair. The woman's name was Zaranella, a large buxom Neapolitan of the neighbourhood, who consented to add the starveling Sofia to her litter of hungry mouths. The child flourished, as did all the others in the district who took delivery from the same Lady Bountiful. But only one of these was to be re-named Sophia Loren, and twenty-seven years later win an Oscar. When Zaranella heard the news and how she, so to speak, had nippled her way to reflected glory, she began making claims, implying there had been more than a touch of magic in her milk.

Reminiscing from a bed alive with grandchildren—her generous service had long been discontinued—she announced: 'Sophia was the ugliest child I ever saw in my life. She was so ugly that I am sure no one else would have wanted to give her milk. It was my milk that made Sophia beautiful, and now she doesn't even remember me. I gave milk to hundreds of children, but none of them drank so much as Sophia. Her mother gave me 50 lire a month. Sophia drank at least 100 lire worth of milk. Madonna mia!'

Just how Sophia Loren could be expected to have total recall, right back to those nourishing hours at Zaranella's breasts, the retired wet-nurse did not say. Musing on it one afternoon at the Excelsior Hotel in Rome, Sophia said to me: 'Okay so she took me to her breast. She was paid for it but I'm grateful to her. She told everybody I looked like a rat.' She laughed, raised two elegant legs on to a coffee table and studied them with evident appreciation. The message was unmistakable. 'Well it shows even rats have a chance in life.'

And then she went on: 'I wouldn't have cared if she just said that she had saved my life. It was probably true. My mother told me that the day she took me to Zaranella she was so ill she almost had to crawl there. But to say that because of her milk she gave me my looks, my body, and my talents, is ridiculous. My looks, I promise you, my mother gave me. After all she did feed me for three months. She is also one of the most beautiful and elegant women I know. My father, Riccardo Scicolone must have had something to do with it. If I have any charm at all, it comes from him. And there is something else. Zaranella had a short memory. The fact that she was able to feed me so well was because she was given the meat of the entire family. My grandmother Luisa saw to that. When the meat was bought she put it on one side and said to my mother, 'Give it to Zaranella. I don't care about her stomach. The babies need her milk. If we feed her, we feed them.' That was the wisdom and the style of the grandmother Villani. Nobody questioned her. She ruled and the family idolized her. They worked harder and were better dressed than most of the families on the street. And all the while Luisa cautiously controlled the family budget as an insurance against the disaster that all Italy knew was coming.

Not that Domenico, his sons and daughters, feared the approaching war. Their one overpowering dread was that Luisa might fall ill and die. And to lose her would stifle the heartbeat of their existence. 'It was my own biggest nightmare,' Sophia recalls. 'She was a marvellous, almost saintly woman. She had the strength of a lion and she fought for us all. Coming home at night to that lovely gentle face was always a thrill for me.'

Romilda Villani, her dreams of being discovered shelved if not shattered, devoted herself to the child she now called 'Lella', preferring that name to the 'Sofia' which was the name of Riccardo Scicolone's mother. She had nothing against Mrs Scicolone of course. Riccardo came occasionally to Pozzuoli, drifting in and out, a fierce-eyed giant of a man who could clown a lot, express decided opinions, but who remained stubbornly vague on the question of marriage. Marriage to Romilda.

Despite the wet-nurse's earlier contribution and all the care Romilda gave her afterwards, the child still looked sick and puny. Romilda looked at the creature and wept.

To pay for her keep and for Sofia's food—the child had now been weaned off the wet-nurse's reservoir—Romilda went back to her piano. She was a good pianist who favoured the classics but could easily give the Neapolitans their own throbbing love songs as long as they were willing to pay for it. She performed at local concerts and in the cafés around the port where the fishermen were happy enough to look at this beautiful piano-player even if they couldn't join in the songs. Those with an urge to give the shapely entertainer a sly pinch or two risked a drenching of vino or having their hands caught under the lid of the piano.

She returned home at night to an apartment teeming with Villanis. The whole family, Domenico, Luisa, Mario, Guido, Dora, Romilda and Sofia had to be distributed in four rooms, two bedrooms, a living room and a dining room. One day Romilda told her mother, Luisa, 'I have something to tell you.' Luisa knew intuitively what the information was. Romilda had been seeing Riccardo, sometimes in Pozzuoli, occasionally in Naples. Romilda said she was expecting another child. 'We'll manage,' Luisa said.

Six of them now slept in one room. Luisa and Domenico in a large double bed, Romilda, Dora, Sofia and, when she was old enough, the newly born Maria, in another bed placed at right angles to it. They were no worse off than most of the families on the Via Solfatara, better off than some. When all the signs of

Mussolini's policies pointed to disaster Luisa intructed the family to get their heads down and not to worry. 'It will pass,' she said.

The war began, for Italy, in June 1940. Its effects soon became apparent on the Via Solfatara when the young men started leaving home, the armaments factory where Domenico and his sons worked hammered on through the night, and when food became ominously scarce. But to Sofia, then barely six years old, the war had little impact at the beginning. There was nothing about her existence that seemed different from any of the other children along the street. She called her grandfather, Domenico, 'Papa' believing him to be her father. After her piano lessons—Romilda was determined that Sofia too would become a concert pianist— Domenico would lift Sofia on to the table and with Luisa playing the guitar, the child would dance for the family. The spell was broken, traumatically, on the day she learned that Domenico was not her real father.

The actress's own recollections of that confrontation have become somewhat tempered by her softening attitude to Riccardo Scicolone. 'Now that I have children of my own,' she said, 'I understand my resentment at the time. You have to live with your parents to appreciate them, love them. How was it possible to love a man who people told me was my father, but who I'd never seen. He didn't see all that much of my mother either. But I don't judge him harshly. Whatever my mother says, she did have two children by him. You don't do that with a man you hate.'

We sat talking in the Villa Ponti with its fifty rooms, ancient mosaic floors. But Sophia Loren projected her mind back to Pozzuoli. 'I was maybe five years old, Maria only a year. One day my mother, looking very agitated, sent me to the bedroom and told me to wait there. She began fussing over me the way mothers do for a daughter who is going to a party. She straightened my hair and my dress. Then she took my hand and led me into the living room. A man stood there, he was tall, seemed like a giant to me then. He smiled at me and took my hand. "Lella," mother said, "this is your father." I'm told I ran from the room sobbing, "He's not my father! I already have a father. Let him go away. I don't want him." I was hurt. But my father must have been very hurt too. He left the child's pedal car he'd bought me in the hall and went away. The car is still there. It was an unhappy day.'

True Riccardo Scicolone had given Sofia his name, in a formal declaration; 'I declare Sofia Scicolone to be the natural issue of Romilda Villani and Riccardo Scicolone . . .' But she was still illegitimate. When she was old enough to go to school she soon discovered what the word 'stigma' meant. 'I always felt a stranger among the girls who had a father. You know how cruel children can sometimes be. They used to talk among themselves, point at me and laugh. I hated it. So I used to go to school either at five minutes to nine when everybody was almost in or at 8 o'clock because nobody was there.' Sometimes when she felt particularly miserable she would climb into the branches of a fig tree outside the house and sit there for hours. 'I seemed to spend my time hiding from everybody,' she said. 'The war was bad but what I remember most was how good and strong my mother was. She cut her best dresses apart to make clothes for me and Maria. When the soldiers came she held me close, daring them to molest us. Although why anybody should have wanted to, I can't imagine,' she laughed. 'I was thin, ugly and dark, almost Arabic in appearance. At eleven I was so skinny the kids used to scrawl *stecchetto* (little stick) on the door of my house.'

There were, of course, thousands of other 'little sticks' who, like Sofia, endured hardship and a nagging hunger which persisted even after the liberation of Naples on 1 October, 1943. Fresh water was scarce. Meat was costly and difficult to get. There were constant epidemics both in Naples and Pozzuoli. Maria was sickly almost from birth and was the victim of an attack of typhoid. Romilda Villani queued for the coarse black bread which turned to glue in the mouth. Sofia would take hunks of it and mould them into animal shapes, gnaw on them in the morning.

Terror came with the air raids, supported by an inferno of shelling from destroyers deployed along the coast. Hunger was the spectre in everyone's home. Neapolitans do not imprison their misery. Keeping the children alive was a collective responsibility and they threw themselves into the task with the same ferocity with which they loathed the Germans. And no one was more resourceful at it than that tornado of a woman, Romilda Villani.

She fought officials, bombarded the shopkeepers and when supplies disappeared completely during the savage air attacks which preceded the liberation of Naples, she unashamedly begged for food. Any other Italian mother in similar circumstances would have done the same, of course. But there was a particular quality to the Neapolitan women during the war. They drove themselves on the internal combustion of anxiety, anger and a venom for anyone who threatened them, their children or their men. They went out during curfews or bombing raids scavenging anything that tasted like food—it did not necessarily have to look like it— from the throwaways at the market and the port. 'We did what we had to do,' Romilda Villani said. The words were more poignant to her when she recalls that Sofia, at the time, was so fragile, 'her bones looked as though they could be snapped like grissticks'.

When the constant shelling and bombing reduced reservoir installations to rubble, the water situation became critical. An Italian driver investigating the owner of a long, attractive pair of legs emerging from beneath his truck was astonished to discover Romilda Villani laboriously emptying the radiator of water. 'Grazie,' she smiled as she sauntered off with the filled can. 'Prego,' murmured the bemused soldier. And once back home, Romilda would spoon out the water for Sofia and Maria, carefully dissecting a crust of bread as though for a shipwrecked crew adrift on a boat in mid-ocean.

The British and American onslaught on Naples was now straddling Pozzuoli less than eight miles away. The prime target was the armaments factory and the town cursed fate for siting it there, more so because of the danger of the bombs triggering their volcano, Solfatara, into a new eruption. Workers like Domenico, Mario and Guido went into shelters during the worst raids but even if they survived, what would happen to them if the factory were destroyed?

'I remember listening to my grandmother and grandfather talking,' Sophia recalls. 'In our family at the time there was no question of not speaking in front of the children. Firstly because we were all living on top of each other. I never slept in a bed that had less than three people in it. And also because hunger, real hunger, is not something that you can conceal too well. So there was nothing else to talk about. I can see them now, the worried face of my grandmother, my grandfather turned away, his hand across his eyes. They would discuss what they would eat to-morrow, or whether there would be anything to eat at all. If the factory had been hit there was talk about whether my grandfather and uncles would be thrown out of work.

'Sometimes my mother would go to the kitchens and when she came back I could tell by her face there was nothing left to eat. We often had no water. No bread. No milk. Nothing. I remember being hungry. Always hungry. But there were many who were worse off. Some were grateful to be alive, others must have wished they were dead.'

The delicious irony to that not unmoving tale is that Sophia Loren's retailing it to me, her eyes occasionally misting over at the recollection, occurred in the week of the publication of her book *Eat with Me*. In it, the former wet-nursed waif of Pozzuoli writes: 'If I were entertaining guests in Rome, for example, my Roman speciality would be *penne all'arrabbiata* (macaroni cut on the slant in a fiery chili-laden tomato sauce), or else *carciofi all Giudea* (deep-fried artichokes as crisp as French fries) or else a flavoured *ricotta*. In my forest farm near the Po, a hunting reserve called Tenuta dell 'Occhio, I immediately think of roast pheasant if the season is right, or a delicious dish of river eel and so forth . . .'

There was to be a long haul for Sophia Loren before she could indulge in those fanciful menus.

Life for the Villanis, as it was for all the Neapolitans along the embattled coastline north-west of Naples, was determined by the relentless rhythms of the air attacks. For Pozzuoli the safest refuge from the raids was the long railway tunnel near the town centre. 'We used to go at night,' Sophia said, 'all of us, carrying our mattresses, what food and drink we had, lying there in the dim light of candles, often freezing. People would be sleeping, arguing, laughing, making love. Then when the first train arrived about 4.30 to 5.00 a.m. we would crawl out with our mattresses and straggle back home.'

During one raid on the town she was hit by a bomb splinter and still carries the scar under her chin. It was a daylight attack. She and her mother were walking together in the street when 'suddenly we could hear the bomber diving down over us. There was this screaming whistle and the explosion. My mother grabbed my hand and we started running with everyone else to the nearest shelter. I could feel blood gushing down my neck. I remember I fell, my mother grabbed me and as we ran towards a tunnel, the plane turned and roared down again. But by the time the bomb exploded we were safe.'

Subconsciously at least, she must have drawn on that experience for her performance in *Two Women*; notably the scene where the mother (Sophia Loren) sinks in torment to the ground, rocking to and fro, her daughter locked in her arms. 'When I think what my mother went through for us, I could weep,' Sophia said. 'I remember one freezing winter she took a camel coat she adored— it was the best thing she possessed—took a pair of scissors to it then sewed it into a winter dress for me. I think, quite simply, that she would have given her life for me and Maria.'

The nights in the tunnel left Sophia Loren with an intense fear of the dark and of being trapped in enclosed places. Her sister, Maria, was less affected by the raid, her memories of it revealing a child's curiously unpredictable reaction to terror. 'It's a bit like a dream now,' she told me, 'but I dimly remember being dragged to a cellar under the house and hearing bombs screaming down. The place was dark and crammed with people praying to the Holy Mother in the special words of the Neapolitan. Everybody expected to die, I suppose, and we all sang the prayer: "*Addesso Nell 'era Della Morte*" ("in the moment of our death"). One very devout woman told us all to prepare ourselves for Heaven. All the time she cried: "*Addesso Nell 'era Nostra Morte*". I remember a man beside her becoming irritated. Finally he said, "Thank you very much but . . ." I remember it better in Italian: "*Per favor, signora pregate per voi non pensate all nostra morte*"—"Please madam, pray for your survival not for our death." Everybody shrieked

with laughter. I suppose Neapolitans are no different from anybody else. It is better to be alive than dead.'

In September 1943, British and American warships began
shelling the port. This bombardment was reinforced by air raids
at night. In the early hours during such an attack, the Villanis'
home was hit. They returned wearily from a night in the damp
coldness of the tunnel to find half the rooms gutted, the roof
ablaze, all the windows shattered. They rummaged through the
debris for their belongings, then dispersed among lucky neighbours along the street. Romilda decided Pozzuoli was no longer
safe for her and her children. There were some cousins in Naples.
The women and children could go there. Luisa, predictably,
stayed with Domenico. Maria, who had a high fever, would
follow later. Romilda packed a case, and with Sofia, took the
earliest train out of the town.

The battle for Naples and the part the Neapolitans themselves
played in its liberation merits more than a passing reference in a
biography of a movie star. Many thousands, either trapped in their
homes or caught in the cross-fire on the streets, shared in the
nightmare. It happens that among them were Romilda Villani
and her nine-year-old daughter Sofia. Their experiences were no
more harrowing—or less so—because the child is now Sophia
Loren. She was a Neapolitan, and it is as a member of that breed
that she recalls the events of the time.

'Once the Germans knew the British and American troops
were approaching they blew up all the water mains and retreated
into the hills. But they kept sniping at people in the town below.
Some Germans remained in the city and I could see the fighting
from the balcony of the house we were in on the Via d'Arsia.
There was shooting from windows, from the corners of buildings
and you could hear screaming and moaning over the fire of the
guns. Sometimes a mother would run from a burning house, a
baby in her arms and a half a dozen people would rush across the
street to rescue her. It was frightening, but exciting too, for a
child. My mother was so marvellously strong through it all. I
remember when the shooting stopped for a while, she went out

into the street, spoke to a woman carrying a shopping basket. I saw her pleading with the woman then pointing up to the window where I stood. The woman took out a loaf, broke it in two, gave one half to my mother, then walked away.' A short war-time memoire from one child of Naples, Sofia Scicolone. She was nine years old, and a spectator. Others, however, decided they had their own account to settle with the retreating Germans.

In the four days before the Allied advance into the town, the urchins and the women of Naples turned on the Germans and delivered as brutal an act of retribution as ever one group of humanity inflicted upon another. It was magnificent and it was also barbaric as they tore into the troops, literally tooth and nail. That event, one of the bravest in the long martyred history of the town, has been immortalized on film in *The Four Days of Naples* and in the bitter prose of Curzio Malaparte's *The Skin*. A remarkable sculpture to the memory of the ragged young heroes stands proudly in the city. It is one of the most moving chunks of masonry in the world.

Two weeks earlier, a similar revolt by the people of Naples had proved abortive and was viciously put down by the German soldiers. The Neapolitans buried their dead, nurtured their fury. In the last week of September, preceded by a thundering overture from the air and from the sea, the American and British forces were on the outskirts of Naples. The Germans began moving out, grabbing what male Italians they could lay their hands on, throwing them into trucks bound for the slave-labour camps of Germany. This was the signal. 'The people of Naples,' Curzio Malaparte wrote, 'fell unarmed upon the Germans, cornered and massacred them in the alleys, crushing them beneath an avalanche of tiles, stones, articles of furniture and boiling water dropped from roof-tops, balconies and windows. Groups of courageous boys hurled themselves at the Panzers raising aloft with both hands bundles of flaming straw and died in the act.' Malaparte adds:

'I myself saw the corpses of many German soldiers still unburied two days after the liberation of Naples with lacerated faces and throats mangled by human teeth; and the tooth-marks could still be seen on the flesh. Many had been disfigured by scissors. Many lay in pools of blood with long nails driven into their skulls.'

Naples was entered by the Anglo-American Fifth Army on 1 October, 1943, giving the townspeople, and Sofia, their first glimpse of a Scottish soldier, complete with kilt. She remembers shoe-shine boys being pressed by other members of the *scugnizzi* to take advantage of their position at ground level to satisfy the age-old curiosity. 'It was one of the lighter moments,' she said.

Equally diverting were the series of 'incidents' in which the military hardware of the incoming forces were inexplicably lost in transit. An American Sherman tank disappeared, was taken apart to the last screw, then reappeared as highly saleable bits and pieces in the junk-yards of the town. One night a Liberty ship which had arrived in a convey of ten, was stolen from the harbour. It was never seen again. As a ship. How it was dismembered, and where the limbs of the corpse were finally distributed, remains, like the mystery of the *Marie Celeste*, just another legend of the sea.

The liberation of Naples brought with it no immediate relief from the permanently installed enemy—hunger. 'The Germans took what food there was, and who could blame them? They had to live too,' Sophia Loren says magnanimously. 'It was at times like that my mother must have missed my father most of all. When her loneliness was unbearable she would write to him in Rome or send him telegrams saying I was dying. I wasn't of course, but it worked. He would drop everything to visit us and bring whatever he could.'

Romilda Villani's fears for her daughter were not merely concerned with food. Prostitution, spawned out of years of hardship and starvation, swept in on the steel-tipped heels of the Allied forces. The women came in bus loads from the South, all shapes, hues and ages. The good-humoured, well-groomed black American G.I.s were their prime target. They paid the most and got the best. Less conventional were the Moroccan soldiers, some of whom had a predilection for the very young, of either sex. Romilda Villani could take care of herself. Any soldier who thought this slim redhead easy game was driven off by a barrage of exquisite Neapolitan abuse to serenade a more accommodating balcony. But Sofia was always vulnerable. Romilda never allowed her to wander on the streets alone. 'Even when I was as young as that she used to warn me, "all men are evil",' the actress laughed. The warning was echoed by all mothers with young daughters exposed to the assorted inclinations of fighting men elated by victory and cheap wine. And Sofia looked much older than her years. She was thin, but tall, her height accentuated by her walk, the erect, self-assured stride of a woman. 'When she came back to Pozzuoli from Naples,' her Aunt Dora said, 'the experience had aged her. Her childhood had gone.'

That view was shared by her school friend, Rosetta d'Isanto, Sofia's *compagna di banco* (they shared the same desk). Now a school teacher, she projected her mind back to the five years they spent together in the class room, presenting a fascinating portrait of a superstar in the satchel stage, of a sex-symbol in the making. 'She demonstrated, we all copied,' Rosetta d'Isanto said, smiling. 'No matter what dress she wore she always made it seem, even in those days, as if it had come from a boutique. She always wore very full skirts and tight blouses. There were those marvellous long, straight legs and she was always glad to lift up her skirts to show them to the girls. But then everybody found something different about her that was quite beautiful. The boys were all captivated by her eyes, the girls by her legs and most of all by the way she walked, the hips moving but never the head. We used to run into the cloakroom after the lesson and beg her to demonstrate. We would then practise it but it was never the same. If she had wanted to be an actress then she didn't show it. All she talked about was getting a husband! And success. It didn't matter at what, she just couldn't bear not being successful. I have never known an ambition like it.'

It was that persistence which, according to Rosetta d'Isanto's delicately expressed reminiscences, made her ex-school chum at the Virgilio Instituto, during an examination, 'take a little look at a book'. That awesome revelation made the engagingly frank Miss d'Isanto blush and she suggested a swift change of subject. In answer to further cross-examination—we thought it best that all other crimes should be taken into consideration—the school-mistress said, 'Yes,' they did steal fruit from outside the porter's garden at a nearby block of flats. But all the children did it to augment the interminable diet of rough pasta and thin bean soup. A change from the minestra, a thinly populated vegetable soup Luisa Villani cooked each morning, and from the Sacred Stew served on Sundays after the family returned from Mass at the church of the Madonna del Carmine. 'Yes,' she recalls the porter chasing Sofia, challenging her and saying 'you have a thief's eyes.'

Sophia Loren admits to the offence and also to filching religious postcards displayed outside shop windows. 'But we only did it to sell them again for ice-cream. It was wrong,' she admitted gravely, 'but at least we were helping to spread the Faith.'

At thirteen the *stecchetto* was beginning to develop the un-mistakable shape, and awareness, of a woman. The transformation was casually accepted on the Via Solfatara where other nubile Neapolitan girls were bursting out of their gym-slips.

But to the husky young physical training instructor who used to exercise the girls in the Roman amphitheatre, the vision of the tall, arresting beauty at full swing, a T shirt tucked meaningfully inside her shorts, was more than he could bear. Unsettled by weeks of this unsolicited provocation he detained Sofia after the lesson, declared his predicament and proposed. 'I remember he had blond hair and marvellous blue eyes. I laughed and sent him off to see my mother. She told him to go away and take a cold bath.'

Sophia Loren met the man in Rome some fifteen years later. He was married with six children, three sets of twins. 'He obviously had been very serious,' Sophia said.

If the horror on the streets of Naples had shocked Sofia Scicolone, the return to Pozzuoli, now under Allied occupation did not instantly relieve it. The Via Solfatara was packed with troops and their wild carousals, with a little bit of debauchery on the side, hardly endeared them to the tight-lipped landladies on the street. 'Some girls were raped, I was not,' Sophia Loren said, putting a Count Basie tape on to change the mood as well as the subject. She rests her case on the accepted fact that the Italian women of World War II were firmly loyal to their menfolk. Prostitution was another matter. But like the earth's atmosphere, it was a global service not the sole preserve of the 'girls' of Naples.

At thirteen, Riccardo Scicolone's daughter Sofia had developed his stature, and the voluptuous proportions of her mother. It was Sofia's grandfather Domenico who increased her own awareness of it. 'You've stopped growing up, you're growing out,' he told her. The whistles from the fishermen in the port confirmed it. Books became less of an attraction for her. Movies, even stuff like the early blancmange of Hollywood's Universal Studios, starring Yvonne de Carlo, sent her home spellbound. She weaved great romantic fantasies around Tyrone Power—'I fell in love with him immediately'—and watching his love-making with Rita Hayworth in *Blood and Sand* was so overwhelming she saw the film three times around. Like thousands of others, she substituted herself for Miss Hayworth, hugging herself ecstatically to sleep.

Her mother, Romilda Villani, clung to her own fantasies too. Though her first attempt to escape from Pozzuoli via that Garbo competition had foundered, the urge was still there. And now here was her daughter, disturbingly attractive and equally restless, demanding more than Pozzuoli was able to provide.

Romilda Villani was driven by two further obsessions; the need for her own identity and self-expression and the simple requirement of survival. Also, Riccardo Scicolone had finally drifted away to marry someone else. On that day, when the news reached Pozzuoli, a disturbed rattlesnake might have been easier to handle than Romilda.

Few Italians understand the inner workings and the surface behaviour of this mother and daughter as perceptively as did Vittoria de Sica. An impressive seventy-two-year-old with silver hair and a charm as smooth as zabaglione, he spoke of Sophia Loren, he said, 'with the love a father might have for a daughter. I am a Neapolitan, so I know how they feel, why they act in a certain way. Sophia's childhood was one of great sacrifice. The mother found herself without a husband. She had no choice but to take advantage of her own beauty and the beauty of her daughter. Everything the mother did for Sofia, and for Maria, and for herself was ... *per guadagnare* ... *per mangiare* ... just to earn, just to eat. Not for reasons of art, not to realize any dreams of success. *Per mangiare,*' he repeated with emphasis, '*mangiare, mangiare.*'

But even with the ending of the war, or at least of Italy's part in it, 'earning and eating' became no easier. The whole coastline was in ruins; the shattered buildings were largely given over to the rats; the black market functioned for the crafty and the rich. The only people who worked with some degree of continuity were the prostitutes and then only for a tin of Spam, a carton of cigarettes or for the equivalent in lire. Mothers could no longer afford to pay Romilda Villani for the piano lessons she gave their children. And starving Naples needed concert pianists as urgently as Pozzuoli required an earthquake. The Villani family shared Romilda's despair. What would become of her—and her two daughters?

The answer came, unexpectedly from Naples. And as usual, it was that resourceful grandmother, Luisa Villani, who did the producing and directing.

3

'Put 'em amongst the slaves!'

The Via Veneto, that mildly degenerate thoroughfare which descends from an old Roman wall down past the Excelsior Hotel to the U.S. Embassy and beyond, is not what it used to be. It was once the most garishly sybaritical quarter of Rome. Fellini immortalized it in *La Dolce Vita* luridly caricaturing those who lived on, or off it, during what might be called its 'hay'-day. Now like an ageing, affluent hooker, it will tell you of the celebrities it used to know and sneer at the current hustlers, male and female, who have driven the 'beautiful people' away. Long ago, at Doney's and the Café de Paris, the famous and the fake would sip their espressos and talk 'deals'. American stars, attracted by the 'sweet life' or the generous tax advantage of spending a couple of years out of their native country, would stroll up one side of the street and down the other, comparing the number of contracts they were offered en route.

Almost anybody with twenty-twenty vision and the faculty of speech could become a producer. Needed for the job—unless you were a Laurentis or a Ponti—was the persistence of a Persian carpet salesman, and the ability to take with a smile the derisory brush-offs from stars or bankers as they shook their heads, leaving you to pick up the tab. Many of these engaging entrepreneurs were emigré Hungarians with no command of the English tongue. They therefore dispensed with the usual formalities, repeating in the manner of a group benediction names like Metro, Fox, Warners or Universal but in a whisper in case Los Angeles could hear them.

Of course, none of the companies concerned had any knowledge

of the said 'producers'. But on the Via Veneto of that era—
around 1950 onwards—everybody's bona fides were as reliable or
as bogus as anybody else's. So you could drop such names as
Frankie, Marlon, Kirk or Ingrid and all enjoyed the joke, knowing that if the issue were forced, you probably couldn't pay the
girl who typed the contract. No matter. It was great parasitical
fun, and when the sun set on your fourth 'café solo' you could
always slide into the bar of the Excelsior and con a drink out of
ex-King Farouk of Egypt. This mountainous rake who spent his
exile pinching Roman bottoms or standing moodily over the
piano at the Hostaria del Orso, was a standard attraction of the
Via Veneto until his money, his glands and finally his life, deserted
him.

At first the street was the exclusive territory of the Italian stars
and starlets. Then Rossellini and Ingrid Bergman had that steamy
rendezvous within its precincts and the world's media packed its
bags, all roads leading to Rome. It was the love affair of the
decade. I remember sitting with Bergman in her apartment on the
Buona Bozzi watching those candid eyes fill with tears as she
spoke of The Affair which burned so fiercely, no accusation or
public condemnation could extinguish it. It was to cool down, of
course, but at the time it dominated the headlines.

No American star crossed the Atlantic without scheduling a
stop-over at the Excelsior or the Hassler Hotel, eager for 'the
action' which included that speciality, fettucini, dished up at
Alfredo's by the proprietor himself with a solid gold spoon and
fork for the selected customer. Brigitte Bardot, Ava Gardner,
Clark Gable, Frank Sinatra, Anita Ekberg and a whole tiara of
contessas, duchesses and princesses turned the Via Veneto into a
kind of safari park in which producers hunted for talent, or for
sport. It was the territory of the languidly rich and of the scandal
magazines who bought candid pictures from the *paparazzi*, those
marauding cameramen who shadowed indiscreet celebrities to
night-clubs, cafés or parked cars for the picture of the week, the
year or the age. The term derived from an actor who played a
photographer in Fellini's *Dolce Vita*. His name, Giuseppe
Paparazzo. During the shooting Fellini yelled it so often when he

wanted the photographers for a scene, that they were soon identified as paparazzi and the name stuck.

The Klondike days for the street began, almost imperceptibly, when Metro-Goldwyn-Mayer arrived at Cinecitta to film *Quo Vadis*. It cost £2,500,000 (a monumental figure in those days); had 235 speaking roles; 32,000 costumes; 150,000 props; 1 bull; 63 lions; 450 horses; 2 cheetahs; 85 doves (white); 10 hogs (for sacrificial purposes) and 30,000 extras—which included Romilda Villani and her daughter, Sofia Scicolone. The studio took over most of the hotel rooms on the Via Veneto and the street became the Sunset Boulevard of Rome.

Their arrival in Rome at the close of 1949 had been a sudden decision. Sofia was then fifteen and sufficient of a physical specimen to enter for a 'Queen of the Sea' beauty contest in Naples. Her grandfather, Domenico, was as hostile to the idea as he had been to Romilda's attempt to become the 'new Garbo'. To him, and to Luisa, there was something immodest about it but Romilda was convinced her daughter had talent and that the competition would open a window on to it. They also needed the prize money. Beauty competitions were springing up all over Italy to cope with the demand for new faces which a big influx of Hollywood coin could pay for.

Romilda finally convinced Luisa, but when they stood Sofia in front of them, in her drab dress and ragged shoes, the disappointment showed in their faces. 'Leave it to me,' Luisa said briskly. She yanked down the pink satin curtains in the living room, ran a tape measure over her grand-daughter, and working through a night and a day, produced a passable dress for the contest. It had to be a long one to hide Sofia's worn shoes. The family budget didn't extend to buying new ones.

Sofia came second. Her prizes were 15,000 lire (then worth about £25), some rolls of wallpaper, a table cloth with six napkins, her picture and a few lines in the local paper. Walking with Aunt Dora around the house on the Via Solfatara I pointed to the paper on the wall of the living room, a dark green background with a beige leaf design spread over it. 'Is this the . . .?' 'Yes it is!' Dora interrupted, her tone as reverential as a guide's in the

Sistine Chapel. 'This is the actual wallpaper won by Sophia Loren in the beauty competition in Naples.' When I mentioned this to the actress at one of our meetings at the villa, she asked me solemnly: 'Did you kiss it?'

'No. But I walked backwards out of the room.'

'That's nice.'

'Think nothing of it.'

The young Miss Scicolone had left the school at Pozzuoli and was now studying drama at an acting school in Naples, the Carlo Maria Rossini. She was determined—as was her mother Romilda —to get into the movies. Thousands of other Italian girls had the same urge. They read the gossip from the Via Veneto of how pretty girls were 'spotted' outside the Excelsior and swept into pictures. An acting diploma in those days was secondary to a thirty-eight inch bust and bushel-sized hips. It was a flesh market and at Cinecitta they needed bodies by the thousand, if not by the ton, and the call went out all over Italy. It reached Naples where, at the drama school, the arresting Miss Scicolone in the back row, felt her heart leap at the announcement.

'The teacher said *Quo Vadis* was being made in Rome and that to anyone who wanted to get into movies, this was the big opportunity. I knew we would only be extras. But it meant we could learn, and we would eat. I ran home and said to my mother, "why don't we go?" I had kept the prize money from the contest. There was nothing to keep us in Pozzuoli. If we failed in Rome, we knew we could always come back.'

Just what that decision meant, for mother and daughter, taking a one-way ticket to Rome and gambling on their looks to sustain them there, acquires a special meaning when Sophia Loren recounts it at the Villa Ponti. This lush palace may be a reflection of Carlo Ponti's adroit handling of his most valued property. It also owes something to Vittorio de Sica who manipulated his friend Sophia with consummate skill. But above all it marks Sophia Loren's personal achievement which could have had no humbler genesis than playing a painted-up courtesan in *Quo Vadis*.

To rebuild and refurbish this remarkable edifice whose

foundations go back 2,000 years, Carlo Ponti engaged the largest army of plumbers, electricians, artists, painters, restorers and horticulturalists ever assembled to gratify the whim of a devoted husband. He announced his intention on the day they were married by proxy in Juarez, Mexico, on 17 September, 1957 saying simply: 'I am going to give you the most beautiful house in the world.'

The urge to compare it to that mausoleum at Agra, in India, the Taj Mahal, which a Mogul Emperor built in honour of his favourite wife, is irresistible. Everything in the Villa Ponti is Carlo's love token to his wife; the sixteenth-century marble fountains; the Louis XVI bedstead and console table made in Tuscany; the priceless Etruscan pottery; the azalea plants bought on a trip to Hamburg; the thirteenth-century granite baptismal font; the gold taps; the white birch trees from Russia and the enormous seventeenth-century style swimming pool. Dominating the twelve-foot high entrance are 400 year-old cypresses which prevent the whole multi-million dollar caprice from getting ideas above its station.

During the war, German officers occupied the villa. They used the delicately painted horses in one of the frescoes (attributed to an artist of the Fragonard school) for pistol practice. The holes are still there, wide of the mark, the officers' aim apparently, on the same level as their taste.

Since the villa houses a fair range of Picassos, Modiglianis, Renoirs and Henry Moores—not to overlook the Pontis themselves—the place is patrolled by day and guarded by Alsatian dogs at night. The sign ATTENTI AL CANE is strategically exhibited and anybody who has seen the dogs knows that the warning has a large complement of teeth to it.

At night, when some canine upstart in a nearby villa starts howling, the Ponti Alsatians respond with a ferocity that shakes the Alban Hills. It jolts out of their sleep everyone from the guests at the Helio Cabala Hotel on one hill, to the monks at the Monastery of San Nilo, on another. But as all the sleepless parties yawn in the dawn they know that Sophia and Carlo, at least, slept safe and sound.

Sophia Loren, of course, is not the only star whose security is guarded by Alsatians. Gina Lollobrigida, who lives a couple of dangerous curves away on the Via Appia Antica, has, or had, two inhospitable samples of the breed. Even if you merely pinched the bottom of the life-sized replica of the lady in an upstairs dressing room, the dogs might just playfully take your hand off at the wrist. The names they fought under, when I last met them, were Elch Von Templebick and Son. During a reported feud between her and Sophia, someone suggested that it might be settled honourably by matching Sophia's Alsatians against Gina's, the contest to take place in the Roman Colosseum. It came to nothing, the wags saying the dogs wouldn't agree over the billing.

But the security of the Pontis and their children does not end with the police, the sensitive fencing or the dogs. Visitors still have to get past Clothilde, a large, deceptively amiable woman who keeps the keys to, and lives by, the huge wrought-iron gates. She knows who is expected and who is not and puts a series of checks into operation before finally permitting entry. Fort Knox could learn a trick or two from Clothilde.

It is not difficult to understand Sophia Loren's almost sensual pleasure as she saunters like some Abyssinian princess through her palace, finally coming to rest in her study which displays a formidable collection of acting trophies, International awards and medals from the high and the mighty. She worked relentlessly for it and luxuriates in it. It is part pride of ownership, and part an unabashed ecstasy at being Sophia Loren. She clearly likes what she is, down to the last sun-bronzed millimetre. When frilled and furbished by some leading couturier, she has an elegance unmatched by any other movie star. When she is suitably stripped for the pool, with, as I recall, more material to her headscarf than to her bikini, the several necklaces bouncing this and that-a-way, one understands why a couple of her co-stars went off their food and bayed at the moon. The bottom half of her black bikini maintained the essential priority at the front, cheekily abandoned it at the rear, and I suggested that had she looked like this, pound for pound, on the day she entered the 'Queen of the Sea' contest she would have won with ease. Miss Loren, never one to give an argument on so serious a matter, conceded the possibility with a smile. 'But at least I won the wallpaper and the fare to Rome,' she said.

It was that train journey, of course, which led to everything; to the love affair and marriage with Carlo Ponti, the two children, the Oscar, the villa and 'Attenti al Cane'. Beneath the round table on which Sophia swung her long brown legs, a stone plaque, inscribed by some sycophant of the era commemorated an equally triumphant journey, this one by the Roman Emperor Marcus Aurelius. The precise details of that excursion have now faded into the stonework. Sophia Loren's memory of her train ride to Rome and *Quo Vadis* is etched more deeply.

'I remember I wore a pale blue dress, white shoes with high heels. When my mother and I got in the carriage we sat opposite each other, both of us knowing what a gamble we were taking. I felt an enormous admiration for her. We had very little money, few clothes and nothing for us at Cinecitta but the right to join the queue. It took a lot of courage. When we got to Rome we moved in on a relative and the following morning took the little train that went direct to the studio. It may sound corny now, but it really was a marvellous feeling getting up at five o'clock in the morning, the sun over Rome, the air so fresh. It was a beautiful experience.'

But they did not walk into *Quo Vadis* at once. No girl, unless she happened to be the instant protégé of the man who put up the money could become an extra overnight. Romilda Villani took brief stock of her daughter's assets and decided Sofia was strong on looks, low on options. Girls desperate to break into motion pictures in the Hollywood and Rome of the early 'fifties knew they'd get more mileage out of their flesh than out of Stanislavsky. To hitch their dreams on walking up and down the Via Veneto—as many did—had dubious advantages. It was also hard on the shoe leather.

The last resort was to enter that Happy Hunting Ground for nubile, but generally uncultivated young females, the model business. And for Sofia Scicolone, that had to mean photographic, not fashion modelling. The latter required aloof, slim, pared-down creatures and Miss Scicolone over-flowed from a vastly different mould. She was big, voluptuous, more pasta than porcelain.

That was part of her good fortune. The rest of it came from the great attraction of the time, the saucy pulp magazines which told steamy tales of lust and love in picture-strips, the dialogue written into cartoon-type 'balloons'.

The magazines were called 'fumetti' roughly translated as 'little balls of smoke' describing the puffs of dialogue emerging from the lips of the characters. They were mainly photo serials with the bosomy and substantially underclad heroines mouthing through agonized lips such phrases as 'Don't leave me—I love you too much', 'If you go I will die', 'How could you do this to me, you brute?' with facial contortions to match.

It was pretty daring stuff for that era. Girls who posed for it gladly raised their hemlines, lowered their necklines and a good time was had by all.

Precisely how far the young and eager Sofia Scicolone went in this direction is difficult to establish since no photographs are available—if ever these existed. There have been rumours of a set of half-nude pictures being offered in New York for some astronomical sum and either finding no takers, or being promptly bought and destroyed by Carlo Ponti. All parties are now tight-lipped on the subject but if it were true it would not be surprising. Rather than allow his beautiful wife to suffer even momentary embarrassment, Carlo would gladly buy General Motors let alone a roll of negatives.

Sophia Loren said simply, 'I was in a business, I had been taught at drama school in Naples how to use my face and figure. The photographer told me what he wanted and I gave it to him.' According to the record, she showed sufficient leg in one magazine cover-picture for a magistrate to declare it as being 'offensive to public morals'. It was, of course, far less revealing than today's trendy calendar or sex-oriented soft drink advertisement, but it led to the magazine being confiscated. It did no harm to the model, however, though she was fined £5 for not turning up as a defence witness.

Inevitably the saucy magazine attracted the interest of a film director—Giorgio Bianchi. He called her to his office, assured her of his best intentions at all times, and gave her a minor appearance in a film called *Cuori Sul Mare* (Hearts of the Sea) starring Jacques Sernas. It was a forgettable picture and a minuscule role. But two things led to another, specifically, *Il Voto* (The Vow) and such sweetmeats as *Le Sei Mogli di Barbablu* (Bluebeard's Six Wives) and *Era Lui Si! Si!* (It was Him—Yes! Yes!) which may give some idea of Sophia Loren's unspectacular beginnings.

But the parts were paltry, the money derisory, the films of no consequence for an actress with the star-struck fantasies of that era. *Quo Vadis* offered more than a chance of a meal ticket. It dangled the opportunity of being pulled out of the crowd. It was this that took Romilda and her daughter on the dusty ride to Cinecitta.

They were in good company. Almost every footloose female with ambitions or hunger pangs joined in the dawn exodus from Rome, chatting eagerly about their chances, swopping the latest gossip from the Via Veneto.

This sad expedition of the indigent citizens of Rome streaming towards *Quo Vadis* with no credentials but their poverty would make today's film unions and Central Casting go puce inside their white collars. Mervyn LeRoy was hiring bodies not talent. It was a bulk order. They required no documents, just the ability to stand, run or shout. At the end of the day the weary mob would be shovelled back into Rome, glad of the windfall to pay for pasta, shoes or the overdue rent.

Romilda Villani glanced at the 'opposition' and steered Sofia to the front. 'Just do as I tell you,' she ordered. Someone announced: 'This way for the girls who speak English. Do you speak English?' Romilda smiled eagerly. 'Sure,' she told the man, 'my daughter speaks English. Don't you speak English, Sofia?' Sofia looked puzzled. Romilda repeated the question in Italian.

'Si Mamma,' Sofia said.

The man again asked, this time of Sofia: 'Do you speak English?'

'Cosa dice?' She asked of Romilda. ('What is he saying?')

'Digli "Yes."' ('Say "Yes."')

52

'Yes.' Sofia obliged.

They were shown into an office. There were thirty other girls in the room. Behind the desk sat Mervyn LeRoy, the short, chunky Hollywood director, at the helm of *Quo Vadis*. He was looking for girls capable of speaking a line or two in the film. Both Romilda and Sofia stood out, dramatically, from the rest. He spoke to Sofia, and the same charade was repeated.

'Have you had any experience in the picture business?'

'Yes.'

'Have you played any special parts?'

'Yes.'

'Do you speak any English?'

'Yes.'

'Where did you learn your English?'

'Yes.'

'How old are you?'

'Yes.'

Mervyn LeRoy turned to his assistant and laughed. 'Put 'em amongst the slaves,' he said.

If Romilda, and her 'English-speaking' daughter were elated at being chosen as extras, their excitement was to be soured an hour or so later. The names of those selected for the crowd were being called by a production man. 'Villani,' he announced. Romilda stepped forward. 'Scicolone.' Sofia walked forward, and so did someone else. Sofia was puzzled. The other girl glared and said, 'You're no Scicolone! That is my name. Scicolone nothing!'

That 'extra' was Nella Rivolta, the woman Riccardo Scicolone, Sofia's father, married in 1943. This unexpected confrontation jolted Sofia right back to the uneasy fact of her birth. Romilda Villani's reaction cannot be recorded here.

Sophia Loren doesn't share her mother's bitterness. 'I suppose she hates that woman, but if she does, she has no reason to. I understand it. My mother, in spite of everything, is a very lonely woman. There have been so many negative elements in her life. Above all she misses not having a man she can love and trust.

It's been a terribly hard, cruel life. You can't blame her if she reacts irrationally.'

As for her own reaction on that day at Cinecitta, Sophia commented wrily: 'It is an extraordinary way to meet your stepmother. I knew about her, of course, because my mother had told me about the marriage. But there on the set, in front of hundreds of women, having someone dispute your right to your name and to discover who your accuser actually was, was quite a shock. Now, of course, I understand her feelings too. She was a Scicolone. She was married to my father. The fact that she was an extra meant that she must have had her problems too.'

Fortunately, with 30,000 slaves Romilda Villani and the two Scicolones were easily lost in the shuffle. The daughter had a slight edge on the mother. While Romilda was consigned to the crowd, Sofia was placed among a group of slaves surrounding Deborah Kerr who played Lygia to Robert Taylor's Vinicius. The film was phenomenally successful despite, or because of, the attacks made on it over the orgy scenes and the too realistic munching of Christians by lions. In the run-up to the burning of Rome, with thousands of gallons of inflammable spirit ready for ignition, Mervyn LeRoy took Nero (Peter Ustinov) on one side and said: 'Okay, now don't forget—you're responsible for all this!' Ustinov remembers the occasion, but not the extra he was later to direct in *Lady L*.

Meanwhile Sofia Scicolone, the slave, continued to stare at Deborah Kerr understanding not a word of the dialogue, but hugely involved. Elsewhere, Romilda Villani rhubarb-rhubarbed with great gusto. At the end of the day, which netted them about five pounds each, she wrapped the money in a handkerchief, and along with the other slaves, they went joyously home on the train to Rome. Every morning, before taking the train to the studio, Romilda untied the handkerchief, laid the money out, and they both stared at it, occasionally with tears. They could eat and they could buy clothes. After five days their extra work came to an end. News had come from Pozzuoli that the younger daughter, Maria, was ill with typhoid fever. Romilda had to leave on a train for Naples.

The scene of her departure was a real tear-jerker which could well have come from one of the 'B' movies much fancied at the time. When Romilda's case was packed, she hugged her moist-eyed daughter (she still used the pet-name Lella), saying: 'I have to go now. You're a big girl, you're intelligent, you're on your own.' If she did not repeat her dictum: 'All men are evil' it was because she knew her daughter had seen the wolves in action at Cinecitta and had the Neapolitan spirit and vocabulary to handle them. 'But I was scared to death,' Sophia recalls. It is understandable.

To be a highly attractive sixteen-year-old girl alone in Rome, on the perimeter of the predatory movie business, was hazardous enough. Nature had added to the perils. Sofia Scicolone was now flamboyantly bosomed, projecting from all points of the compass that sheer sexual bravado which diverted startled errand boys and their bikes into the nearest ditch.

She had also become a model, been spread anonymously over the *fumetti*; worn five days' worth of greasepaint in *Quo Vadis*. True, when she saw the film, all trembling at the thought of seeing herself in that epic, all she saw of her scene was a close-up of Deborah Kerr, and a busty blur in the background which could have been her, or merely a couple of hills of Rome. But she consoled herself with the thought that during the lunch breaks it was she, and not the cool Miss Kerr, who drew the glances from the crew. Moreover, she knew instinctively that when she weaved provocatively between the café tables on the Via Veneto, all eyes homed in on her retreating figure like S.A.M. missiles on their targets. She had had a short flirtation with the movie business and was hooked. But *Quo Vadis* was over. It had moved back to Hollywood, leaving Cinecitta and Rome as empty as though the circus had wrapped up and gone.

Other film parts were slow in coming. Sofia received several propositions as she walked around agents' offices but it was straight barter and she wasn't interested. She badly needed a change of luck. Maybe it would happen under a new name.

There were those who candidly informed the girl that 'Scico-lone', pronounced 'shickoloney', sounded like a chunk of Italian sausage. It was hard to say, difficult to spell, and was no name to put above the title. (Years later, Sophia Loren winced at such thoughts as 'Sofia Scicolone in the *Fall of the Roman Empire*' and 'Sinatra and Scicolone in *The Pride and the Passion*'.)

It was the editor of one of the *fumetti* magazines who suggested she change her name. He came up with 'Sofia Lazzaro', lifting the idea from the story of Lazarus in the New Testament (John XI). Lazarus of Bethany, brother of Martha and Mary, was said to have been raised from the dead after four days. Precisely what this miracle had to do with Miss Scicolone, now Lazzaro, is a fair question. His answer was that this able-bodied creature had such sexual sorcery she could even arouse a Lazarus from the dead. The story acquired some interesting permutations at the time, but no actual tests were conducted.

The raw but enthusiastic bit player who ricocheted from one pot-boiling movie to another, looked nothing like the elegant creature who was later to head the Best Dressed Female lists of the world. Nor did she behave like her. The starlets who were paraded on the Via Veneto like promising fillies in the saddling enclosure, were not expected to be strong on etiquette and finesse. Their ankles, legs, breasts and hindquarters were scrutinized if not thumbed by film men who might just as well have been farmers at a cow auction. If they said anything at all to these nymphettes, it was unlikely to be more than 'turn around' or 'get your teeth fixed'.

The eighteen-year-old Sofia Lazarro was more than a match for these merchants. As Romilda Villani's daughter she had inherited that redhead's Force Nine fury and the rare Neapolitan vocabulary that somehow clinched the argument. Those who retain a vision of this sulphurous beauty at full spate, her eyes blazing, bosom heaving, one hand on hip, a long, menacing finger leading the attack, do so with a kind of rueful admiration. Undeniably, she desperately wanted to be a success in movies. But it was not going to be on the unequivocal terms which applied at the time.

'I needed money—but not that badly,' Sophia Loren said as we examined early material in the vast depository of film stills, cuttings, letters, records, which occupy an entire upper section of the villa. 'I still wasn't taking the business seriously. I didn't think I was good looking. I had all the wrong features, and I was bigger than I should have been. But I was making enough money to send some home to Pozzuoli, where Maria was still recovering from the effects of typhoid fever. I remember writing to my mother saying: "I am not spending anything. Everything is all right. I have bought a black skirt and black sweater so I can go out in the evening. DON'T WORRY!"'

The closeness which exists between Sophia, her mother Romilda, sister Maria and Aunt Dora in Pozzuoli, is due to the actress's own flair for sharing her well-earned goodies around. Her generosity, controlled though it is, ensures that nobody in the family need deny themselves the basic luxuries. This is no new development, the regal hand-out from a Croesus-rich movie queen. 'Right from the very beginning,' her Aunt Dora impressed on me in Pozzuoli, 'Sophia gave what she could. Once she started earning money, she said to us: "Whatever happens in the family, there's always me, I am behind you."' If this meant working solidly from film to film, 'lobbying' for work at night among film directors, producers and agents, Sophia had the peasant strength for it and it was worth it.

Maria has several reasons for being grateful to her elder, more celebrated sister. But the overriding one—and it has a touch of poignancy to it—is that, in her view, at any rate, she owes her name to Sophia.

For the illegitimate Maria Villani to have 'Scicolone' written on her birth certificate required the same sort of declaration Riccardo Scicolone made in the case of Sophia. There appears to have been some reluctance on his part to do so in respect of Maria. 'Sophia paid for my name,' her sister said simply. 'As soon as she started earning money in films our mother said to her: "Listen you are sisters and I am ashamed that you have different names." So Mama went to Riccardo and asked him to declare his name, officially, for me too. He asked for two million lire. Sophia paid him. He signed a paper, then my mother went into a judge's court in Rome and came out with my name. It was quite a present from a big sister!'

Sophia's beaver-like passion for work is no different today when she hardly needs the cash, from what it was in the early years. She goes into film after film with barely a break to change costume. 'I always seem to be working as though I'm starving,' she says with a hint of annoyance. 'I wish I could get out of that feeling. In the early days, before I met Carlo, I don't think I realized how exhausted I was.'

But it was all effort and no direction. She continued to farm herself out to producers for films whose titles may give some indication of their substance. *Il Mago Per Forza* (The Reluctant Magician) was one. *E Arrivato L'Accordatore* (The Piano Tuner Has Arrived) another. In *La Tratta Della Bianche* (a white slavery melodrama) she played alongside Sylvana Pampanini and another Italian beauty, Eleanora Rossi-Drago. They played prostitutes, she did not, although it is generally accepted that nobody can play a tart with greater zest than Sophia. Shirley MacLaine made a pretty good show if it in *Irma La Douce* but she was more tinsel than tart.

Sophia, when she puts her mind to it (as in *Marriage Italian Style*) can be the perfect harlot from leer to rear. She had seen them at work and play as a child in wartime Naples, and remembers the tricks, adding a few nuances of her own. She was being labelled in magazines and newspapers as 'The Sizzler', 'The Roman Rocket' and other incendiary devices, but like Raquel Welch in her formative years, it induced a greater interest in her phone number than in her curriculum vitae.

Sofia was dissatisfied with herself, anxious to break out of the straitjacket of bit parts in second features. She wondered whether the *fumetti* editor had been all that helpful in his choice of the name 'Lazzaro'. She was finding it difficult to raise parts, let alone raise Lazarus. The Italian producer, Goffredo Lombardo, who had cast her in one of his films disliked the name, saying it sounded more like the corpse than its resurrection.

He had been working with the Swedish actress Martha Toren on the film *Madelaine*. The association had been a success. Maybe it would work again. He took the name 'Toren' and worked through the alphabet stopping at the letter 'L'. 'Yes, "Loren"—

it suits you,' he decided. Sofia became 'Sophia', the changed letters intended to add a touch of class.

The name Sofia Scicolone was to remain on her birth certificate. Sofia Lazzaro had had a short and happy life. She was cordially thanked and dismissed, along with the dubious *fumetti* layouts which had flourished under her name. Lella the girl from Pozzuoli was now re-catalogued as Sophia Loren. An eighteen-year-old Amazon with, as the late Clark Gable was to murmur as she left us talking in a Naples hotel, 'plenty of meat on the bone and every ounce of it choice enough to eat!'

It was certainly choice, but under-employed. As before, the options were few. A question of meeting the right people, being seen in the right places, grabbing the right opportunity. Fortunately for Sophia, and she frequently offers suitable prayers in recognition of the miracle, all three elements were powerfully combined one fascinating night in Rome. All incorporated in the short but forceful figure of a Milanese lawyer named Carlo Fortunato Pietro Ponti.

4

Carlo Ponti Enters

Ask any of the old inhabitants of the Roman film colony of the early 1950s about Romilda Villani and her two daughters, Sophia and Maria, and the response is three parts a smile of admiration to one part knowing wink. It is kindly, though there is the implicit recognition that in those lean years the undiscovered film starlets of Rome were forced, in the words of Damon Runyon, to do the best they could. Not that the situation has changed very much. Film starlets without the benefit of an Actors' Studio diploma or an irrepressible talent, have often been obliged to take the easier route between the covers. Beauty, an eager sensuality and no fear of strangers were a surprisingly successful substitute for the conventional haul to stardom.

Fortunately for the two daughters of Romilda Villani, they had talent too.

Maria had joined her mother and sister in Rome. Though four years younger than Sophia, and shorter, she was strikingly built, and when all three were of a mind to saunter out into the sun, the wolf-whistles on the Via Veneto were drowned only by the appreciative honking of motor horns. Romilda taught them how to dress and make the most of their physical inheritance—the sexual fortissimo which came to them, courtesy of Romilda Villani.

Their looks were hers. Their determination was hers. Their flouncing hostility to men—in the early days—was hers, and she rarely let them forget it. If she encouraged them, promoted them, steered them, all lacquered and spangled into the most influential quarters, it was simply to give them the confidence and invulnerability which she never achieved herself. Embittered by her own experience, she relentlessly hammered home the warning to them, 'all men are evil' until a producer's inoffensive 'Buon Giorno' seemed like a prelude to rape.

Over the years, Romilda's concern for Sophia—cynics described her as 'The Marshal'—has earned rich filial dividends. She told an interviewer recently:

'Sometimes I feel like her daughter. She'll phone me in the mornings, before she goes to be with her children. She always wants to know if everything is all right with me, if I'm *tranquillo*. I say "yes" to reassure her, but I'm not a tranquil person at all. I can't fool her; she hears it in my voice when I'm down. But she has spent her life among people who must act a certain way, and as a result she has become so constrained that I can no longer be sure when she is upset. Sometimes when I'm desperate and lonely I call her and she calms me down. "That's life, Mammina," she'll say. She's a marvellous woman, with incredible humanity and sensitivity, and I feel secure with her.

'Sophia is sweeter than I am; I'm too impulsive. But I had to be that way to survive, and she always understood that.

'I have no friends. I'm a strange character. Everything that I wanted for myself happened to Sophia. I live in her reflection.'

First-term psychology would indicate that in spite of the pyrotechnics of a jilted woman, Romilda loved Mr Scicolone. Now she doesn't, bringing Fate in as a guilty third party, for ending a promising career as an actress. And so she said she renounced everything for her daughters. They would be what she could not be. But if Sophia was to make it big, then in spirit at least, Romilda was going to be up there taking the bows with her. The role she gave herself in her daughters' frisky apprenticeship in Rome was to spell out the objectives, lead them from the front. They would make wrong marriages over her dead body.

Sophia's success, and the fierce, armour-plated affection these three beauties have for each other, suggest that Romilda Villani has played her role well.

In the absence of work film starlets played, wherever the action was. If the Via Veneto represented the day shift of their operations, a few selected Roman nightclubs took care of the after-dark activities. The Hostaria del Orso was one. The Colle Oppio, an open air spot on the Esquiline Hill overlooking the Colosseum, was another. Both were favourite playgrounds of influential producers and of the *paparazzi* who fed off them like tick-pickers on rhino.

True there was a glut of beautiful young girls on the market at the time. But they looked at the success of one of their breed, the sturdily built Silvana Mangano, and argued that if it could happen to her it could happen to them.

Miss Mangano's launching pad had been the film *Bitter Rice* in which she squelched around, the water lapping at her thighs and tight wet pants. It introduced a new, damply erotic element into motion pictures and was a sensation across the world. She too had been an extra when producer Dino de Laurentis met her, fell in love with her, and threw all his energies and cash into making her a star. Hers may have been a slightly less coy version of the Cinderella story although the basic plot was the same. If the producer liked what he saw and the shoe fitted, then it was all systems 'go' with a chauffeured carriage at the door.

There have been many such successful liaisons between aspiring actresses and their grateful sponsors. Melina Mercouri and Jules Dassin. Vadim and Bardot (followed later by Annette Stroyberg and Catherine Deneuve). Antonioni and Monica Vitti. Fellini and Giulietta Masina. It adds zest to the relationship and halves the overheads.

But none of these fruitful twosomes, nor Silvana Mangano's triumph, can match the landsliding good fortune which came Sophia Loren's way following a chance visit to the night-club, Colle Oppio. There are several versions of what happened that evening, some writers adding a few fanciful notions of their own. To reduce the scenario to a sentence, Carlo Ponti caught a glimpse of Sophia, and if the earth didn't move, it was clearly faltering on its axis.

Sophia's own feelings burned more slowly at the time. 'I didn't look at Carlo and see the skies open up,' she admits. 'I had gone to the night-club with some friends,' she said. 'A man stood at the microphone and announced that a beauty competition was about to take place to find the most beautiful girl of Lazio Roma which covered the whole region. There always seemed to be a beauty competition taking place somewhere. My friends suggested that I enter just for the fun of it. I said I'd much sooner sit and watch others trying their luck.

'But someone on the jury seemed determined that I should enter. He sent a press agent over to my table who said: "the gentleman over there thinks it would be a good idea for you to enter the contest."

'"Which gentleman?"

'"Signor Ponti. On the jury."'

Sophia laughed loudly, self consciously covering her teeth with her hand. 'I thought to myself, "Listen, Sophia, if a member of the jury thinks you should enter a competition, that must give you an edge on the rest." There's no point in being a Neapolitan if you don't think like one! So I entered, just like the "Queen of the Sea" contest in Naples I came second. It didn't bother me too much then. I hadn't gone there to participate, so I didn't care. But Carlo came over to my table afterwards. He started to talk exactly like a producer, you know, "Listen, I've launched many actresses like Alida Valli, Gina Lollobrigida; it was for me that they made their first appearance in films, I can do the same for you . . ." But I was sceptical. It was too much like the cliché situation. I just sat there listening with a smile on my face. But he had very kind eyes. He just didn't look at me the way most men did.'

Ponti told Sophia, 'Come to my office tomorrow, I'd like to make a test of you for a film.' Sophia went back to her room that night, her mind in some turmoil. It was either an authentic offer or the old-fashioned ploy from a producer–seducer.

The confusion persisted when she arrived the following day at Ponti's office on the Piazza d'Ara Coeli: 'I went to what I thought was the correct address,' Sophia smiled, 'but it turned out to be the Carabinieri. I hadn't looked at the number properly because I was so excited. When I saw where I was I thought: "Here we go! You, Sophia, falling for a line like that!"

'One of the carabinieri asked me what I wanted. I had to say

63

something. I felt very foolish. "I don't suppose," I said, "that a Carlo Ponti has his office here?"

' "It's next door," the officer said. I walked up the stairs, into a large office, and there was Carlo, surrounded by film people. He smiled, and I felt guilty for not having trusted him.'

It would be naïve, however, to suggest that Ponti's first view of this tall, full-figured beauty did not evoke something more than a detached 'Bon Giorno'. She stood there, all five feet eight of her demanding to be noticed. Nobody failed her.

The test was a disaster. The cameraman who was paid to oblige Ponti exploded afterwards: 'She is quite impossible to photograph! Too tall, too big-boned, too heavy all round. The face is too short, the mouth is too wide, the nose too long! What do you want, miracles?'

(Ten years later, the *Daily Mirror* film critic was to write of Sophia's performance in *Marriage Italian Style*: 'Watching the irresistible Sophia Loren in a film is like peeping at a kaleidoscope of every quality in a woman dreamed of by any man. She is by turn radiant, funny, tender, provocative, earthy, pathetic, dignified, tough, saucy, desirable, obstinate, gay, cunning, sensuous, helpless, formidable, forlorn, maddening, lovable and oh so stunningly attractive!' (Quite a talent spotter that cameraman).)

Hearing his recital of her deformities did not make Sophia Loren feel that a Venus had come to the Piazza d'Ara Coeli. 'Would you consider,' Ponti asked her gently, 'doing something to your nose and maybe losing twenty pounds or so off your weight?'

Sophia's fuming rejection of the idea gave Ponti an interesting foretaste of their relationship in general, and the hazards of matching a Milanese with a Neapolitan in particular.

Her refusal to give an inch let alone lose one, impressed him. He liked the style of this bumper-sized vixen and placed her under contract. His associates, however, were privately convinced that he was out of his mind and that in time the starlet would soon be back making faces in the *fumetti*.

They were not the first to mis-judge this shrewd little powerhouse of a man. He made *Blow Up* with Antonioni in the face of tough opposition from everyone at MGM with the exception of

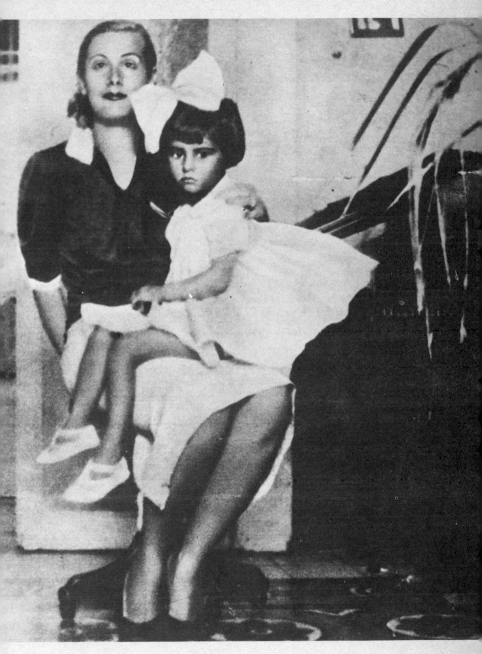

Aged three on the Via Solfatara, Pozzuoli, with her mother
Romilda Villani.

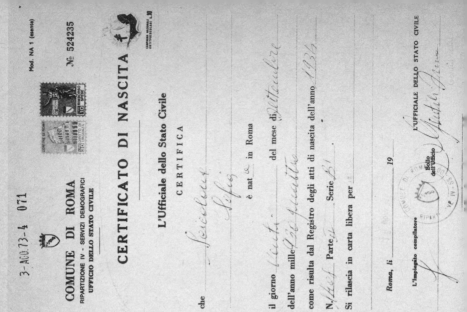

Top Born Scicolone, Rome, September 1934.
Left The girl from Pozzuoli – Sophia aged twelve.
Right First communion, with her godmother.

Early days and an aspiring Miss Italy.

Top In Spain for *The Pride And The Passion* (1957) with her sister, Maria, who married a Mussolini. (*Interfoto*)

Bottom Sophia's mother, Romilda Villani . . . an astonishing resemblance to Greta Garbo.

Domenico Villani, Sophia's grandfather (*right*).

The pin-up.

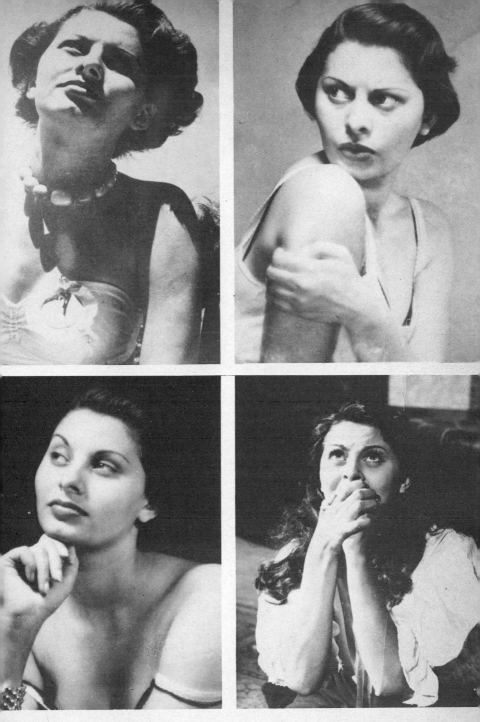

Sophia, a range of suitable expressions, during her 'Fumetti' days.

Left Carlo Ponti and Sophia – pride of ownership. (*Associated Press*)

Bottom Sofia Scicolone and Carlo Fortunato Pietro Ponti – marriage, French style, 9th April 1966. (*France Soir*)

EXTRAIT
DU REGISTRE
DES ACTES DE MARIAGE

de 1966 n° 27

MAIRIE DE SÈVRES
SEINE-&-OISE

ARRONDISSEMENT
DE VERSAILLES

CHEF-LIEU DE CANTON

Le Neuf Avril, ————— mil neuf cent soixante six, ——————
à Dix, —— heures ——————; devant Nous ont comparu publiquement
en la maison commune :

Carlo Fortunato Pietro PONTI, docteur en droit, ——————
né à Magenta (Italie), ——————————————————————
le Onze Décembre mil neuf cent douze, ——————————————
domicilié à Paris (8ème arr.), 32, Avenue Georges V, ——————
fXxxxlxx

xXxXxx

d'une part ;

et Sofia SCICOLONE, artiste, ——————————————————
née à Rome (Italie), ——————————————————————
le Vingt Septembre mil neuf cent trente quatre, ——————————
domiciliée à Sèvres, 36, Avenue Eiffel, ——————————————
fXxxdxx

xXxXxxx

d'autre part.

Les futurs époux déclarent qu'un contrat de mariage a été reçu le Trois
Avril mil neuf cent soixante six, par Maître Jérôme GASTALDI, notaire
à Paris, 15, Avenue Victor Hugo.—

ILS.—

ont déclaré, l'un après l'autre, vouloir se prendre pour époux, et Nous avons
prononcé, au nom de la Loi, qu'ils sont unis par le mariage.

POUR EXTRAIT CONFORME délivré le Vingt Avril, ——————
mil neuf cent soixante six./

L'Officier de l'État-civil

its then president, Robert O'Brien. At one time, Jack Valenti of the Motion Picture Association, refused to grant the picture a seal. The film was an enormous success, critically and commercially. *Doctor Zhivago* opened in New York to appalling notices. It cost twelve million dollars. At the last count it had grossed in excess of one hundred million dollars.

Watching Ponti operating in his first floor suite over Rome's Government centre is reminiscent of Brando in that opening sequence in *The Godfather*, with a procession of characters arriving to pay tribute or ask favours. Not that there is anything menacing or ominous about Carlo Ponti. He does not insist you agree with him instantly—just take your time. But the slim, neat-suited lieutenant who marshals the endless flow of visitors in an outer office, does so with the stern devotion of a court usher. Young writers, failed producers, 'experimental' directors, out-of-work cameramen, disillusioned actors, eager starlets, penniless artists, join the queue of well-known agents and their lawyers all hoping for a few indulgent moments with the Master. He rarely fails them.

He sits behind a large antique desk surrounded by some tasteful stone pieces, a chunk or two of ancient Rome, several artfully displayed film awards, some valuable paintings and a large, exotic, black-and-white sketch of Sophia. Ponti is not a tall man and seems even smaller behind the several phones, scripts and bound books on his desk. There is the immense intensity of the Northerner, relieved occasionally by the slow-forming smile which can be read as charm, agreement, anger, or contempt depending upon the accompanying caption in the eyes. His phone conversations are a production in themselves. His gestures, rising baritone voice, the thunderclap of laughter or choice Milanese oaths, have onlookers enthralled, almost calling for an encore. I sat through five consecutive performances in which he disarmed, or disillusioned, various characters around the globe, disgorging a daunting array of figures—and in different languages—which left little to say at the other end except a numb 'Merci' or resigned 'Auf Wiedersehen'.

The dominant feature of the North Italian—Milan has produced the country's leading industrialists—is his driving, relentless energy. 'Ponti has to build, build, build,' one of his associates said. 'The deal is the attraction, not the profit.' Thus Ponti rarely turns anybody away from his office. He works on the sound theory that today's hustler could be tomorrow's Fellini. And what would pain him more than losing such a genius would be the thought of someone else hiring him.

This subtle amalgam of lawyer, charmer, kindly sponsor and wheeler-dealer, has made Ponti one of the richest and most powerful film-makers in the world. His company, 'Compagnia Cinematografica Champion' is sustained by its own resources, backing his hunches, adding a string of noughts to his intuition. I have seen him in eyeball-to-eyeball confrontation with the toughest Hollywood heavyweights and watched them cave in under his genial onslaught. His technique is patience. He out-waits them into the ground.

But powerful moguls, particularly those with someone like Sophia Loren to sweeten them, can be generous on the grand scale. In the autumn of 1973 when all was ready to start filming *The Journey* with Sophia and Richard Burton, the director, Vittorio de Sica, collapsed with a critical lung illness. The Burton–Taylor shennanegans at the time had already thrown the production into turmoil. Now there were serious delays which might have meant cancelling the picture because of Burton's several other commitments. But Ponti reacted as de Sica's lifelong friend, not as the producer of an important and costly motion picture. He chartered a private plane in Rome, alerted a surgeon and team of doctors in Switzerland, flew de Sica there with a doctor and nurse and organized the intensive surgery required.

When the director was well enough to return to Rome and work, Ponti arranged for medical assistance to be discreetly deployed on the set, had the shooting schedules designed to give the director maximum rest.

But the question which has lurked in more than a handful of minds and dominated acres of newsprint for almost twenty years, is, to put it crudely: 'What on earth did this magnificent, goddess-like Loren see in this short, balding producer who was old enough to be her father with a few years to spare?'

'All I can tell you,' Sophia said to me on an occasion when Carlo was out of earshot, 'is that when I am without him it is as though I were without oxygen.'

That is one answer to the question. A closer look at the said oxygen supply provides another.

Carlo Ponti's entry into the movie business at the age of twenty-two was an accident. His father was a leading Milan lawyer with a substantial practice in that city. Carlo displayed a considerable flair for law and when he passed his finals went straight into the family concern. A client of theirs had invested some money in a film company in Milan but was forced by other pressures to leave it for a year. It had a staff of twenty, one film in the making, but no principal who could reliably take it over in the client's absence. He asked Ponti senior to fill the breach. Carlo's father replied that he had enough problems of his own and anyway wanted nothing to do with the caprices of Italian film production. But Carlo would run it and hand it back at the end of twelve months.

His first picture, based on the Italian masterpiece by Antonio Fogazzaro, was *Piccolo Mondo Antico* (Little Old World). It was directed by Mario Soldati and provided the then unknown quantity, actress Alida Valli, with a formidable debut. It turned out to be a dramatic overture for Ponti too. The film, released in 1939, centred on the Austrian occupation of Northern Italy in the mid-nineteenth century. Its violent anti-German, anti-dictatorship flavour was regarded by Mussolini as an oblique swipe at the Fascists.

They had tried earlier to coerce him into making movies, whitewashing Il Duce. Ponti's answer *Piccolo Mondo Antico* infuriated the régime and they threw him briefly into gaol as a warning to him and to others. But Ponti was not easily scared off. Facing him across the desk in his office or watching him deftly spoon-and-forking the steaming spaghetti for guests at the villa, you see a mild, middle-aged lawyer, soberly dressed, his entrepreneurial hustle concealed behind an all-purpose affability.

But he conceded, drily, 'Whatever I have done in my life always

SOPHIA

seems to have been against something or somebody!' His command of English was not as good as Sophia's but his points lost none of their emphasis as he continued. 'They tried, the Fascists, to persuade me to do this, to do that. But all my life I fight like a dog. What happened for Sophia and me is unbelievable. But I fight. I fought the priests, the Church. And now,' he shrugged, 'I am being sued by the Pope's niece. But I am a Milanese. If we believe we are right we fight like an animal against the world.'

The phone rang. 'Scusi . . .' he murmured, 'Pronto? . . . Ecco . . . va bene, bene, bene, si si . . . Ciao.' (He had probably underwritten a million dollar deal in those few seconds. The Ponti day was starting well.)

The suit, from the niece of Pope Pius XII, Countess Eleha Rossignani, was brought against Ponti, Richard Burton and Marcello Mastroiani. She claimed their film *Death in Rome* was an unfair picture of the Pope's conduct in World War II. Was Ponti worried about it? 'I am a free man,' he said tersely, 'I care only for the freedom.'

Before the end of 1939, the company Ponti was heading produced half a dozen pictures of which *Piccolo Mondo Antico* was the most important. He had now decided to stay in the business. 'I loved the challenge of it,' he said. 'It is truly creative because it begins from nothing—and sometimes ends in nothing—but it is an exciting conspiracy of talents and I love every moment of it.'

In 1946 he made *To Live in Peace*. He won a Critics' Award for it and established himself as a producer of class. In 1949 he went into partnership with the equally shrewd but more excitable Dino de Laurentis, and together they corralled some of the best brains and talents of the Italian movie industry.

Determined to break into the world markets they hired Federico Fellini to direct an arty epic called *La Strada* which starred Anthony Quinn although it was said that the film's main objective was to create a good role for Fellini's actress wife, Giulietta Masina. The picture won the Oscar for the Best Foreign Film of 1954.

'But in our business though it is good to have awards,' Ponti said, 'you cannot take goodwill for granted. When *Zhivago* opened in New York it was a gala night—torchlights, the mounted police, all the celebrities with their jewels—everything. But when the reviews came out they were not just bad they were insulting. It was then I realized I was in a business where, if you were a success, the others can't stand it. If you have a flop they kill you. They watch from the sides and hope you die the death. It was the first time in my life,' he grinned, 'that I realized the truth of what Ingrid Bergman had said to me many years ago. She had been making a picture with Rossellini. One morning during the filming of the picture she was reading a morning paper. Suddenly she laughed: "Ah good! An actress I know has just opened in a new picture and it's a huge flop. We're all entitled to a bit of good news now and again!" Now it is very interesting,' Ponti laughed. 'This from Ingrid Bergman, one of the nicest, most generous and sympathetic women in the world.'

If Sophia Loren's first test for Carlo Ponti on the day she visited him at his office on the Piazza d'Ara Coeli had been a disaster, ten more which he subsequently made of her were not much better. Film cameramen who were now under the direct supervision of Carlo Ponti moaned that they could not, in effect, fashion a silk purse out of a sow's ear. Their complaint was not that the whole effect of the woman wasn't stunning—merely that they didn't know how in blazes they could capture it. As scripts came in and Ponti suggested Sophia for the lead, so directors took one look, whistled, but shook their heads. Stubbornly, Ponti declared: 'One day she will be one of the greatest actresses in the business.' 'Grazie mille,' they shrugged, 'but not with us.'

Though they had reservations about her talent, and about capturing all her unsymmetrical features on film, they had no complaints about the body. In 1953 producers hunted around for an actress who could swim and fill a bathing suit with some style. Sophia could do both and the result was a daft trifle about a white woman in darkest Africa called *Africa Under the Sea*. It wasn't *Bitter Rice* but it was a beginning. Sophia looked with envy at Silvana Mangano and the now famous Gina Lollobrigida and

challenged Ponti with 'when am I going to be the star you promised I would be?' Ponti's soothing reply, 'Wait five minutes,'
has been the catch-phrase of their whole relationship. 'That,'
Ponti smiled, 'and a lot of love.'

After *Africa Under the Sea* he sweetened her awhile by putting
her in a film version of *Aida*. Her contribution to the Verdi opera
was to crinkle her hair, black-up her face and mime to the sublime
singing of Renata Tebaldi. Fortunately for Sophia, most people
recognized the familiar curves behind the borrowed voice and the
sepia spray-job. She was being talked about. Directors were now
asking to test her. And Ponti was slowly playing Professor
Higgins to her un-smudged Eliza Doolittle, diluting the exotic
make-up, toning down the clothes, persuading her to take her foot
off the sexual accelerator. After a handful of small parts in Italian
films, in one of which (*Two Nights With Cleopatra*) she was virtually bare-breasted, Ponti and his partner Dino de Laurentis, were
confident enough to match her with an internationally known
star, Anthony Quinn. The film was *Attila the Hun*—a piece of
average hokum in which Quinn, as the Barbarian, goes clumping
after the female Honoria, played by Sophia Loren.

Quinn had in fact seen her before they began work on *Attila* and
recalls the occasion with some relish. 'I had come to Rome to start
filming *Cavalleria Rusticana*. (He did not mention it followed the
Oscar he won for *Viva Zapata*.) The studio were casting around
for someone to play the part of the young girl. I remember walking across the lot and seeing this fantastic, statuesque girl. It
wasn't so much the body, which was incredible, but the amazing
walk. The face was beautiful but she seemed to be minus one
tooth, had a gap there, or maybe,' he added discreetly, 'it was the
way the sun was throwing a shadow. Anyway I ran upstairs and
said to Dino (de Laurentis), "Hey, I've just seen the perfect girl
for our movie."

' "Who?" Dino asked.

' "Come to the window and see for yourself."

'Dino looked down and shrugged it off saying she was just a
girl his partner Ponti had under contract.'

Anthony Quinn's account of their second confrontation, this

time on *Attila*, is presented the way he told it to me. He drove from his home at Albano and we talked on the terrace of the hotel Helio Cabalo, Marino, with its bird's-eye view of the Ponti villa. 'I hate to say that I was ever naïve,' he said, 'but I guess I must have been. One day I was going to do this love scene with Sophia when a character comes up and says, "look here, take it easy in that love scene." I said, "why do you want me to take it easy?" And this feller repeats, "Just take it easy. That's all."

'I said, "Come on—what kind of shit is this? What do you mean? I play a love scene, so I play a love scene! Okay?"

'But I notice nobody is saying anything. As it was, it was going to be a terrible scene because I'm eating lamb chops at the time. I'm supposed to be the Hun, the Barbarian, and suddenly when I see this girl, I have to grab her, kiss her and start making love to her with a mouthful of lamb chops. Anyway I'm still getting these warnings to take it easy, so I take an interpreter, and I can imagine it sounded terrible, because what the interpreter says to Sophia, is: "Mr Quinn says somebody has told him he has to take it easy with the love scene, was that your request?"

'Sophia says, "No, I've got nothing to do with it. What specially do you want to do anyway?" Which is much worse. I said, "No, no, I'm just asking if it's not she, then what the hell do they mean take it easy?"

'I then went over to the director and there was a big, big hassle. He took me aside and said, "Listen, she's a friend of the producer," I said, "Fuck you", nobody's going to tell me how to play a love scene with this girl. And I grabbed her and kissed her the way a Barbarian is supposed to kiss, except I've still got this lamb chop in my mouth. And it's a hell of a kiss. But I must say Sophia takes it very sweetly, she knew that what I did was out of defiance and she pulls back, starts to laugh, and says, "You don't have to take it out on me because they told you to take it easy!" and that was that.'

Despite the film's junk content that shrewd showman, Joe Levine, bought it for American distribution. 'I can say without any fear of contradiction,' he said to me beaming chubbily behind his horn-rimmed spectacles, 'that it was one of the worst pictures ever made in the history of the film business. It was so amateurishly done, I believe I could have shot it better myself with a hand camera—and been shot myself for my trouble. I paid eighty thousand dollars for it, took it around the country myself, and it did terrific business.' (At that stage Joe wasn't too familiar with the Italian set up. He thought Carlo Ponti and Dino de Laurentis were one and the same person—Ponti de Laurentis, and he addressed Carlo as such when they met for the first time in a New York elevator.)

Sophia Loren saw nothing in *Attila the Hun* to make her feel anything more than a piece of the scenery. She envied other Italian actresses who worked in bigger pictures, were treated like celebrities and mixed with the American film colony on equal terms. She noticed too that Silvana Mangano, married to Carlo's partner Dino de Laurentis, had become an international star on the soggy foundations of *Bitter Rice* alone. Mangano, however, loathed the business and retired from it as fast as she could. But she was a wife. Sophia Loren had no such security. In 1946 Carlo Ponti had married Giuliana Fiastri, the daughter of an Italian general. They had two children. It should be said that in the barrage of accusations and counter charges, the years of protracted wrangling over the Loren–Ponti affair, this quiet, elegant woman has remained discreetly in the shadows. As Carlo and Sophia saw more and more of each other, Giuliana Fiastri knew that one day, legally or otherwise, she would lose her husband. In the event, it was her willingness to become a French citizen which finally paved the way for Carlo and Sophia to marry. But in the early stages, she merely watched from the side-lines as Ponti plunged into the serious business of turning his impatient protégé into a star.

Italian actresses, due to the Italian movie industry's determination to break into the world markets, were now being featured prominently in the international media. They were given a considerable boost by the then reigning champ, Gina Lollobrigida. 'La Lollo' was queen of them all, her fast but leaden quotes being given almost as much space as the bouncy super-structure from which they were launched. When the young new-comer, Sophia Loren, arrived on the scene, gossip writers and other interested parties concocted some gamey publicity on the 'my bosoms are bigger than your bosoms' theme.

An Italian Film Festival which took place in London in October 1954 was the catalyst for this drawn-out piece of mammary match-making in which the two protagonists played a most unwilling role. I was vaguely involved in the affair myself, remembering it only because it was the first time I met Sophia. To launch the film week, Unitalia, the official organization of the Italian film industry, flew two plane loads of actresses into London. On seeing the first batch I wrote a chauvinistic pot-boiler suggesting that these homely Romans hardly justified the great drum-roll which had preceded them. This irked them all and I have fond memories of a well-stacked beauty named Clelia Matania shaking her fist and snarling at me: 'So you don't think we're beautiful eh? I am just wondering whether your throat is worth cutting.'

The following day, the second contingent flew in, were installed at the Savoy Hotel, and dominated by Gina Lollobrigida and Sophia Loren, were unveiled for the British press. In answer to a question about her bust and hip measurements—old Chinese proverb has it, he who sees a mountain invariably inquires about its height—Sophia replied in metres, the English equivalent being, 'thirty eight inches, thirty seven inches.'

'Is this bigger than Gina's?' the reporter persisted.

'What you ask?' Sophia demanded, her command of English at the time being pretty weak.

'Your bosom,' the oaf continued, miming two half-moons on his chest. 'Is bigger than Lollobrigida's? Y'know, molti grandi?' He was pleased with himself. She understood.

'Si. Is true,' Sophia replied. 'But is not important.' (The same dazed inquirer had a minor Freudian slip as he reeled away from his encounter with the bold-fronted Sophia. 'She's great, aren't they!' he said to a colleague who had taken the pictures.)

Sophia's candid information about her superior bust measure-ment (superior to Gina's but not necessarily a world record) was simply an answer to a question. But by the time the agencies and correspondents had added a few stings of their own, it had acquired sufficient venom to sustain the argument for a year. Place two highly volatile explosives close to each other and you risk what the experts call 'sympathetic detonation'.

The phenomenon applied to Gina and Sophia. They were professional rivals and that was all. They even admired each other. But the press relentlessly bore down on both of them with Gina being quoted, or misquoted, as saying: 'Sophia is a very pretty girl but she cannot threaten me because she is incapable of playing my roles.' To which Sophia is alleged to have responded (but now denies): 'She is good as a peasant but incapable of playing a lady.' It was good bitchy stuff in which *Il Messagero* finally took a hand, offering this advice to the two contenders: 'Never think aloud, it might be dangerous.'

It was all of twenty years ago, but my first view of Sophia is still firmly grafted on the retina. Romilda had artfully swaddled her daughter in a green two-piece outfit of body-hugging wool which must have been painful on the warp and the weft. Sophia had strategically placed herself dead centre in the Savoy suite so that onlookers could view the property on a three hundred and sixty degree circuit.

While her homesick compatriots looked moodily out of the window, or quizzed the Italian waiters hoping to find a relative or a town in common, Sophia held her slim waist between her hands, pulled her shoulders back, and virtually bulldozed her way on to the front pages of the afternoon editions. She smiled, she giggled, looking deep into everyone's eyeballs with an effect so devastating, Italian waiters from the Strand hotel opposite were flocking in carrying the odd ice bucket or other unsolicited items. I had called in an Italian-speaking friend named Frederick to act as interpreter. It took a little while to establish that his intimate conversation with the lady had nothing to do with our questions. He was blithely inviting her to dinner.

Nevertheless in the bar of the Excelsior and on the sun-drenched pavement outside, 'The Feud' was the scintillating topic of the day. (The rest of the country was preoccupied with lesser problems like a Government crisis and unemployment, but the Via Veneto never failed to get its priorities right.) At the end of it all, Gina complained: 'This comparison of anatomies between Sophia and me makes me sick.' To which Sophia replied pleasantly: 'I have been falsely reported as having criticized the acting abilities of Gina. I am now ready to meet her to clear up any misunderstandings. She can name the date and the time.'

The offer was declined, no doubt for the cautious reason that one does not dignify the opposition by standing, profile on, alongside it. There was also the nagging thought that on those terms Miss Lollobrigida, as Mr Sinatra might say, had two chances—slim and none.

Meanwhile Sophia's publicity-rating, already high, soared as a result of this unsolicited boost. But Carlo Ponti took a stern view of it all. His 'discovery' was playing it for laughs, straight out of burlesque. Her language was still kerbside Naples. She had shrugged off small-town Pozzuoli and was having a ball. If the critics hadn't yet noticed her, the magazines repaired the omission. She cornered the cheesecake market by the acre, that huge, admirable bosom as pneumatic as a Michelin advert, and just as eye-boggling. If the criteria of the movie business was size, shape, weight and a seething flair for pushing it all around, Sophia Loren, under the tutelage of Romilda, was the best there was.

But Ponti hadn't invested his time, money and his growing affections just to create a Jayne Mansfield Italian Style. In his book, this beautiful, intuitively intelligent creature had more to offer than the biggest pair of boobs at Cinecitta. He took her aside, talked to her and she listened. 'Don't push it, let the world find it,' was roughly his advice. In this he had the edge on Professor Higgins. His 'pupil' learned fast, was always ahead of the lesson. The quality was there. Dormant. Ponti, the lawyer turned film producer, addressed himself to the subtle and, as it turned out, highly enjoyable, task of breathing it into life.

In his office, looking with evident pleasure at a portrait of Sophia, he gave this account of his first impression of her: 'I saw in her all the best that is Italian. She has the Neapolitan gaiety and artistic feeling. But also there is a vitality, sensitivity and sense of rhythm that no acting school can teach. She is not an actress, she is an artist.'

At his insistence she went easy on the pasta, began acquiring the finesse which distinguished a Sophia Loren from a Sofia Lazarro. And when he decided she was ready he presented her to the Italian director, Vittorio de Sica, as though putting a chunk of virgin marble in the hands of Michelangelo.

So this tawny-skinned Trilby acquired two Svengalis for the price of one. From that powerful alliance came the first significant picture of her career. It was *The Gold of Naples* directed by Vittorio de Sica, a marriage between his unerring flair for handling raw talent and her infallible instinct for getting into the intestines of a character. It was to lead to her first American picture, that brave, hilarious disaster *The Pride and the Passion*. And Sinatra. And Hollywood.

Everything looked good for the realization of her limited objectives—to become rich, famous and acquire a kind of middle-class respectability, fair aspirations for a girl born poor and illegitimate. If there was a danger of her personality becoming embalmed in Givenchy fossilized by Cartiers, it was too far ahead to worry about. Professionally, she was destined, or doomed—depending upon how you evaluate the package—for success, Hollywood-style. Emotionally, there wasn't quite the same equilibrium. The strands of her relationship to Ponti were becoming tautly interwoven. The private preoccupation was about to explode into the Public Affair.

5

'You'll Get Yours'

The film director who flunked Sophia's film test for Carlo Ponti
was surprised to hear that Vittorio de Sica had signed her for
The Gold of Naples without bothering to try her out in front of
the cameras. What had de Sica seen that he hadn't? Wasn't one
camera's eye view of an actress the same as any other's? Not to
de Sica. Sophia was brought down on to the half-lit set at the
studio to meet him. She was then barely twenty years old. From
the start the electricity between them sang like overhead wires in a
high breeze. De Sica had in fact seen her around the studios a
couple of years earlier. But apart from marvelling with some
amusement at the well-displayed equipment, he merely wished her
every good fortune for the future, and went musing on his way.

This time, they exchanged a few pleasantries about such shared
enthusiasms as Naples, pasta, poker and the movie business. He
had seen enough. He spoke to Ponti: 'Magnificent. There's no
other woman to put in the part.'

Well what had he seen? He replied to that question by turning
his hands palm upward, declaring simply, 'A revelation. She was
created differently, behaved differently, affected me differently
from any other woman I have known. I looked at that face, those
unbelievable eyes and saw it all as a miracle.' But having delivered
that hosanna he was clearly bothered by the effect of his words.
His tone changed from lilting guitars to the diplomatic bag. 'I
would like my judgment of Sophia,' he said cagily, 'to be taken
not as of a man who is in love with her, but from the paternal
point of view. I am fond of her. She is fond of me. I am a very good
friend. But I repeat, I love her as a father.'

'Understood,' I said, 'please continue.'

'The outstanding quality was her impulsiveness. Neapolitans are extroverts. All her gestures and statements were always outgoing. Nothing is held inside. No internal reflection. I don't say this only of Sophia, all we Neapolitans are the same. We improvise. We speak first, think later. The women are not particularly elegant. In fact they generally have bad taste in clothes. They go by instinct. With Sophia, in her private life, in her love, in her work and in her passions, she is always instinctive, never calculating. When she came to me,' he said, 'I already knew about her early life and what it meant, because I had come from the same environment. And I knew about her love for Ponti. But she wasn't able to express it then. He was married with two children. It was an impossible love for her, and so she waited and worked. With me from the very beginning the rapport was perfect. Perhaps,' he smiled, 'I am not really a director, just a teacher of elocution. I know how to make people say their lines. And Sophia is clever. She understands this so well with her intuition. So, nothing needs to be explained in words. She gives herself completely into my hands, like clay. I mould her. She has trust, blind faith. And when the material is as willing as that, I respond. And so I can say that Sophia gives me a joy which few actresses have ever done. I make an expression on my face and she translates it immediately. With Silvana Mangano and Gina Lollobrigida, I also had success. But Mangano was the complete introvert. Everything locked inside. Gina Lollobrigida was more like a little doll, beautiful, but superficial, without any internal or external force.'

Undoubtedly, de Sica's rhapsodies on his first impressions of Sophia had acquired an afterglow of hindsight. More likely he regarded this bouncing, Botticelli-style female as ideal for the role of the flighty Neapolitan shopkeeper in the film.

But though the picture had great moments of fun and de Sica's special flair for irony (as seen in *Miracle in Milan*) it did not match those earlier masterpieces *Umberto D* and *Bicycle Thieves*. By the time it was cut and dubbed in English it had lost all the flavour which de Sica had so painstakingly stirred into it. It was a hit in Italy, not so abroad. But everybody remembered the girl. Ponti's girl. It slowly dawned on producers that there was more to this creature than merely a leggy front-cover or a brown-bosomed centre-fold. She could act. She had a real comedy-sense. And her sexual deployment had a delicious self-mocking quality to it. (It still has. When disturbed males are driven to declaring, 'You're so terrific, it's unbearable,' the lady smiles gravely and sighs, 'I know.')

It's just a trick of course, designed to hide a gigantic nervousness which, when Ponti is not around, makes her even today as vulnerable as a range animal deserted by the herd. She knew that *Gold of Naples* under de Sica's direction could take her out of the two-bit movies into the international scene. She went on the set shaking with terror. And de Sica knew it. He placed both his hands over hers. 'Listen, there's nothing to worry about. Don't act. I show you.' He did not direct her. He wooed a performance from her. That seductive technique was to continue for seven more pictures—a flawless fusion of talents.

Ponti was delighted with Sophia's performance, but she still couldn't equal the international level of his partner's wife, Sylvana Mangano, now Mrs de Laurentis. On the basis that anything Sylvana could do, Sophia could do sexier, Ponti leapt at the chance of making *Woman of the River*. This steamy tale of primitive passions involving sex and smuggling would enable Sophia to repeat Mangano's sensational formula in *Bitter Rice* putting on a tight, wet shirt and hot pants which shrunk provocatively in the drying sun. The film was given world distribution. Loren, hitherto no more than a sexy cover-girl, was now short-listed for the major league. Ponti who had parried her constant demands for an international picture with 'wait five minutes' was finding it less easy to placate her. She was not merely a restless thoroughbred eager to be tried out in a classic race. She was also totally in love with him. She was now saying openly: 'Men never approach me simply for friendship. Everybody wants to be my lover. Well I am engaged. I cannot tell you his name because he is a married man, eighteen years older than I am. I hope one day we will be married. I am created for motherhood. I have made up my mind I must have my first child by the time I am twenty-three.'

Romilda knew what was happening and was perturbed by it. Ponti saw the apparent hopelessness of it, but he was no longer the disinterested producer. On the last day's shooting of *Woman of the River* he walked on to the set, took Sophia aside and handed her a package. She opened it and found a ring. They exchanged a momentary glance, then Ponti turned and left. 'It was a marvellous yet frightening moment,' Sophia recalled. 'It was the first time I sensed I meant more to him than just an actress under contract. Every moment of my day, all my thoughts and feelings were concentrated on him. I knew he was married with two children. Yet at that age you don't try and rationalize passion. I loved him deeply, and he had given me a ring. He hadn't kissed me. He didn't say "I love you, and want to marry you." Nothing. But it was a ring just the same. I went back into my dressing room and wept.'

Success, Italian style, was now thrusting Sophia into all the raddling, gimmicky activities which shove movie stars into the public eye. With the Loren–Lollobrigida feud still good copy, both parties lost no opportunity in keeping it on the boil. The advantage swung dramatically in Sophia's favour when on an April afternoon in 1956, the word got around that she had called to buy a brassière in a shop in down-town Rome. The huge crowd which assembled outside the plate-glass windows looked like a scene from a de Sica comedy with maybe Marcello Mastroiani playing a bra-salesman. Tourists, pilgrims and a couple of passing priests hovered around as a police riot squad and the Rome fire department sirened into the scene, having been alerted by the nervous proprietor. When Sophia emerged from the fitting booth she was ashen right down to her thirty-eight inch cups. The crowd threatened to crash into the shop. 'Loren, Loren, Loren. . . .' they chanted. 'Is a murder?' a latecomer inquired. 'No, is a brassière,' was the cheerful reply.

The police and firemen cleared a passage for Sophia to her car. Unlike the James Bond cocktail, she was both shaken and stirred. It was a taste of honey, and she loved it. More and more she saw her name in print and she adored that too. When a fashion designer bearing the portentous title, Count Lelio Galateri sued her, claiming she broke an undertaking to publicize his dresses, she dismissed it all with throne-room disdain. She became even more withering when the said merchant raged, 'The girl could not even walk or talk properly when I first met her.' He went on to claim that he coached her Pygmalion-style, giving her the sheen and elegance she would otherwise never have possessed. In return (the dresses were on the house) she was, he said, to have put his name in the credit titles of her films. His complaint finally filtered to nothing, but like the riot outside the bra shop, it concentrated the public's mind most wonderfully on the significant area of the Loren architecture.

The demands for her to make personal appearances, open fêtes, pick lottery tickets, judge contests, were flooding in. She said 'yes' to almost everything. They were the essential booster rockets to the global lift-off to the stars. The theme was an intensely sensual body-worship—hers—and she was no less enthusiastic about it than the rest of the appreciative onlookers.

In her large, splendidly arranged salon at the villa, a brief glance around the walls is a bizarre experience. All the paintings or drawings are of women. Nude women. Voluptuous women. Loren-like women. Many of them are by the Belgian surrealist, Magritte. Others by Matisse and Modigliani. Not far away are the concealed loudspeakers on which she hears the tapes, transplanted from the originals for her, by Peter Sellers. She will lie outstretched on a couch, listening to some cool Bacharach, securely cocooned by those familiar and reassuring contours around the walls. An anatomical Nirvana for an audience of one.

Her eagerness to play the sought-after movie queen led her to accept—then decline an invitation to appear at a charity ball in Brussels. 'I don't like flying, it frightens me,' her mother said. In those days, Sophia went nowhere without Romilda. 'Okay, we won't go,' she said. A young actress, Marcella Mariani, who had won the 'Miss Italy' title two years earlier, went in her place. The plane crashed on its return flight to Rome. All the passengers were killed.

The effect of Sophia's narrow escape did not last long. A

month later she entered for the 'Motor Rally of the Stars' a fancy publicity jaunt which ran from Rome to San Remo. At the end of the first stage of the trip her silver grey Mercedes was mobbed by the crowds. The car was pushed off the road, the windscreen shattered. Her wrist was cut by the broken glass. A predatory fan bit her bare shoulder. Trembling but smiling weakly she was helped out of the car by police. If she had been given to keeping a diary, the incident might have appeared in it as 'was mobbed, cut and bitten—a good day'. In the Mercedes as her co-driver in the rally, was a swarthily handsome Sicilian-born writer, named Basilio Franchina. Besides Ponti and de Sica, this volatile character has been one of the most potent influences in Sophia's life. But always behind the scenes, operating in the shadows, as elusive and uncommunicative as a secret agent. Basilio's role in her life has never been precisely defined. When he has been on film location with her he has, to his Sicilian fury, been described as her 'bodyguard' installed by Ponti to keep a watchful eye on the Adored One. Sometimes he has been listed officially among the screen credits. As a writer, intellectual and talented film-maker his services have frequently been called upon by Ponti. But often, like Sophia's secretary, Ines Bruscia, he is simply *there*, encouraging, arguing, protecting. There can be no doubt that any actor who dared to go beyond Sophia's clearly marked out defence lines would have this temperamental aide to deal with. Basilio now hedges on the point but Peter Sellers candidly admits: 'I was never in love as deeply with any woman the way I was with Sophia. One day Basilio came to me and said: "when the husband he finds out about this there will be trouble." '

Like all the friends and colleagues inside Ponti's royal circle, Basilio takes the self-denying ordinance of silence when strangers' questions become too probing. But then his loyalty goes deeper than most. He has always loved Sophia. His respect and admiration for her is just as passionate. When both have their tempers at furnace level, his smelted in Palermo, hers near the volcano of Solfatara, onlookers take to the catacombs with their fingers in their ears. Basilio is not the plaything of a rich, self indulgent movie star. He has been around to see Sophia tear her way through the jungle of the starlet days to the exotic landscape of a superstar. He has a stake in the triumph. He may live in Switzerland, work in Cannes. But if Sophia needed him, it would take more than a troublesome film script to keep him from leaping into his sports car and come screeching to a halt, say a thousand miles later, at the door of the Ponti villa.

During the last two years of World War II, Basilio hid in the mountains, living with two escapees from a prison camp, an Englishman and an American. When Italy's part in the war collapsed, he became active in politics, was the first National Secretary of the Film Union. At the time, Italy was still split in two, with the Germans and Fascists occupying the north. Like Ponti, he developed a loathing for the régime, identified himself with left wing groups. At the end of the war when Sophia came to Rome, Basilio was already engaged on films. 'The legend has been created that I was always hired as her bodyguard,' he said. 'This is all bullshit. Really bullshit. If I don't feel something inside of me I don't do it. It's true that I like her very much and I try to protect her. Maybe I love her too. Many people do.'

And so, either as a writer, associate director, friend, or what you will, Basilio Franchina has glided soft-footed through several of Sophia's films. Officially, no bodyguard he. Just the unpaid dragon with his eye on the princess in the castle.

It was Basilio, playing Pickering to Ponti's Professor Higgins, who began the process of converting Sophia from a pizza-munching sex-bomb to the more svelte-like creature demanded by the international market. After *Woman of the River* Sophia was loaned out for a couple of Italian pictures, but she was restless for better things.

On one of his trips to America, Ponti wired Sophia: 'There could be a wonderful future for you if you learn English.' She wired back: 'Okay, I learn.'

She hired an Irish teacher, Sarah Spain, who happened to be living in Rome. It was not the action of a dilettante filling in time between photo sessions and cocktails at the Excelsior. Sarah Spain went to Sophia's home on the Piazza Colonna, bullied her dizzy with grammar and pronunciation. For booster shots she pursued Sophia to the film studios and battered her further between takes. 'She was not a teacher, she was a persecutor,' Sophia laughed, 'but I am grateful to her.' (Before there is some well-modulated howl in erudite quarters, it is conceded that there were other teachers involved in Sophia's elocutionary achievements.)

When Ponti returned from America he was delighted at Sophia's quick progress.

'You will have to start reading serious things,' he said, tacitly implying that the mind ought to keep pace with the body.

'Okay, so I read.'

Carlo and Basilio consulted the literary lists and marked her card. At the end of a day's shooting at the studio, Sophia scrubbed the make-up off and settled down to read. She launched herself into Prosper Mérimée's *Carmen* and continued with Stendahl, Balzac, Thomas Mann, Defoe and Shaw. She read them in Italian, and continued her basic English when some of the heavier stuff exhausted her.

'Hello, how are you? Good morning. I wish to cross the road. I am ill, fetch a doctor. Sing a Song of Sixpence' and similar phrases were thrown at Romilda and Maria whenever they were in earshot. Sophia read the overseas edition of the London *Times* aloud to her mother who sat woodenly, and uncomprehendingly listening to reports of Chinese infiltration into Central Africa, pulping operations in Newfoundland and other topics not absolutely vital to her Neapolitan soul.

Today, Sophia has a remarkable command of the language with an incisive appreciation of its several nuances. She is hilarious at Cockney slang, having learned the basics from Peter Sellers over candlelit chicken almond at Fu Tong's in Kensington, London. Occasionally, particularly when her nerve falters, the words become thickly accented in Italian. David Frost had this effect on her during a programme he did with her which was clearly too adoring even by his over-reverential standards. He invited her to recite Hamlet's speech to the players which she did well enough, with just a hint of verbal Parmesan like 'treepingly on the tongue' and 'beget a tamperance that may geeve it smoothness'. The subject turned to the anatomical side of speech projection and

Frost, now floundering in a cream-topped ocean of 'terrifics' and 'wonderfuls' continued gleefully: 'I was fascinated when you said yesterday that Italians, English and Americans all speak from a different place . . .'

'Not from a different place,' Sophia said brightly. 'They all speak with the mouth, don't they?'

It ended Shakespeare for the evening.

Sophia's verbal agility at being able to proclaim, unaided, 'Good evening, hello, sit down, don't mention it,' hardly made her an instant candidate for an English-speaking movie. But the day it was announced that United Artists were looking for a girl to play opposite Cary Grant and Frank Sinatra in *The Pride and the Passion* she immediately called Ponti and asked, 'Why not me?' For once Ponti did not fob her off with 'wait five minutes'. He had already suggested her name to Stanley Kramer the distinguished Hollywood film-maker who was to direct the picture. Based on C. S. Forester's novel *The Gun* the original story had no heroine as played by Sophia, in it, but on seeing the script, the novelist said with some finesse: 'If the changes are intelligent and sensitive as they are in this case, then the author should be grateful, and I am.'

Two hurdles had to be jumped before Sophia could realize that ecstatic dream of rising actresses, a co-starring role opposite two legendary figures of Hollywood movies. United Artists didn't want her. Nor did Cary Grant. From the studio's cautious standpoint the idea was ridiculous, bordering on the insane. This was going to be a multi-million dollar epic. How the hell could they gamble on an Italian Amazon who would have to ape the English words and hope for the best? Better to get someone like Ava Gardner, who knew Spain, who could guarantee a sizeable profit at the box office, and whose estranged marriage to Sinatra offered intriguing publicity spin-offs.

Ava Gardner was not averse to the idea of making a film with Sinatra despite the problems. 'Why not? I like him very much,' she said, 'and he's a fine actor.' But Metro-Goldwyn-Mayer, with whom she had a three year contract had her earmarked for *The*

Little Hut and so Kramer, now installed at the Hilton Hotel in Madrid was still without his star. But that was to turn out the least of his problems. He knew what Sinatra could be like, having directed him in *Not As A Stranger*. He also knew what Sinatra, despite the impulsive behaviour and unpredictable temperament, could offer to a picture. In publicity alone he was worth upwards of a million dollars. It would not be with his eager assistance, of course. Before Sinatra arrived in Madrid a phone call to Kramer from the States warned that if so much as one newspaperman showed up at the airport he would take the next plane back. This was typical of Sinatra, consistent with his attitude to the press generally. (My last telegram from him, complaining about a mildly critical piece, declared: 'I considered you . . . to be one of the fairest journalists I have ever met, which from my experience is saying a great deal. As of this morning you blew it. Sinatra.')

So Kramer saw what he was in for. Or thought he saw.

Sophia was unaware of the front-office politics. She would cross those egos when she came to them. Carlo had told her there was a possibility that she might be starring with her two idols, Grant and Sinatra, and the resourceful beauty intensified her assault on the English tongue. Kramer had seen Sophia in a couple of Italian films and like most other Hollywood directors, he could recognize the physical bonuses but doubted the presence of any real or potential talent. 'She had this great physical thrust,' he said, 'but nobody suspected, thought or dreamed seriously that she could take on a major acting role. But I needed someone to play this Spanish girl who wouldn't be overwhelmed by Grant and Sinatra.'

Kramer took a plane to Rome, invited Sophia to lunch.

'Do you speak English?'

'A leetle. Sometimes good, sometimes bad. Yesterday was Thursday, tomorrow is Saturday. Pass the salt, I geeve you pepper. What else you want to know?'

Kramer was amused, but hardly listening. He was marvelling, as most men do, at those arresting eyes, the mocking innocence, the whole bag of tricks. He convinced himself it wouldn't matter a damn if her only language was Serbo-Croat. The eyes and the body would have to say what the tongue could not.

'Will you trust me?' he asked her.

'Completely,' Sophia said.

'In that case,' Kramer said, 'we'll overcome the language problem this way. You just repeat the words the way I want them, and to hell with whether you understand them or not.'

That was half the problem solved. Back at his hotel, Kramer decided on his strategy with the studio. 'My case was very simple,' he said, 'it was that with a beauty as stunning as this, the words could kind of take care of themselves.' He sold Sophia to United Artists.

But when the studio chiefs told Cary Grant that his co-star was to be a virtually unknown Italian actress named Sophia Loren, he recoiled with the familiar rolling eyeballs and high-pitched indignation. He got her name mixed up with Gina Lollobrigida's calling her Sophia Brigida, Sophia Lollo and similar permutations. 'My God!' he said to Kramer, 'you want me to play with this Sophia somebody, a CHEESECAKE THING!? Well I can't. I won't.' He called his agent, M.C.A., and repeated his objection, stating flatly, 'Kramer wants this girl in the picture. I want out.' His agent said: 'Wait a minute, Cary, you haven't met her. She's gonna be the biggest star in the world.'

'Are you kidding?' Cary asked.

'No we mean it. She's wonderful. She looks fantastic. Don't take any notice of the publicity stuff. Just meet her that's all.'

The meeting between this English-born charmer and Sophia then, tacitly, Ponti property, took place at a party in Madrid, just before she was signed for the picture. Grant was an hour late in turning up and Sophia, as precise as a jewelled movement, was angry. But when he ambled in, sleek, dimpled and suave, mumbling apologies saying, 'Ah yes, Miss Lorbrigida . . . er . . . Brigloren . . . I can't remember Italian names,' Sophia adored it. And him.

Grant left the party with a galloping pulse beat. He went to Kramer. 'My God, Stanley, you were right. I can't understand my prejudices. This girl is magnificent. What is the matter with me!'

The answer was that Mr Cary Grant had looked into those

large green-flecked eyes of Sophia's and had gone visibly weak in the knees. He filled her room every day with fresh roses. Whenever they were free he would sweep her off to mountain top restaurants for dinner. He became less attentive of course when Carlo Ponti flew in for a few days at a time, when Basilio Franchina was in close orbit, or when Romilda and Maria joined Sophia on the picture.

'I knew he loved me,' Sophia said, 'though he never said so outright, that isn't his way.' She was sure, had she chosen to, that they would have married. But Cary had to compete with more than merely her devotion and deep affection for Carlo. It was the immense feeling of security Ponti gave her. Grant, whose own psychological turmoil had made it difficult for him to sustain a happy marriage, didn't offer the same confidence. But Sophia's unspoken rejection of him did not diminish his hopes which persisted with increasing ardour, years later rocking *Houseboat* to the embarrassment of all aboard.

But that was to be another director's problem. Kramer had a harder nut to crack.

The Hollywood version of *The Gun* centred on a huge cannon, dragged across Spain by a ragged army of partisans, aiming to blast Napoleon's soldiers out of the fortress of Avila. Sinatra, black-fringed with burnt features, led the guerrillas. He conflicted with Cary Grant, a captain of the British Navy who feared that the gun might fall into the hands of the French bombardiers. Their animosity is brought to a torrid head of steam by both parties falling for Sophia, whose swirling flamenco under the blazing sun, adds further to Cary's private dilemma.

It was a tough location employing nearly ten thousand extras, 1,500 animals and a squadron of helicopters for the costly air shots. Kramer took his production team to the countryside around Avila, had them uproot telegraph poles, demolish the odd house which might have spoiled the landscape shots. He sweated over the script, concealing an uneasy feeling that he was being irresistibly edged over into a ravine.

When he had directed Sinatra before, in *Not As A Stranger*, the tale had been put around that he would never have Sinatra in one of his films again, even if he were forced to go begging in the street with a tin cup. Kramer denied it. But halfway through *The Pride and the Passion* he was tempted to review that retraction. He talks about it now with the wry humour of a man who has been nudged safely out of the path of a falling chimney stack. 'The film was a disaster, though oddly enough Frank Sinatra quite liked it,' he said. He pressed a switch in his private office in Hollywood, instructing his secretary not to disturb us for a year or two and went on: 'Cary Grant never did well in costume drama. He was really a drawing-room character. But with one of my more blatant bursts of creative misjudgment, I cast him in a role and it was not for him. You know, in the tight military pants, the frilled shirt of the British officer tradition. To compound the problem, Frank Sinatra's rather stormy career was taking one of its profound dips. I had thought: "I shall personally return him to star stature." He personally walked out of the film in the middle of Spain with weeks of work still to shoot.' (The full story of Sinatra's abrupt departure from the production might benefit from Frank's own interpretation of it. On this, as on most other matters, the actor prefers to keep his own counsel.)

'There was Sophia, caught between that and Cary Grant, who was deluging her with flowers and taking her to little hilltop cafés. When an actress has had a very rough, tough beginning, she either turns out to be terribly bitchy in a retributive sense, or as joyous as a touch of spring. We had the joyful version with Sophia. But it wasn't easy for her.'

At the start of shooting, out on the Spanish prairie, Sinatra was the prankster, the joker. He was reasonably happy. Ava Gardner visited him occasionally. Pastrami and dill pickles were flown from the Stage Delicatessen in New York to give him salivary contentment. And there was Sophia, big, bosomy and eager, great raw material for Frank, who took over from the late Humphrey Bogart as the genial needler.

'He played the American joke,' Kramer said, 'saying all the time to Sophia, "All right honey, you'll get yours."'

'For a long time, Sophia, unaware of the implied promise—or

threat, would ask: "What means that? What means, 'you'll get yours'?"

'I told her it means, "He'll get you, Sophia. He'll get you."

'Well even then, with her poor English, Sophia showed she had a pretty good sense of humour. One night, a very rainy night, we served supper in the tents. The wine was being poured —I didn't want it but the Spaniards wouldn't work without it— and there was Sophia at one end of the table, Sinatra at the other. Frank was in a baiting mood. He rose on to the table, looked down on Sophia and he said, "Hey, Sophia, you'll get yours," but she was ready for him this time. She got up on a chair and said: "Not from you, you guinea son-of-a-bitch!"' '

This coarsened freemasonry between two volatile characters of the same national bloodstream only temporarily relieved Sinatra's yearning to return to the more familiar pastures of Vegas and Palm Springs. 'He was away from his cronies, away from the main stream,' Kramer said. 'He was in the middle of nowhere for weeks and weeks and weeks.' Kramer understood the pressure he was under, but there was a multi-million dollar movie to complete. He spoke to Sinatra in a Madrid hotel room. 'You know, Frank,' he said, 'it's different if you are dealing with—in your own language—a fink, or somebody who doesn't have the integrity or is basically just not a nice guy or a guy not worth his salt in his work. But in every case I have filled the bill right up to the end with you.'

Sinatra replied with some anguish, 'Don't you understand? Do you want me to throw myself out of the window?'

It was the familiar vulnerability syndrome of the superstar. Marooned out there in the searing scrubland with the flies, the interminable paellas, no flip-talk from close buddies, it was torture to Sinatra and he ached to get home. Cary Grant, borrowing a little additional gallantry from the character he was playing, took the Sinatra problem like an officer and a gentleman. But the atmosphere on the location became tense and miserable. Some actresses caught in a verbal crossfire they couldn't comprehend might have been thrown disastrously off balance. But Sophia had a movie to make. She was scared and was struggling with the words.

In the walled city of Avila where the climactic scene of the film occurs, Sophia went through the scenes, parroting the words under Kramer's direction, at night unburdening her soul to him in the bar. Kramer could see her dilemma. She was desperate to give a good performance and needed the help of her two co-stars to achieve it.

'All I want to do is prove I can act,' she said to Kramer. 'It is terribly important to me. But I need an atmosphere of tranquillity—yes, even love. I build bridges. I hate trouble.'

But trouble there was. Ponti flew in occasionally to find everybody feeding off everybody else's nerves. He also heard rumours of Cary Grant's persistent wooing. 'Leave it to me, I can handle it,' Sophia said to him. Ponti hardly needed the reassurance. Romilda Villani's daughter, case-hardened on the streets of Naples could easily cope with Cary Grant's middle-aged version of calf love. Anyway Basilio was there performing the extra-curricular function of a friendly observer. Besides, the situation had sufficient piquancy to remove some of the sourness caused by Sinatra's brooding restlessness to finish the picture as fast as was feasible and get the hell out of the place.

If Kramer and his assistants found Frank hard to manage at the time, Sophia, whatever her private feelings, managed to take the edge off Sinatra's misery. On the rare occasions when she found him alone, he was still woefully missing Ava Gardner, playing suitable heartache music to himself, drawn from Puccini, Verdi and Mascagni. But he brightened when Sophia entered the room, switching the sound track to Tony Bennett and Ella Fitzgerald. 'I knew he was terribly unhappy, what with the terrible heat, the script, and because of Ava Gardner,' Sophia said. 'But he taught me a lot about films and music.' When I asked her about Sinatra's taunting, 'You'll get yours!' she replied. 'He's a smart man. He knows when he can talk and when he can do.' Sinatra's departure was abrupt. 'He had nothing against the film,' Kramer said. 'But he'd had enough of the windmill country. He just said, "You've got lawyers and so-forth," and left.'

Kramer returned to Hollywood to finish the picture. He did a deal with Sinatra and his lawyers, he said, with Frank working on all the close-ups against a background of potted plants and stuff to represent the Spanish locale. But Kramer knew the picture was doomed. The critics generally treated the film with derision. 'There was not a shred of integrity left to the story. I thank God Sophia was there. She was like a breath of fresh air. If she had problems nobody knew about it. She was prepared to work until she dropped.'

Kramer always throws a big party at the end of a production. He did so on *The Pride and the Passion*—a costly shindig, part wake, part exorcism. But when they looked around for Sophia they discovered she had quietly left for Rome. She had achieved what she wanted, a major Hollywood film in which she acted in English opposite two of the most famous names in the business. Now there was a more pressing personal matter. Was Carlo Ponti going to marry her or wasn't he?

6

Mecca

The fiasco of *The Pride and the Passion* might have persuaded Sophia that it was better to be a success in Italy than to be internationally known in an English-speaking flop. But there it was, her name alongside Cary Grant's and Sinatra's. Anyway, if the critics were unanimous in their hostility to the picture, all agreed she was better-looking than the Gun—one of them was convinced that she and the cannon stole the picture.

Sophia returned to her penthouse in Rome to find a sack of fan mail, requests to do cover stories from *Vogue* and *Time Magazine* and more bouquets from the persistent Mr Grant. If Cary had known that Carlo and his wife Giuliana Fiastri had already called it a day and were now discussing an annulment, he might have gone a little easier on the wooing. But he was in deep. He thought he had a chance. Back home in Beverly Hills, in between the morning press-ups and the nightly gulps at the Pacific air, he slotted such verbal posies as, 'She looks so sensuous that most men would long to tear the clothes off her on sight, but . . . (there was a bashful slamming-on of the brakes) . . . no one would dare to contemplate even laying a finger on her sleeve because of the natural dignity with which she holds herself.'

Ines, Sophia's secretary, brought these American clippings in with the morning coffee, and their giggles were joined with those of Romilda and Maria who also had a percentage of the general ecstasy. Sophia Loren was now playing the superstar role with relish. She examined herself in a full-length mirror and decided to refine the whole package. She removed some of the slave-girl paint from around the eyes, softened the shape of her lips so that they no longer appeared to have been moulded around the top of a Coca-Cola bottle, and cut down on the pasta and mozzarella until it hurt. She was still voluptuous but manageable. She began buttoning up where before all was spilling out.

She had earned 25,000 dollars for the Kramer picture and when Romilda, Maria and the family back home in Pozzuoli had received their share of the cake, Sophia began to spend, star-style. Shoes were ordered from Ferragamo, one of Italy's top cobblers, a dozen pairs at a time. He came to fit them in person. Sophia's experience at the bra-shop with half of Rome trying to peep inside the cups, made public shopping a hazard. It was a minor extravagance by a major film property. She began going to the top Italian couturiers. That paddyfields look was buried under a mountain of sleek poses in glossy magazines. She was no longer to be caught off guard, hair down, slip showing. From now on she would be presented as a smooth, plucked and oven-ready chick. Ponti was delighted. He was proud to be seen with her, and if she happened to be a head taller than he, their eager appetite for each other redressed the balance. He was, despite the Spanish disaster, totally dedicated to making his amorous protégé into the biggest star in the world. He was as industrious as Sophia was restless. One afternoon he phoned to say: 'I've got another American picture for you. A co-starring part with Alan Ladd.'

This was bizarre casting even for Hollywood. The film was *Boy on a Dolphin* in which she played a Greek peasant, diving alongside Ladd for sunken archaeological treasures. Two more contrasting types were never imprisoned in the same dreary production. But Sophia decided, with Sinatra and Cary Grant notched on her career, a millionaire producer as her lover and hopefully all set to be her husband, that it was all part of the game. She was as usual, her flamboyant outgoing self. Ladd, on the other hand, couldn't get the measure of this Italian broad who came on so strong and voluptuously. He told a crony on the island of Hydra, 'It's like being bombed by water-melons.' That was the least of his problems. When the director, Jean Negulesco mounted the first two-shot of them on the beach, he turned to his assistant and murmured, 'Do you see what I see?' On level ground Sophia was inches taller than the slim, fair-haired hero of *Shane*—she clearly towered over the then biggest box-office draw in America.

'I'll tell you what we're going to have to do,' Negulesco said to them pleasantly, 'When you're both together we'll dig a hole for Sophia to stand in which should bring you eye to eye and lip to lip.'

It was a by no means unusual production trick. But out on Hydra with the Greek islanders grinning behind the cameras, to go into a love scene with your co-star being lowered into a ditch, soured Ladd to his intestines. 'Shit that,' he muttered to his friends in the bar at night. 'Why did I have to put myself opposite a frigging giraffe?'

But Negulesco had no complaints. Bewitched by this large accommodating creature, he filled the time between shooting and getting holes dug, painting scores of portraits of her. It was clearly another case of face-and-figure worship by a film-maker unaccustomed to sun-bronzed sexuality on so overpowering a a scale. He imported canvases, oils and brushes from the mainland by the crate-load. He could hardly wait to say, 'Print it,' so that he could get back to his easel and the mutual appreciation of artist and model. He told her she had marvellous eyes and a fantastic figure, and Sophia gracefully conceded the point. Inevitably rumours blew up suggesting that Sophia was responding to Negulesco with more ardour than is customary for an actress who just happened to be doubling up on portrait-sitting. They were bitchy and untrue. Long afterwards, when the film opened to tepid notices, Negulesco nailed them further by saying: 'She (Sophia) would be a hellish girl to fall in love with. There's too much of her. And she never stops loving herself. Always at the mirror.'

When Sophia read the report she broke into tears. For all the poise and apparent composure, adverse criticism and personal stabs invariably strike a nerve.

Halfway through the production it became obvious to the more discerning observers that the Ladd–Loren chemistry was about as volatile as blancmange. The main contenders kept to their own camps just pawing the ground waiting for the whole agony to end. Away from Carlo, and still struggling with her English, Sophia played poker with Ines, made passionate phone calls to Ponti begging him to fly in. He did so on 27 September, 1956. Sophia was waiting at Athens airport. It was a memorable encounter for both of them, though for different reasons.

When Carlo, balding and beaming walked through the barrier, Sophia leapt at him as though he'd returned from a long stint in a prison camp. They clung to each other in a reunion kiss that appeared to continue all the way through customs, immigration, baggage compound and out into the afternoon sunlight. Both were oblivious to the audience of Carlo's fellow travellers and the hordes of cameramen who had hoped for some fun but hadn't bargained on a field day. Only when one of them began shouting, 'Encora, encora!' did it occur to Ponti that he had quite a situation on his hands. He turned fiercely on the photographers, angry at the intrusion.

Until that moment, his relationship with Sophia had been kept gracefully under wraps, largely out of respect for Mrs Ponti and the two children, Guendolina and Alex. Unofficially, at least, the marriage was at an end. But nothing had been resolved. Ponti was now going through the motions of seeking an annulment of the marriage, but he knew, as did his wife, that the application was mounted on quicksand. His lawyers argued on his behalf that he did not conscientiously believe in the sacrament of marriage at the time of the ceremony. The declaration carried little force and the annulment was denied. But the denial failed to diminish Ponti and Sophia's love—and need—for each other. 'I want to marry you,' she told him, 'I can't go on for ever this way.' Ponti flew back to Rome hoping to stem the tide of newspaper reports and speculation. Romilda Villani flew in to have a few straight words with her daughter.

'What are you getting yourself into?' she asked sharply. 'He is a married man with two children. You know he cannot be divorced. So how will you end up, like me, unmarried with maybe children?' (The problem of course, had been easier for her. She just had a reluctant lover on her hands. Reluctant bridegroom at least.)

Sophia replied tersely, 'I don't know what will happen. All I

96

Blacked up for her first film as 'Sophia Loren'. She is 'Aida', the voice was Renata Tebaldi's. *Aida* (1953).

Left Sophia Loren and Trevor Howard, *The Key* (1958).

Meeting the Queen at the Royal Première of *The Key* (1958).

In *Desire Under The Elms* with Burl Ives (1958).

With Cary Grant on *Houseboat* (1958).

Top With Cary Grant, and a wedding on *Houseboat* (1958).
Bottom Sophia is the mother in *Two Women* (1961). (*Pierluigi*)

Sophia with Peter Sellers, celebrating the release of
The Millionairess (1961).

Sophia during her 'epic' period – Charlton Heston is *El Cid* (1961).
(*Antonio Luengo*)

know is, Carlo is my whole life. He wants me and I want him. There has to be a way out for us.'

She smiles now when she remembers her confidence at the time, before the first explosions began. 'I didn't know what I was being caught up in. How could I? When we first met he was just a kind producer who gave me a chance. But the more we were with each other, all kinds of bonds held us together. He was a friend, counsellor, lover, father, teacher, everything . . . without him I was never a complete woman. Everybody frowned at this relationship between a man nearly twenty years older than the woman. But how would they know? How can anyone ever understand the real intimacies of a man's relationship with a woman, a husband's relationship with his wife? My need for him has always been total and uncompromising. It took him a long time before he decided he would marry me. Think of his situation. He had a wife, two children. He was a famous producer. I was just as troubled as he was. If he had sacrificed them to our love so easily, so quickly, then perhaps, I thought, he might one day do the same to me. All I knew was I adored him. He was my man. My only man. I wanted him desperately as a husband and as the father of my children. Finally it had to come to the point when I knew that he was not going to make the decision unless I put him on the spot. After all,' she laughed, 'it's universal, not just Italian, for a husband to try and get the best of both worlds— a nice situation with his family, and just as nice a situation going for him with his mistress. That was not what I had in mind for Carlo and me.'

But there were no ultimatums. The Neapolitans are too soft-hearted to make them, the Milanese too inflexible to be impressed by them. Moreoever the path was smoothed for them by Ponti's wife, Giuliana. She had been trained as a barrister. Matrimonial problems were no novelty to her and she understood the hopelessness of trying to breathe life into a dead marriage. But neither she nor Ponti had any illusions about the hostility the Establishment would mount against the guilty party or parties. While Carlo and his lawyers prepared for the opening skirmishes against the stern moralities in Rome, Sophia, in Greece, tried to generate some ignition between herself and the handsome but leaden Mr Ladd.

It was hard going. By contrast with say, Marcello Mastroiani whose love scenes with Sophia have an exploratory candour to them bordering on frenzy—with Alan Ladd, the mercury never seemed to rise in the bulb. Negulesco finally put his faith in the basics—Sophia's. Whenever she emerged from the water he had her photographed, her clothing wet, tight and transparent. It was a hopeful variation on a theme of *Bitter Rice* and *Woman of the River*. But in the event, *Boy on a Dolphin* like *The Pride and the Passion* was submerged under a tide of critical disapproval. 'Slow and stodgy' . . . 'Alan Ladd looks more mummified than most of his discoveries' . . . 'Clifton Webb gives a bad caricature of himself' . . . were what some of the critics said of the film. But almost all of them found Sophia ravishing, with 'gorgeous' . . . 'vibrantly believable' . . . fair samples of their reactions. That, and a gallery of portraits by the director Jean Negulesco, was about as much as a percentage Sophia drew from the film.

At the end of the shooting, she and Alan Ladd exchanged cool farewells. He went back to America nurturing a private resolution never again to make films with much taller girls in general, Italians in particular. Sophia merely added his name to the leading co-stars she had captured, and flew back to Rome to deal with the more pressing matters of her love affair with Carlo. The world was asking questions and she was running out of answers. She was now wearily repeating herself. 'Yes I am in love and I would like to marry but the man is married so I cannot tell you his name.' There was a slight embellishment to it when she made a short trip to Nice to discuss a film with some Columbia executives. A friend of mine working as a correspondent on the Riviera was a shade more persistent than his colleagues. She told him crisply; 'I not only know the name of the man I am going to marry—but when I will marry him. It will be in 1958. And to prove it I have written the name on a scrap of paper, put it in a small bottle and placed it in a safe deposit. On 20 September, 1958 I shall be 24. Between January and September of that year I shall be married. I shall produce the paper and you will see the man's name written on it.' Why she should have to put the name in a bottle since it was going into a safe deposit and not to be flung from a desert island into the open sea, was never fully probed. But the interview revealed how convinced Sophia was that she had finally baited, hooked and landed the genial Signor Ponti.

That achieved, admittedly unofficially, she could now get on with the business of carving further steps up to the summit. Alan Ladd had now been nudged aside by John Wayne as the biggest box-office draw in America, and also in Japan where he won points for size as well as star quality. It was thought that both his and Sophia Loren's careers would benefit from the booster shots of acting with each other. The argument ran this way: a partnership between the tall, leathery Westerner of a few words and the unquenchable Sophia, would, as expressed to me by a Hollywood Agent, 'have more balls to it than all the pin-alleys of Pennsylvania'. (Since women's lib and Jane Fonda, producers are now wary of seeing all sex potential in terms of testicles.)

There was a story on hand which was considered ideal for the earthy pair. It was set in North Africa and involved a search for a 'Lost City' and the treasures within. The third character in the triangle was entrusted to Rossano Brazzi, playing a plausible rogue, but very dashing from his charcoal waves to his Cuban heels. He was also Italian and the notion was that his presence would alleviate Sophia's yearning for home during the lonely Libyan nights.

After juggling with several titles, the studio named this sand-blown melodrama *Legend of the Lost*.

I flew to Tripoli, then on across the Libyan desert to the oasis village of Ghadames which straddles the borders of Libya, Tunis and Algeria. By the time I arrived, the Tuaregs, the Berber Arabs who form the larger proportion of the village population, had become accustomed to the finer idiocies of a Hollywood film company going native in a remote oasis on the edge of the Sahara. Few, if any, had ever seen a film camera before. Yet with that naïveté which separates press agents from their fellow men, David Hanna who was covering the movie, had brought along a stack of press handouts giving details of the production, the

synopsis of the film, and biographies of the stars. All this for publication in local papers which didn't exist, for an adult audience
which substantially couldn't read, and certainly not in English.
But something happens to movie crews when they arrive in
darkest Africa (it is always 'darkest' Africa to them even though
there may be a jam of 1975 Chevrolets at the main intersection,
honking to get into the drive-in movie).

But Ghadames was primitive enough. Here the women did the
work, while their menfolk, their headscarves drawn like veils
beneath their eyes, sat around—I mean fell about—as director
Henry Hathaway played ringmaster to the high-stepping antics of
John Wayne, Rossano Brazzi and Sophia Loren. As often happens, the incidents on location were hilarious to everyone but the
inmates. Had some enterprising amateur secretly filmed the unit
at work, his effort might well have grossed more than did the
actual picture. It could scarcely have been less funny.

I arrived to find Hathaway peering through a viewfinder,
apparently dissatisfied with the footprints some character's safari
boots had left in the sand dunes. He wanted these to have that
pristine, untouched-by-human-foot look. He turned to an
assistant who grabbed a megaphone and bellowed to the shimmering horizon: 'GET SOME MEN AND DUST THEM DOONS!' A moment
later the squatting Tuaregs almost wept as six chanting Libyans
began rhythmically sweeping the desert. They may still be there.
One does not cross the Sahara in a day.

To their right a crewman sent a message over the two-way
radio. 'LOCATION TO BASE. LOCATION TO BASE. IMPORTANT DIS-
PATCH. URGENTLY REQUIRE TWO BOTTLES OF BRANDY, SIX CANS
OF BEANS, AND SOME MULE FODDER. THE BRANDY IS FOR THE DUKE
(WAYNE) THE FODDER FOR THE MULE. OVER.' As I recall it the
story had Wayne as some kind of adventurer—Joe January they
called him—hired by Rossano Brazzi to lead the trek to 'Lost City'.
Sophia is an Arab girl who is somehow caught up in the safari,
with Wayne and Brazzi competing for the action. Taking refuge
with them under the same tarpaulin during a twenty-four-hour
sandstorm, she staggers out to declare—'I hate men,' giving rise
to all kinds of notions as to what happened under the tarpaulin.

The mandatory love scene with Wayne, was shot one scorching afternoon. Sophia relished it on two counts; the first, because they did not need to dig a hole for her as required with Alan Ladd, the second because she believed that she was kissing her way to greater glory.

Wayne, who had synthetic perspiration squirted on him to emphasize his ordeal, was doubly grateful. His company had a big percentage of the picture. When the scene was over, his face creased into the familiar sag-mouthed grin. He slapped her appreciatively on the rump. 'Oh! you gorgeous investment you!' (If he'd had a vision of the disappointing returns at the box office, he might have kept the gesture, revised the dialogue.)

Sophia was delighted by this rough but generous stamp of approval from the Number One Star of America. Her friend, that inscrutable minister without-portfolio, Basilio Franchina, shared her pleasure but had private reservations about the outcome of the picture. To this serious, radical scriptwriter (and to most critics), *Legend of the Lost* was a piece of equatorial tosh which even Victor Mature might have baulked at.

At night, in the no-star hotel which housed the film's principals —and Wayne's King-sized bed brought by special bearers from Rome—we sat around under dim lights listening to the Tuaregs murmuring in their underground tunnels outside. Rossano Brazzi complained that the African night brought on acute depression. 'Sometimes the silence is so unbearable I have cried,' he said. Against this, however, was a greater self-awareness which, he confided to me, had given him an entirely new attitude to women. What he meant, he said, was: 'I now make them feel more important than I am.'

Wayne was less forthcoming, but he did break a leg, falling in the Roman ruins at Leptis Magna. Sophia flew back to Rome, glad to get back to the silk sheets, the Italian food, the cooler Rome nights and to Carlo. The loyal and attentive Basilio delivered her from the airport to Ponti, then drove off in his sports car to work on a script in Cannes. The delivery was less ceremonious than the handing over of the Keys at the Tower of London. But the similarity was there in security terms. Ponti's precious property had to be untouched and unmolested from Ghadames to the Palazzo Colonna.

Each blessed their own good fortune as they broke for air in the magnificent apartment Ponti had lavishly furnished for Sophia and her family in Rome. Ponti stood back, looked at his mouth-watering goddess, and decided she had never looked more beautiful. Sophia, long exposed to the traumas and tantrums of the first batch of Hollywood leading men, was glad to get back to the package deal security of lover, father-figure and friend. 'Just being with him made every fear, every tension, every problem melt to nothing.' Sophia said to me in Ghadames. 'He made some of the young men who made a play for me seem like a joke.'

When their reunion had enthralled itself to a standstill, Sophia could see that Ponti was beaming with more than ordinary delight. He had given her some jewellery—a sizeable trinket followed every film—but now he had some news. The latest tax returns showed that Sophia was now worth exactly the same amount of money as her formidable screen rival, Gina Lollobrigida. The figure then (December 1957) was forty-six thousand pounds. Sophia would hardly accept that sum today to pay for her studio incidentals. More important, Carlo had signed a deal with the huge Paramount Film Corporation of Hollywood for Sophia to make four films there.

Hollywood! So here it was at last. What her mother Romilda had missed (despite the Garbo image), Sophia Loren, formerly Scicolone, Lazzaro, starlet, and runner-up in the Naples beauty contest, had finally achieved. It was no longer a mirage. Paramount had laid it on the line. There would be a chauffeured limousine. A suite at the Bel Air Hotel. More money in expenses than she earned as a star in Italian films. Publicity men to tell her what to say. Parties at Romanoff's and the Beverly Hills Hotel. Lunches at the Brown Derby, week-end swimming off Malibu beach. The whole soundless, smokeless, palm-fringed New Jerusalem west of Coldwater Canyon to the Pacific ocean was hers for the taking. Sophia called in the finest Italian couturiers in the manner of Sir Edmund Hillary detailing his Sherpas for the assault on Everest. The aim was not merely the conquest of America. 'I thought it would be nice to knock its eye out.'

Whether Carlo Ponti should have been so eager to submit Sophia for the bland re-programming by the studio machine, is arguable. Certainly at that time, international star-rating demanded not merely a leading role in a major American film. You had to be seen there, to be one of THEM, reachable and touchable to Hedda and Louella; on call for the Debbie Reynolds' charity shindigs, clucking away at the baby 'showers' for the celebrated infant of the week: 'In', 'Hot' and a 'Winner'.

Sophia Loren, her uneasy love life aside, qualified in all areas. But was it a wise route for her to take? When her friend de Sica heard about the Paramount contract and the imminent debut in Hollywood, his reaction was an anguished, 'Sperduto! I felt complete despair. All the producers knew at that time were formula pictures.' He struck his palms together in a gesture of distaste. 'Always the happy ending. Always commercialism. I once went to Hollywood and worked with the greatest of writers. But nobody could understand what we were saying. For the backers the cinema was only a question of profit. For me it is life. It is poetry. To surrender a fragile, subtle talent like Sophia's into their hands was to invite its destruction.' Maybe George Jean Nathan was right when he said: 'Hollywood impresses me as being ten million dollars' worth of intricate and highly ingenious machinery functioning elaborately to put skin on baloney.'

But de Sica affectionately sped Sophia on her way, hoping privately that Hollywood would eventually return her to him undamaged, partially recognizable at least, as the Neapolitan he used to know. It was a tall order. Paramount's hired praisers were already at work, introducing her to the American millions.

The overture was loud, brash and effective. When Sophia and Carlo checked into their Beverly Hills hotel, the flowers, gifts and invitations had spilled over on to the wall-to-wall carpet. 'Miraculoso!' sighed Sophia as she looked around the lush apartment, caught a glimpse of sun-bronzed bodies beneath overhanging palm trees which fringed the vast pool. She and Carlo sorted through the party invitations. To the Hollywood of the period

Italian women were mostly sex-dominated, ran to fat and ate pasta. Some of the cards read—'Please come and join us for a spaghetti dinner'; 'Monday's our Macaroni night—we'd love to see you'; 'If you want to taste real Fettucini, we're up at Cold-water Canyon,' and so on. Sophia giggled at Carlo. 'I suppose if I'd been a Chinese actress it would have been Chop Suey seven days a week.'

The scene was now set for the great splurging extravaganza of a party given in Sophia's honour the second night of her arrival. It was held at the famous restaurant of that spoof of a Royal Russian, the late Mike Romanoff. The host was Clifton Webb, who, with Tony Perkins, was to film Eugene O'Neil's *Desire Under the Elms* with Sophia. The welcoming committee which greeted her as she entered the restaurant in a chic, tight black dress included all the top seeds at the studios. Gary Cooper blushed, shuffled his feet and kissed Sophia awkwardly on the hand. George Raft bowed, produced a sleek smile and said 'Buona Sera' to prove he had the language. Gene Kelly, Barbara Stanwyk, Jeff Hunter, Ann Miller, Robert Wagner, Tony Perkins, Fred MacMurray, June Haver . . . Sophia received them all regally. 'Not bad for a Scicolone,' she whispered to Carlo as the stars jostled to be photographed with her. The party proceeded on its elegantly torpid way. The background music was Sorrento-oriented and the conversation with Sophia was roughly on the level of 'can you drink the water at the Excelsior', and 'my houseman, Alfredo, comes from Bologna, I don't suppose you'd happen to know his family?'

But Sophia, charming, tactful and delectable, played it straight. Hollywood was clearly going to fall for this 'Neapolitan broad'. But the records show that the more classy the party, the more vulnerable it is to the kind of sensational intervention which occurred halfway through the proceedings. It was made by that large and lamentable creature, the late Jayne Mansfield who had cornered the market in heaving herself on to promising band-wagons.

I witnessed the first of her brash, unsolicited entrances at Silver Springs, Florida, many years earlier. I had flown there with

Jane Russell in a Constellation, courtesy of Howard Hughes, for the opening of a film called *Underwater* which, in classic RKO style, was actually screened under water. All was primed for Jane Russell's bosomy immersion into the lagoon, when who should gambol across the scene but this sugar-plum fairy, Jayne Mansfield. The result was a triumphant debut in the morning papers, and some unprintable but understandable observations from Jane Russell.

Now in Romanoff's, the place Kleig-lit and alive with reporters, Jayne Mansfield took the mandatory deep breath for bulging starlets, and launched herself like an Intercontinental Ballistic Missile, towards the centre table. She had prepared herself well for the confrontation, wearing a flimsy dress, the neckline dropping to her navel. She also announced to newsmen within earshot—she was coming through loud and clear at a distance of fifty feet—that, 'All this is me. I got absolutely nothing under this dress 'cept what Nature intended.'

This said, and adding, 'Watch this!' which was as close as she could get to 'Geronimo!' on the night, she lolloped over to Sophia's table.

Sophia was startled, more so when Jayne took up a position behind the star, then bent over so that cameras could zoom down through the canyon between her mighty bosoms then return the same way, right up to the moistened parted lips, which murmured: 'Welcome to California, I'm sure glad to see you Miss Loren,' which for an uninvited guest had more gall than gush. Sophia looked up at the overflowing intruder, and casually turned back to resume her conversation with Clifton Webb.

Jayne Mansfield pouted back to the bar. 'She's a silly girl. I only wanted to make her welcome and prove to her we've also got bosoms in Hollywood.' Those photographers who had missed the first shot were anxious to get into the act. They invited Jayne to repeat the intrusion. This time Sophia was prepared for her, quietly delivering a choice Italian epithet. Miss Mansfield failed to grasp the meaning but got the message. She picked up her mink and flounced off. She said she was going to a Bavarian sausage party.

The initiation rituals over, the news pictures of Jayne Mansfield's mammary invasion of Romanoff's being wheeled away with the breakfast things the following morning, Sophia got back to the business of making films. As her personal Cadillac swept her past the crew-cut lawns which border Sunset Boulevard she experienced that shiver of excitement foreign stars feel as they approach the main gates of a major Hollywood studio for the first time. By comparison, arriving at Pinewood studios, Bucks., England, is like visiting a rich old uncle for tea, while working at Cinecitta, Rome, is an exercise in mass hysteria.

But the Paramount complex, like MGM and Twentieth Century Fox before the auditors dismembered them alive, was vast, important, and the centre for some of the most successful films ever to emerge from Hollywood. If you were a star, the 'treatment' was absurdly lavish as long as you obeyed the rules and showed a profit on the front-office's investment. Sophia's reception there, as they polished up one of the largest dressing rooms and filled it with flowers, exceeded the customary back-scratching. But then, she was not only a star of increasing potential. Ponti was a powerful producer, invaluable to Hollywood on the distribution of their product in Italy.

So the studio executives called her 'Miss Loren' and treated her like visiting royalty. Those with a predilection for handling the company's merchandise—especially when there was plenty of it to go round—were advised to keep their hands in their pockets.

The role Sophia had come to play was of Anna, in the film version of Eugene O'Neill's sombre play, *Desire Under the Elms*. The picture featured Burl Ives as a ranting, domineering farmer with two wives deceased, and three sons he loathes. He brings the Italian woman, Anna, back home as his third wife where one son, Eben (Anthony Perkins) sees the woman as a threat to his inheritance. With their mutual hostility no less savage than their lust, the situation is neatly poised for the sexual interplay and child murder which is the chilling centrepiece of the story. It was a good part for Sophia, more suited to her gifts than some of the candy-floss which was to follow. Her performance was well received by the critics, one London reviewer declaring, 'Sophia Loren creates a lasting impression . . . her love scenes with Anthony Perkins were beautifully handled.'

But Vittorio de Sica disliked Sophia's entire Hollywood adventure, saying: 'She made bad pictures, it was a bad period for her.' Yet he excluded *Desire Under the Elms* from the general condemnation. 'It was the only picture in which Sophia was very good. Delbert Mann's direction was excellent.' Many will regard de Sica's comments as being unduly harsh. The films she was to make with Cary Grant and the late Clark Gable, had sufficient Neapolitan charm and comedy-sense, to offset the less successful elements in the pictures.

So Paramount were pleased. So too was Ponti. He'd taken Sophia to Hollywood to prove his contention that she was a much better actress than her first English pictures indicated.

Meanwhile Sophia, the film over, was sending urgent messages to Romilda and Maria, on the 'wish you were here' theme. It was no fun for the girl from Pozzuoli making it big in Hollywood if she couldn't share the goodies with them. When her mother and sister arrived, the three of them buzzed around Beverly Hills like Queen bees taking over a new hive. Maria was now demonstrating that she could sing and act, though she hardly had the beauty, let alone bone structure, of her sister. Paramount offered her a script on condition she had plastic surgery to remodel her face which they considered to be too broad. It was Frank Sinatra who told her to resist being a studio re-mould. 'Don't bother with the cinema, Maria,' he told her, 'you were born to sing. Follow your own road.' Hollywood's loss was to be Romano Mussolini's gain.

When the last scene of the film was wrapped up, Sophia and Carlo sat by the hotel pool and pondered their situation. American reporters were now challenging Sophia about Ponti. 'Is he your lover, or isn't he?' 'When are you going to get married?' 'What's the score, Sophia?' They do not equivocate in the City of the Angels.

The same situation was now blowing up in Italy. The couple knew that an army of *paparazzi* would be waiting for them at Rome airport. The 'just good friends' syndrome would be a belly-laugh to the Italian reporters who well knew the score.

'We needed some peace and quiet to think out our lives,' Sophia said. 'They were asking too many questions in Hollywood getting too close to the truth in Italy.'

They had no wish to re-visit the scene of the 'crime'.

One morning in late July they checked out of their hotel, and flew direct to Geneva. They moved into one of the grander hotels in Burgenstock, that chic haven for movie stars with a taste for privacy, the mountain air and considerable tax advantages. The hotel boasted a genuine Rubens on one wall and a discreetness as tight-lipped as a numbered bank account. Reporters who converged on the hotel noticed that Carlo and Sophia both wore rings on the 'marriage finger'.

When the Italian papers traced them to their hideout, they launched into print, suggesting that both were taking out Swiss citizenship as a prelude to marriage. It was a hasty conclusion and a false one. Ponti had no such plan. In fact he had already begun preliminary proceedings to obtain a Mexican divorce from his wife Giuliana. With that achieved, he and Sophia could finally marry.

At dinner a week after their arrival, he gave Sophia some documents to sign.

'Is this for Paramount?' she asked.

'No, for Ponti,' he chuckled. 'That's if you still want me.'

She wrote, 'Sofia Scicolone, spinster' on the dotted line, flung her arms around his neck and kissed him fiercely.

It was a memorable night in Burgenstock, and they slept long and blissfully the following morning. Only Ponti's lawyers lay awake.

7

The Grant Connection

On 17 September, 1957, Senor Antonio Lopez Machuca and Senor Mario Ballesteros, were married before Judge Jorge de La Fuente, at Juarez, Mexico. It was a quiet wedding. And a drab one. The couple wore frowns, perspired visibly in the heat and were clearly anxious to get the proceedings done with and move to other business.

Both were attorneys, male, and only 'bride' and 'groom' by proxy, standing in for their clients, Doctor Carlo Ponti and his fiancée officially named as Sofia Scicolone. Senor Machuca announced that he spoke for Mr Ponti and produced documents showing that in August, also in Mexico, the eleven-year-old marriage between Carlo and Giuliana Fiastri, the general's daughter, had been terminated. He was now free to marry Miss Scicolone—the lawyer smiled in the direction of his bride-for-the-day, Senor Ballesteros—all the necessary papers being in order. Two thumps of a rubber stamp later, Carlo and Sophia were man and wife, at least at a spot 32 degrees N.–106 degrees W. in Juarez, that quick pull-up for divorces and marriages conveniently within shotgun range of the United States.

It was not the ceremony Sophia Loren had visualized in her childhood fantasies over the vinegar factory in Pozzuoli. For all her poise and craving for sophistication, she was a middle-class sentimentalist with the conventional yearnings to be married in a white veil, followed by the scramble through a blizzard of confetti to the waiting limousine. But she and Carlo had little choice. A month earlier when they had left their mist-screened sanctuary at Burgenstock for Rome, they found that the love affair was no longer confined to the table-talk on the Via Veneto. Their amorous deadlock had triggered off the expected reactions of envy, bitchery and sympathy. The film colony took the conciliatory view that if Ponti's marriage was, unofficially at least, at an end, if he could land so superb a creature as Sophia, twenty years younger at that, as his woman and most valued business asset too, then Mamma mia!—good luck to the winner. But the moralists and the Vatican press sharpened their fangs and their knives, waiting for their prey to make the first official move.

Sophia, now that the marriage papers were being prepared, decided that the identity of her lover need no longer be kept under wraps or imprisoned in that bottle allegedly incarcerated in a safe deposit box. Standing on a balcony in Rome, symbolically looking out towards the Vatican, she said to me at the time: 'I can no longer hide the feelings that are tying me to Carlo Ponti. He is the only man in the world of whom I am absolutely sure. This man has been my support in the most difficult and delicate circumstances. Without him I am nothing. I have no intention of giving myself to any other man.' She considered it hardly necessary to spell out what those 'difficulties' were.

Mr Ponti, however, with a fine show of Milanese wariness, hinted to well-wishers and detractors alike, that La Signorina was unique, an original, and a very agreeable girl to have on a round-the-clock basis. The more cosmic his feelings for her, the more firmly he kept them to himself. Her surrender to him, of body, soul and career, was as total as a patient's in the hands of an anaesthetist. The woman and the star belonged to him. He had the music. Others could provide the words. He confined his talking to discussions about film deals which, now that Paramount had invested millions in her, were cascading in. All the major studios, scared they might be missing out on some big discovery, were keen to get into the act.

Sophia had always wanted to make a film in England. That formidable writer-producer Carl Foreman, had a subject called *Stella*, later renamed *The Key*, which he considered perfect for her. The story was a sea tale in which several ships' captains had one thing in common, the key to Sophia's flat—with William Holden the preferential shareholder. The idea of going to England attracted Sophia for compelling reasons. She had an urge to test-run her assiduously acquired elegance on British society. She craved the acceptance and prestige which she saw as the hallmark of British aristocracy. The superstar image was a joke compared with tinkling the teacups on the lawns of the nobility. When Duchesses later entertained her, their Dukes stuttering in admiration, Sophia was ecstatic, convinced that she had purged herself of Pozzuoli. The two distinct personalities which were emerging were not the familiar dichotomy of star image and private persona. They were the ungarnished Sophia of *Woman of the River* or *The Gold of Naples* against the more high-toned lady which the public really didn't want at all. The contrast was subtle but noticeable to her friends. They said her voice was quite different on television, notably on the David Frost show. It had an archness to it which was more prissy than Pozzuoli. But with a past inhabited by war-time squalor and the tarts of Naples, Sophia's yearning for the Grace Kelly touch seemed not unreasonable.

Making *The Key* for Carl Foreman offered another advantage. With William Holden and Trevor Howard as her co-stars, she could now chalk up more international leading men to her credit than could Gina Lollobrigida. No small bonus to the Sophia Loren of those days. The feud had ended but the rivalry lingered on. Her English was improving rapidly. She had attacked this (to her) awkward, eccentric language with the unrelenting zeal of a Kamakaze pilot. 'I was absolutely determined to learn it well enough,' she said, 'to joke in it, argue in it, and swear in it.' She might had added 'and wheel and deal in it', as money was becoming as important to her as it was to Carlo.

She consented to play the role and left Carlo to work out the deal. This took much longer than Foreman anticipated. Eventually, as the October starting-date of the picture loomed nearer, still without Ponti's signature on the contract, Carl sent the script to Ingrid Bergman in Paris.

It was an adroit move, having the dual effect, intentional or otherwise, of cornering Sophia and jogging the elbow of Carlo's reluctant writing hand. (Carlo was now demanding the kind of money for his client and partner which had the Columbia account-ants complaining he was attacking them with a blunt instrument.) When the Italian actress heard that Bergman was reading the screenplay, she leapt at Carlo: 'Darling, get the picture for me.' (It may not have been darling but Melanzana Parmigiani—her 'little eggplant'—Sophia tending to name her favourite people after her favourite dishes. Peter Sellers was to become goat's cheese to the lady, Doctor Christiaan Barnard immortalized as Lasagne Pasticatta, while Marcello Mastroiani is for ever Salted Pigskin in Sophia's eyes.)

The deal over *The Key* settled, Sophia could now leave for Hollywood to make *Houseboat* with Cary Grant. Her feelings as she kissed Carlo goodbye at Rome airport had all the conflicting overtones of an afternoon TV romance for housewives. Here she was, having signed documents for an imminent Mexican marriage, flying off to make a picture with Cary whose passion for her had gone into verbal orbit. 'She is a woman no world, terrestial or astral, can afford to be without,' he said. Moreoever, when Sophia read the script and noted their tender love scenes with Cary's pressing (and finally successful) demands for her to marry him, the resemblance to their real-life situation was too close for comfort. His and hers. Mr Grant was having problems too. Sophia could not know, could hardly be expected to know—the effect her rejec-tion of him would have on this immensely likeable but complex character. Like everybody else she refused to believe that the celebrated Grant dimple was already eight years old when Scott, the explorer, reached the South Pole in 1912.

He was fifty-three (thirty years older than Sophia) when she arrived in Hollywood to renew the professional relationship begun on *The Pride and the Passion*. But age and Cary Grant is not an equation which can be viewed in ordinary terms. A sun-bronzed Peter Pan, he is clearly the vitaminized, vitalized, weather-proof phenomenon of motion picture history. Mr Grant's intense toning-up procedures begin with early morning press-ups and conclude with mighty intakes of the Pacific air before the last glass of milk of the day. He tried to get Sophia involved in the

cult, saying, 'Treat your lungs right and they'll never fight you.'
'I've never had a fight with my lungs that I didn't win,' Sophia told
him.

Whatever else his four wives might have accused him of, they
could never have reproached him for being unhealthy. Sophia,
before she and Carlo had made it legal, called him 'the world's
most perfect male'.

What amused Sophia, as it did me to witness it, was that a star of
his calibre, with a fortune last calculated at around 25 million
dollars, should choose to hand-wash his own shorts in transit
around the globe. Ladies panties, I recall Cary explaining, dried
more quickly.

Nobody, and certainly not Sophia, could accuse Mr Grant of
reckless spending. In fact he has always boasted that he saves
upwards of forty pounds a year just by checking restaurant bills.
Waiters who have had to stand by while the cautious superstar
bends over the check, lips moving silently as in prayer, hardly feel
they've been serving the Last of the Big Spenders.

But in spite of his immense popularity the two Rolls-Royces and
the palatial weekend home in Palm Springs, Cary Grant has had
periods of excruciating torment, much of which he poured out on
Sophia during breaks in shooting. Self-doubt, emotional insecurity
and an apparent inability to sustain permanently a happy and
totally fulfilled marriage, have generated much private despair
behind his public image. He tried the usual palliatives, had a brief
honeymoon with hallucinatory drugs, but finally gave these up
in favour of auto-hypnosis which at least helped him to kick
the tobacco habit.

His fourth wife, Dyan Cannon, provided no solution to his
problems. Her Spanish-style home on Malibu beach, California,
houses its own padded cell, about five feet square, in which the
lady retreats for Primal Scream Therapy. This bizarre but apparently fruitful activity involves letting herself go to the extent of
screaming like a demented witch, punching and kicking the well-
insulated walls until she subsides in a tearful but subdued heap on
the floor.

But when Sophia Loren checked into the exclusive Bel Air

Hotel near Hollywood, to start *Houseboat* for the gifted writer–director Mel Shavelson, Dyan Cannon and her upholstered cell were still to make their appearance in Cary Grant's life. This may have been Mel's bad luck. When script problems and Cary's heart pangs over Sophia became acute, Shavelson might have welcomed a short session of Primal Scream Therapy, maybe in a padded duplex with the film's producer, Jack Rose.

The behind-the-scenes scenario of the setting up and making of *Houseboat* would have made a much juicier epic than the film itself turned out to be. Somewhere between Day One of the pre-production activities and the last shot in the studio, Cary Grant's marriage to Betsy Drake had begun to founder beyond the salvaging; Mel Shavelson and Jack Rose worked so many permutations on the script, they were re-writing in their sleep, re-casting in their nightmares; while Sophia was frequently in tears both because of Cary's persistence and her own uneasy position over the proxy wedding.

The story of the film as it eventually staggered from the typewriters of Shavelson and Rose was of a government official (Grant) who hires Sophia as a housekeeper to look after his three kids when their mother dies in a car accident. The original plot had been written by Cary Grant's wife, actress Betsy Drake, who saw herself playing the leading female role opposite her famous husband. Cary had worked for the successful Shavelson–Rose partnership before and had said that he'd be glad to make another picture with them. He also said he had this story written by Betsy about a family living on a houseboat and hinted that if they bought the story he would make the picture.

'We knew this was the only way we could get Grant committed,' Shavelson said. 'It's always very difficult to pin him down. Sometimes you didn't know until the cameras actually started turning whether you had got him or not.'

They bought the story for a sizeable amount of money, but as they feared, Cary slid away without warning, or signing. Paramount executives became agitated and finally tailed him to the airport where he was waiting to fly off to make *The Pride and the*

Passion in Spain. They caught him on the plane. He laughed and at last agreed to make the picture. With Betsy Drake. He had not yet met Sophia Loren.

Shavelson and Rose settled down to write the screenplay, sometimes in the studio, occasionally in Mel's spacious house in the San Fernando Valley. By the time they got to page three it was clear that the original plot had to be sunk for one reason or another. 'Barely the only thing we kept from Betsy's story was the houseboat,' commented Shavelson wrily. 'Then we got a call from Spain and Cary told us he had met such a wonderful girl, she's going to be the new Garbo, and would it be much of a change to make the heroine an Italian girl instead of an American girl? We said "of course not Cary", but in fact we sat down, tore up the script and started all over again.'

So the two master-minds set about Italianating the story. 'Not so unreasonable,' they told each other cheerfully. 'We've got this beautiful Italian broad, and Cary, maybe the fact that she's Italian adds something to the movie.' They finished the screenplay, now re-styled with touches of *fetuccini* and Puccini, Sophia's screen father being a Toscanini re-mould. Then Cary returned from Spain. All three met for lunch in the executive dining room at Paramount studios. When all had ordered, the tanned Mr Grant smiled and said, 'Okay, tell me the story.' Shavelson began outlining the plot of the widowed husband looking for someone to act as housekeeper and nanny, continuing, 'so then he meets this daughter of a famous Italian conductor who encounters one of the children who is lost . . .'

'But you've got an Italian girl as the heroine,' Grant frowned.

'We thought that was the whole idea, Cary,' Shavelson said crisply. 'Remember it was your suggestion—Sophia Loren, the new Garbo . . .?'

Cary Grant put down his fork. 'I will not make a picture with Sophia Loren,' he said tersely. He gave no reasons. But it was obvious that Cary was apprehensive that his emotional entanglement with Sophia might cripple the picture. 'There was a terrible time,' Shavelson recalled. 'I suppose, though I wasn't that close to Cary to be sure, that he felt he had done her a big favour by putting her into an American picture with him and then she had rejected him. He obviously didn't want to have to go through the torment of being on the set with her every day. And he had to take it out on somebody and I was the most convenient, although after the picture was over he apologized for giving me such a hard time. He tried to get out of the film, but Paramount were determined not to release him from the contract. Finally, Grant, who is a good professional, realized he had given his approval. He'd approved the script because Betsy Drake had written the story. He'd approved me as director and he'd approved Jack Rose as producer and he'd approved Sophia Loren as leading lady, so he had no approvals left and there was no way he could get out of the picture. So the deal was set.'

Even in less turbulent circumstances, producers who sign Cary Grant to a contract soon discover they are not merely taking on an actor, but come away as though from Sinai with a list of covenants chiselled into forty uncompromising legal pages. In addition to the usual perks of dressing room on the stage, private phone, chauffeur, secretary and similar sweeteners, he has approval of the leading actress's body make-up. I wondered about this until Mel Shavelson explained: 'He asks for this because he frequently wears his own clothes in a film and doesn't like to get the actress's body stuff on them. We were doing a scene in a picture where he's dancing with Martha Hyer, when he stopped it because the make-up was coming off on his clothes and it wasn't the stuff he'd okayed.'

But Shavelson and Rose would gladly have settled for a cartload of similar eccentricites just to keep Grant happy. The film, after all, was meant to be light-hearted and gay, and Mr Grant, normally unequalled in this territory, was obviously miserable and rattled. Shavelson who declares a considerable respect for the veteran actor, found that once the cameras started turning, it was not the amiable Cary Grant of yore. 'He objected to the photography, he objected to portions of the script, he objected to things which in normal situations he would not have minded at all. Here, his problem was with Sophia. And that's what made this particular picture hard going.'

But with Cary Grant's mortifying dilemma hanging over the picture, Shavelson was more than grateful for the resourceful way Sophia Loren reacted to it all. She had her problems too but she exorcised them between scenes, playing poker with Ines or making long phone calls to Carlo. She was struggling to extricate herself from the Grant connection well aware of the possible dangers of offending a man of his influence in Hollywood. She was wrestling with her English trying to give meaning to words still barely understood. And then there was the matter of the proxy marriage, news of which was due in a matter of weeks. When Italy and the Vatican press got hold of that, all hell would be on their backs.

Yet when the picture started she walked on the set ahead of the rest of the cast, joked with the crew, grimaced when, in rehearsal, the dialogue coach made her take some of the parmesan flavour out of the English vowels. Cary sprawled down on the canvas seat beside hers. They smiled at each other, both instinctively casual on the 'show must go on' principle. Whatever the emotional temperature had been on *The Pride and the Passion* during those candle-lit dinners with the anguished Flamenco singing in the background, there was no hint of it in their preliminary exchanges on their reunion.

'How's Carlo?'

'He's fine. How's Betsy?'

'She's okay.'

'Thank you for the flowers, they were beautiful.'

Cary grinned. 'It was a pleasure I assure you.'

Behind the cameras Shavelson added his own ten cents worth of assumed nonchalance. 'You both look terrific. Let's make a movie.'

As the first week's shooting got under way it seemed that Cary had succeeded in defusing his feelings. When they lunched alone together he joked a lot though he rarely took his eyes off hers. If Sophia found his probing glances disturbing, she concealed it, adroitly playing the distance game. But she was glad of the occasional respite when the scenes involved just her and the three child performers, Mimi Gibson, Paul Peterson and Charles Herbert.

Shavelson had worked with a fair assortment of movie actresses and therefore was familiar with all the permutations on temperament, petulance and plain egotistical hogwash. By contrast Sophia demonstrated a degree of professionalism which on one occasion drew a hug of appreciation from Shavelson and a spontaneous burst of applause from the crew.

A key scene between her and the boy Peterson, called for him to break down and weep. Shavelson called 'Action' but the child's performance was stilted and lacked conviction. After several retakes, Shavelson became irritated, Sophia infuriated. She grabbed the youngster and slapped him hard. 'Listen Paul,' she hissed, 'they're giving you a lot of money to do this and if you don't pay attention then they shouldn't pay you. I'm working hard, why don't you? Eh . . .!' that Neapolitan finger was now stabbing him remorselessly. It worked well. The boy blubbered effectively and the shot was in the can. She hugged him. Shavelson hugged her. The crew shouted, 'Bravo.'

She then took everyone back into her dressing room, Ines opened a bottle of Chianti and Sophia cooked spaghetti for all.

If Shavelson had a problem at all with Sophia, it was over her make-up. When she started the picture the director studied her face and decided she was too tanned. He called over the make-up artist who lightened it. Cary Grant never uses make-up, preferring to let the Californian sun do the job for him which gives him an extra hour in bed and takes a little off the overheads. But as the picture proceeded, Shavelson noticed that Sophia's face was becoming noticeably darker each day. 'She had begun looking comparatively white and halfway through was beginning to give a passable imitation of Al Jolson. Then it dawned on me I suddenly realized that back in Italy only a rich girl and one with social standing can afford the time to sit in the sun and get a tan. And putting this dark make-up on to match Cary's was Sophia's badge of prestige. She even did the same thing with her voice, high-pitching it on an aristocratic level and I practically had to bang her on the head and say "you're a Neapolitan remember, talk like Pozzuoli not Park Avenue".'

All then promised fair sailing for *Houseboat* until the script threw Cary and Sophia into each other's arms. This delirious encounter takes place at night in a small row-boat which, owing to the size of the two cavorting contestants, all but rolled them into the river. This climactic love scene, in which Cary realizes that it's really Sophia and not Martha Hyer he's wanted all along, coincided with his own renewed aspirations towards the Italian star. Sitting alone with her in her dressing room before the night sequence was set up, he re-stated his position. He was in love with her. If and when he were free, he would like to make her his wife. He had fallen in love with her in Spain and his feelings hadn't changed. This was no film-set caprice. He took her hand, but she pulled it away. 'I can't marry you, Cary,' she said with some anguish. 'I think you are a marvellous man, kind and wonderful to me. But I am already in love with Carlo Ponti. Soon, when his divorce is through, we will get married. I am sorry, it's just not possible . . .'

She ran from the dressing room, sat down with Mel Shavelson and wept. 'I had to do quite a lot of hand-holding on that picture.' Mel smiled, 'Sophia often came to me crying, largely because of what was going on between her and Cary on the studio floor. She made it clear so many times to him that Carlo Ponti was her man, but apparently Cary just couldn't understand it. He couldn't comprehend this father-fixation that Italian women have, this need for the care, the comfort and the guidance which Sophia certainly got from Carlo.'

It was in this overstrung mood that the two stars took up their positions in the boat. 'I want you to slide your arm underneath Sophia's waist,' Shavelson instructed Cary, 'you'll be lying against her on your left side, then embrace her fiercely and you go into the kiss.' It was a tantalizing moment and Cary and Sophia lay locked in position while the lighting men, make-up artists, the art director and the stills man, busied themselves on the shot. 'Okay let's try it,' Shavelson said. Cary lowered his face against Sophia's, kissed her fiercely on the lips. There was a pause. 'I think that looks good,' Shavelson said smiling quizzically. 'We'll try the shot.'

The directions in the script acquire a special piquancy when measured against the actual torment of the two leading performers. They read as follows:

DOCK: MED SHOT.

As Cinzia runs out on the dock, Tom finally catches up with her. He tries to grab her, but she pulls herself free, runs to the end of the dock and climbs into a rowboat. We hear the sound of the fireworks.

DISSOLVE TO: INT. CHILDREN'S BEDROOM—MED. CLOSE (NIGHT).

Robert and David are sleeping. All we hear are the night sounds of the river. Then a bell tinkles. David opens his eyes, sleepily. The bell tinkles again. It is the one attached to the fish line. David climbs quickly out of bed and hurries to the window.

THE RIVER. FROM DAVID'S ANGLE. MED SHOT.

The rowboat has caught the fish line in one of the oar-locks. No one is rowing. Instead, Tom has Cinzia in his arms and they are locked in an embrace. Tom kisses her. The bell tinkles (the kiss rocking the boat, the boat ringing the bell).

As he watches them, David slowly withdraws from the window.

The bell goes on ringing for quite a while. Shavelson and other interested parties noted that even after the signal 'CUT' Mr Grant continued kissing his co-star. A superstar's co-operation had rarely gone to such lengths.

If that sequence offered some encouragement to Cary, a later scene where she appears to reject him, took the edge off it. She faces him and says, 'It was a lovely interlude. I enjoyed every minute of it—until we both had too much champagne and spoiled it all.'

Tom It was just an interlude was it?

Cinzia Yes, an interlude.

Tom For a girl who's had so much experience lying, you're not doing very well at this moment.

The words were too loaded to have no effect. When the scene was over Grant stared painfully at Sophia then swung round without a word and returned to his dressing room. When Shavelson called 'Cut' on the final scene, their wedding, with the white veil, Mendelssohn, confetti and all, he felt, like Mark Antony that it was the unkindest cut of all.

But it wasn't the coup de grâce. That came the following morning in Sophia's suite at the Bel Air Hotel where Carlo had flown to join her.

A waiter wheeled in the breakfast trolley with a copy of a Los Angeles paper placed alongside the flowers. Sophia munched on a gristick, turned to the Louella Parsons' column (it was dated 27 September, 1957) and read: 'Here is a surprise. Sophia Loren has been married to Carlo Ponti since 17 September' . . . 'She and Ponti were married in Juarez, Mexico, in a proxy ceremony by Judge de la Fuente. This is her first marriage and she has been in love with him for years. It is his second marriage.' They had hoped to keep the proxy wedding a secret buried in Mexico. Now fifty million readers were sharing it.

Sophia looked up from her bed. Carlo was by the window. 'I've got news for you darling,' she said.

'Oh. What news?'

'We're married.'

'Who says so?'

'Louella Parsons.'

'Give me the paper.' Ponti read the column and noted that Louella had mis-spelt the name of one of the lawyers.

'Aren't you going to kiss the bride,' Sophia laughed, holding out her arms. An hour later she went to the studio for the wind-up shots on the film. Cary had also read the papers. 'I hope you'll be very happy,' he said kissing her on the cheek. 'You too,' Sophia said, turning abruptly to say her goodbyes to Mel Shavelson, Jack Rose and the crew.

She was sad for Cary Grant. Elated for herself and Carlo. She could now brandish a piece of paper legitimizing a union which had been joyously established for years. No more camouflage. No more denials. No more 'I am in love with a married man but I cannot tell you his name.' When the tornado came she and Carlo would just have to lean into it and hope for the best. She could write 'Mrs Carlo Ponti' on hotel registers now, talk about a husband instead of a lover. 'But since we were deeply involved with each other long before the proxy wedding,' Sophia says now, 'when the papers finally came through it was an anti-climax. Seeing it in Louella Parsons' column was almost like reading about two other people. We were already man and wife in our eyes. Passionately joined to each other. A paragraph in a gossip column hardly did it justice.'

When I raised the subject of Cary Grant, she was less forth-coming. The episode was long over. He and Betsy Drake had been divorced; Dyan Cannon became the fourth Mrs Grant, and that marriage too had collapsed. Cary, now seventy years old, sees his daughter Jennifer under 'visiting rights', that forlorn ritual of broken marriages. Sophia, still immensely fond of him, has no urge to revive the more painful aspects of the episode. 'I was really very sorry for him at the time,' she said. 'He had his own special problems of insecurity and the mixture with my own would not have made for a lasting marriage. He thought psychoanalysis might help me,' she laughed, 'but I know as much about myself as any psychiatrist could possibly discover. Anyway my complexes have been good to me. They help to make people what they are. When you lose them you might also lose yourself.'

With *Houseboat* completed there was relief all round. Cary's ordeal was over. He walked into Shavelson's office, shook hands, expressed his regrets for any difficulties he might have caused and departed. Shavelson and Jack Rose were glad to get off the rack, pleased that the picture had turned out as well as it did. As for the martyrdom of coping with the emotional convulsions of movie stars, Shavelson instances the Truffaut film *Day for Night* which itself is the story of the making of a movie. The director goes through so many problems on the set he's a nervous wreck during the day, is unable to sleep at nights. 'What can we do?' Shavelson asks ruefully, 'it's a vocational disease. It's terrible but not terminal.'

Sophia and Carlo had a week of tying up loose ends, saying their farewells to the stars who had entertained them. They were now man and wife, and Hollywood which can be as prudish as any other socially incestuous village, was able to wine and dine them less self-consciously. When Shavelson drove over to Bel Air to say goodbye to Sophia, he asked her, 'Aren't you going to take a vacation?' She laughed grimly. 'A vacation? I've never had one. I've been working ever since I was twelve. What would I do with the spare time anyway?' Curiously, the treadmill still turns as relentlessly as ever. What began as a compulsive ambition has now become an obsession. Work is her sole addiction.

Carlo booked passages on a boat to take them back to Italy for a brief intake of breath before she was to begin work on *The Key* in England. But a letter from a friend in Rome, which arrived a day before they were due to leave, pole-axed the entire operation. It did more than that. It gave them both a curtain raiser to the great chorus of abuse and condemnation which their proxy marriage had induced.

The friend urged them not to return to Italy. 'The ugly word "bigamy" is being mentioned. Everyone is talking about it. It will be very embarrassing for you both if you returned here now.' The letter enclosed a newspaper clipping.

The first warning shot across the bows had come from the Vatican paper, the *Osservatore Della Romana*. It made no direct reference to Sophia and Carlo, but merely published a reply to a reader's query demanding to know the Church's attitude to the wedding of a 'noted film star'. Why the paper was so coy about naming Sophia was mystifying since there was no sudden epidemic of Italian movie stars marrying by proxy in Mexico in September–October of 1957. However, Signor Pio Ciprotti, a lawyer on a Vatican tribunal which ruled on marriages, wrote: 'Civil divorce and a successive civil marriage are gravely illicit acts and have no judicial effect whatever before God and the (Catholic) church. Those responsible are public sinners and may no longer receive the sacraments.

'The code of Canon Law regards as bigamists those who contract a new marriage—even if only a civil one—although they are bound by a valid marriage. It punishes both parties with the penalty of infamy (a stigma attaching, in Canon law, to the character of a person). If they set up life in common, this is termed concubinage and may be punished even with interdict and excommunication.'

'Bigamy', 'Infamy', 'Concubinage', 'Excommunication', the hair-raising severity of the words turned Sophia, in her words 'to ice'. She read, and re-read the words with 'a terrible feeling of dread and indignation. I was being threatened with excommunication, with the everlasting fire, and for what reason? I had fallen in love with a man whose own marriage had ended long before. I wanted to be his wife and have his children. We had done the best the law would allow to make it official. And here was a paper calling us "public sinners". We were supposed to be on our honeymoon but I remember weeping for hours.'

Carlo Ponti, as always, squared up, fists up, to the problem. It was going to be a rough, protracted battle. He knew that accusations and abuse, in public and in private, would reach gale force as their controversial marriage sailed out into rocky waters. But he turned to the weeping Sophia; 'Don't worry. They won't destroy us. If I have to I will fight like a dog. You are my wife, and you will always be my wife.'

But there was no returning to Rome. Instead he booked seats on a plane to Paris. They were mobbed by a crowd of reporters and photographers at Orly airport. This was no ordinary movie star with a 'quickie' Mexican marriage to her credit. The Pontis were now celebrated fugitives on a collision course with the Church and other powerful enclaves in Italy.

From Orly, Sophia went on to London, Carlo going quietly to Rome by train. He'd had enough of airport interrogations. But he stayed only a few hours in Italy. He sensed the ominous deployment of the forces against them. As he went from his office to his apartment and to restaurants he had the uneasy feeling he was being shadowed. He took another train, bound for Calais and England, felt a sense of relief when it trundled slowly across the Italian frontier.

L'Osservatore and others could do their worst. The newly-weds, Mr and Mrs Carlo Ponti were going to have a honeymoon. In England, and hopefully, in peace.

8

Sinners in Transit

Sophia Loren's entry into Britain as the debatable Mrs Carlo Ponti had none of the jaunty self-confidence which marked her previous visit to England for the Italian Film Festival. Then she was just a sexy, somewhat limited starlet raiding Gina Lollobrigida's undulating territory. Now, despite the limp impact of *The Pride and the Passion* she could claim Cary Grant, Frank Sinatra, Alan Ladd, Tony Perkins, John Wayne and soon William Holden as her co-stars. But impressive though this was, it hardly explained the hordes of cameramen and reporters who swarmed into the V.I.P. lounge at London Airport to cover her arrival.

News of the Vatican's severe reaction to her Mexican marriage had been given wide coverage in the British press, and picked up around the world. The tabloids hadn't had so magnificent a coconut since the Rossellini–Bergman affair. They were going to milk it dry. Sophia, with her shrewd appreciation of the role and the occasion, wore a tight-waisted, plunging black dress, held the mandatory glass of champagne in her hand, and crossed her legs as only film stars know how. She was clearly baffled by the sensation her proxy marriage had blown up, but also defiant. 'What is the situation?' she asked angrily. 'One minute I am married, now people say I am not. They call me a sinner. Do I look like a sinner?' she demanded, to the embarrassment of the reporters who prefer to ask the questions. 'Come on tell me,' she persisted, 'is my husband a criminal? Have we done something wrong to get married? There are many others in the same position but they don't get talked about. Why then do they talk about us?' The photographers, unacquainted with the vagaries of the

Italian law on divorce, made sympathetic noises and said, 'Could you lift your skirt a bit higher, signora, and if you lean forward a bit . . .' Sophia cooled down and smiled. She was back in a safer and more familiar corral. She took care to display her engagement ring with its grey and silver pearls, and also the plain gold band alongside it. Pressed on the subject, she said that she and Carlo hoped to have seven children, 'or mebbe nine' she added quickly when the questioner seemed a shade unimpressed.

In the car to her hotel she was informed by a studio aide that the Catholic Men's Union in Rome had issued a communiqué urging its members to pray for her soul. 'That's kind of them,' she said, smiling grimly. They also demanded a boycott of her films. She was pained by that, more for Ponti's sake than for herself. It was a taste of the sourness to come. 'A star in Hollywood is not above the moral law,' the communiqué thundered, ignoring the fact that thousands of couples in Italy, some distinguished names among them, were living in what the law called 'established concubinage'. Sophia Loren and Carlo Ponti were rich, famous and in the dubious world of films. Scores of self-styled defenders of the nation's morals elbowed each other to cast the first stone.

Sophia arrived at her hotel, for the short stopover before going on to the Edgwarebury Country Club, Herts, to find her suite ablaze with flowers. They were from Carl Foreman, Sir Carol Reed and her two co-stars William Holden and Trevor Howard. Carlo was due a day later. She was glad to hear his voice on the phone. 'What is happening, what are they doing to us?' Carlo replied, 'Forget it, it will blow over,' his voice carrying more conviction than his feelings. He decided not to mention that day's gibe in an Italian paper, quoting a Vatican source, 'These poor people are not only victims of their lack of morals but also victims of their own ignorance. In the eyes of the Church, Ponti and Loren are living in concubinage.' Had the change in the divorce laws of Italy occurred then instead of thirteen years later, it would have saved them both a load of misery, and Carlo about a million pounds paving the rocky route to French citizenship and a legal marriage. But in 1957, the Pontis like Rossellini and Bergman before them, were not only victims of archaic marriage laws.

Theirs was the paradox of two people trying to function in the liberated life-style of the international movie world, within the boundaries of the repressive codes at home. On the subject of love and marriage the Vatican and Cinecitta walked backwards towards each other.

Ponti's last decision before leaving Italy was to apply to the Church's highest tribunal, the Rota, for the annulment of his marriage to Giuliana Fiastri. He knew, privately, that the application was likely to be scoffed into the street. But the request made, he was glad to slip into his camel coat, pleasantly aware that soon he and Sophia would be in each other's arms, safe from Pontifical accusations, in the English countryside. Sophia's own pulses were similarly jumping, but for additional and intriguing reasons. A large official envelope in her suite disclosed an invitation to be presented to the Queen at the Royal Film Performance. She phoned Romilda, who told Maria, who transmitted the ecstatic message to the Via Solfatara in Pozzuoli. 'A Scicolone to meet the Queen of England. Not bad, eh?' said Aunt Dora from her doorway on the street.

Meanwhile in London, Sophia hugged the satisfying thought that illegitimacy was no obstacle to shaking hands with English royalty. Anyway, the state of being 'Figlio Naturale' was not unknown to the British monarchy.

She was excited by another invitation which had been handed to her at London airport—to dinner that evening with Sir Carol Reed who was to direct her in *The Key*. Also invited were the producer, Carl Foreman, and her co-star William Holden. All three were distinguished names in movies. She knew Carl Foreman but had not met Reed or Holden before. Sophia was determined not merely to capture their goodwill. It was essential for them to adore her, if not on sight, then she might concede them an hour or two to be caught within the spell. Sophia assiduously prepared for the conquest—the locale was Carol Reed's house on the King's Road, Chelsea—positively shimmering in soft chiffons and expensive jewellery. Other actresses are content to see their leading men for tennis or swimming on Sundays, exchanging sun-oil and gossip, then back to the studios on Monday. Not Sophia.

She demands a soul-to-soul relationship, hoping to be loved, or at least liked by her co-star. She sees this as the antidote to her intense vulnerability, which no amount of husbandly adoration, film awards or hard cash seems capable of diminishing. One harsh word, as when Jean Negulesco implied she was vain, destroys her. A deep appreciative look into her green eyes swiftly resurrects her.

That evening, in Carol Reed's home, Miss Loren cornered the market in male adoration. Carl Foreman, very much the spectator that night, recalls the situation with some amusement. 'Both Bill and Carol were, of course, happily married men. But the impact Sophia had on them was so devastating, without realizing it they began to compete with each other. They were clearly both excited by this stunning Italian creature, each determined to achieve, platonically of course, THE RELATIONSHIP with her. 'What was happening,' he laughed, 'was that they were fighting for the possession of her psyche.'

If the gentlemen concerned had but known it, Sophia Loren's psyche was, in the parlance of the trade, 'up for grabs'. However, she soon became aware of the subtle competition being waged across the table. She balanced the two protagonists, superbly bestowing her favours equally upon them both.

The faithful Basilio had arrived in England with her, fulfilling, as Carl Foreman delicately put it, 'the role of dialogue coach and valued friend, although most people understood him to be her bodyguard'. There was a minor but ominous moment when the unions threatened to strike because Sophia insisted on using her own hairdresser instead of the one on the production. But when that was resolved by Sophia ruefully capitulating, the picture got under way.

The pre-production sparring between Ponti and the Hollywood distributors putting up the money, throws a fascinating light on the care and skill Carlo exercised on her behalf. It was laid down in unequivocal clauses in her contract that the director had to be selected from six of the top men in the business. The same insistence applied to her co-stars who had to be in the Gable, Grant, Holden bracket. In demanding this, Ponti was merely following

Louis B. Mayer's edict at MGM; 'If you want to build a female star you have to put her with the aces in the pack.' Carlo never departed from that principle. Studio bosses who tried to glare him out of it soon found they were challenging the wrong eyeballs. On contractual matters Signor Ponti is about as easy to cow as a cornered bull. 'He never shouts,' one old campaigner said to me. 'He just opens his hands, shows all his teeth and you find yourself programmed into doing what he asks with a doltish grin on your face.'

With Foreman as the producer, Carol (*The Third Man*) Reed as the director and the superb British actor, Trevor Howard, joining Hollywood's William Holden, neither Ponti nor Sophia could have any complaints. It was in line with their rule on escalating status. What impressed Foreman, as it was to impress other producers later, was Sophia's almost obsessive determination to break out of the Italian sex-symbol mould and be accepted as an accomplished, English-speaking superstar. Every off-studio moment was dedicated to improving skills she already possessed or acquiring new ones. She learned fencing to give her poise. She took dancing lessons, French lessons, English speaking lessons, read the London *Times* and badgered anyone within earshot to explain the intricacies of the British political system. It was all basic to her drive for prestige and acceptability which she was convinced would improve her as an actress, make her more exciting as a woman.

Confronted by this cerebrally-oriented Amazon, actors react in various ways. When Bill Holden talked to me about her, in a rooftop bar overlooking Hollywood, it was fifteen years after their first meeting. But the memory of it was sufficiently vivid to bring on that familiar, guilty schoolboy grin. 'Beautiful women have always thrown me,' he said. 'I really don't know how to handle them. She didn't walk in, she swept in. Never saw so much woman coming at me in my entire life. I have always made it a rule as far as actresses are concerned, to play it absolutely cool, almost cold on the outside. Beautiful actresses, particularly in Hollywood are subjected to some pretty dangerous invasions not only by their fellow actors but by other assorted characters in the profession. I just don't want anything in a relationship with an actress to be misunderstood at the time. You have to work with them terribly intimately, particularly in the love scenes, and unless you play it neutral you may well have a situation on your hands. I've had that difficulty with Jennifer Jones, Grace Kelly, Audrey Hepburn and Kim Novak,' he said, and reading my laugh conceded that it was probably better than being held prisoner by the Viet Cong. 'All I'm saying is that in all the relationships I've had with leading ladies, and I consider the one with Sophia a very important one, I found that the less involved I was with them, the better. Oh listen, I have people I absolutely adored—two women, three—I just think the world of, and if they had ever been willing to change their way of life and say "I'll go with you", it would have been fine. But we never stepped over the boundaries. So after all these years we have the same kind of respect for each other that we had in the beginning. I'll tell you, it's worth a lot more to me than a piece of ass.'

Holden's initial indifference on the set worried Sophia and though they worked competently together, neither was completely at ease. The breakthrough came from a most unexpected source. The film-maker Bryan Forbes, on the set at the time, had picked up an Italian *Confidential* type magazine which had published a bare-breasted picture of Sophia taken years earlier when she was working as an extra. 'Have you seen this one Sophia?' Forbes asked. Holden stared at the magazine, his reaction of contempt and anger just about reflecting the attitudes of 1957. Sophia came over to him. 'What is it?' she asked. Holden thrust the magazine under her eyes. 'This,' he scowled, 'isn't it dreadful?'

Sophia Loren reacted in character and in style. 'I don't think they're dreadful,' she said solemnly, 'they look pretty good to me.'

Holden laughed. 'Later on I got to thinking about it, and I thought "God dammit, they *were* beautiful." What the hell was I doing knocking it. It was just my moral concepts of the time. I realized how chic Sophia had been about it. From then on we began to get through to each other. But it was a long time before we showed any affection. It was always there as far as I was concerned but I never wanted to express it because of her bloody beauty and everything else, I don't go out of my way to place myself in jeopardy.'

Sophia soon established the same kind of rapport with Trevor Howard. This gravelly, versatile performer who has acted some of the world's finest talents into the ground, helped to give the film much of its impact. In this tale of the wartime tugboats which went to the aid of torpedoed merchant vessels, Sophia played Stella, the girl whose door key was passed around the officers' mess. (Wags said it was a new version of *In Which We Serve* to the un-amusement of the late Sir Noël Coward.) Some critics found the film novelettish, though all agreed that the performances were excellent, and the action stuff exciting. Sophia came in from a game of snooker with Carlo at the country club where they were staying to read: 'The heroine (in the film) is Lollo's great rival, Sophia Loren. And Loren does what Lollo found beyond her power—after an hour or more of tedium she rescues the last forty minutes from disaster. Sophia Loren alone rises superior to the script—she manages it beautifully, even movingly. Just when I had given up the picture for lost she brought it captivatingly to life.'

'What is "captivatingly" Carlo?' she asked.

'Is very good anyhow,' he replied, smiling doubtfully, screwing his eyes up at the print.

The Royal Film Performance which brought Sophia that prestigious royal handshake from Her Majesty the Queen, sent her home weeping with assorted emotions. In England the following morning, papers were full of her pictures, the elegant curtsy and the shining-eyed glance up at the Queen. But on the day of the Royal performance she and Carlo had received disquieting news from Italy. A woman living in Milan, Signora Luisa Brambilla, had registered a formal *denuncia* for bigamy against the Pontis, saying that she did so 'as a mother of a family, to save the institution of matrimony in Italy'.

By Italian law any citizen may denounce another for a crime. Once this is done the Public Prosecutor is forced to take action. In the case of Carlo and Sophia, their situation was so complex, it was unlikely that the authorities would have acted at all at that time. But Signora Brambilla's denunciation could not be ignored.

Moreover, other citizens, given Dutch courage by the accuser in Milan, howled into the act. A lawyer in the town of Chieti added his accusations. This was swiftly taken up by a male hairdresser in Genoa who worked himself up into a fair lather of indignation. A group of 'anonymous Italian mothers' (most of the accusers fired their missiles from submerged positions) said they were protesting to safeguard 'good morals'. But the cruellest blow to Sophia was the protest which came from—of all places—her home town of Pozzuoli. A group of housewives there, a touch of envy and malice distilled into their general wrath, demanded that 'action be taken'. In the event, at the preliminary hearing some months later, not one of the critics turned up in court. Nothing has been heard of Luisa Brambilla for some years. She is said to have vanished to a convent. 'I bear her no ill-will,' Sophia says. 'She did what she felt she had to do. We did what we had to do. But she caused us a great deal of pain. She drove us into exile, with the threat of a gaol sentence hanging over us.'

But exile, English style, was proving an agreeable exercise. It was a warm autumn and the classy contacts of Carol Reed and Carl Foreman brought the Pontis invitations from government ministers, and to parties on the lawns of English stately homes. One night Sophia was guest of honour at a party at the Italian Embassy given by the then ambassador, Count Vittorio Zoppi. The occasion was kept secret because of anxiety over Sophia's position with the Church. To have as your chief guest a woman threatened with possible excommunication, whose husband faced bigamy charges, was hardly in the best tradition of diplomatic dinners.

If the short grey-haired ambassador thought Sophia would tacitly accept the delicacy of the situation by remaining silent, he was swiftly disillusioned. As she was presented to him, she drew him to one side. 'Can nothing be done to get my husband's first marriage annulled?' Sophia pleaded. He raised her hand to his lips. 'I can make no promises,' he said, 'but I will do what I can.'

The Ponti's leisure hours in the sedate Edgwarebury Country Club were hardly spent in the manner expected of superstars and their rich husbands. When she swung hippily into the dining room for meals, Sophia had to weave her way between apple-cheeked retired admirals and wealthy widows peering critically over their lorgnettes. At one point, an elderly gentleman approached Sophia, cleared his throat and said, 'Um . . . er . . . excuse me madam, I fear you are sitting on my *Times*.' If a resident could be more concerned with his paper than with the formidable posterior that was unknowingly warming it, then clearly, Sophia reasoned, this was the place to be. As we were driving away from there one evening, Sophia, despite the limited impact of her first English-speaking films, displayed a firm confidence and a rare degree of prophecy. 'I know everything I've done has been more bodywork than acting. Fine, that's all they think I have to offer. But you'll see. One day I will prove myself and win an Oscar.'

We had been driving to the Savoy Hotel, London, for a private dinner party I had arranged as a piece of journalistic whimsy designed to off-set the gloom of a protracted November fog. Finding my column three inches short, I hit on that old standby, a competition, which fills space and saves effort. I tossed out an invitation to readers (around fifteen million at the time)—to write, in a few sentences why they would like to have dinner with Sophia Loren and William Holden and what they would say. (In the easy-going Britain of the time one could engage in sprees of that sort without blushing.)

Selecting two of the most promising letters from the thousands of replies, I arranged for the winners to be brought to the hotel. Mr Holden had 'won' a Mrs Patricia Dyer of Frinton in Essex; Sophia, Denis Doyle of Bilston, Staffordshire. I sensed, over the oysters, the turtle soup, the chicken and the Niersteiner wine, that Bill Holden had had a hard day. Mrs Dyer was nervous and stared into his face from her position on his left. Bill stared back without speaking. It was going to be quite an evening.

Finally, Mrs Dyer, drawing on the inspiration of all the sages, leapt in with 'what is your favourite film?'

Holden twisted his lips into a dangerous smile. 'It hasn't been made yet,' he said.

'If you quit show business altogether,' faltered the lady, 'what would you do?'

'Die,' Bill Holden said pouring himself another drink.

Mrs Dyer's voice was now a whisper. She geared herself for the final question which had won her this scintillating, forthcoming, informative superstar for the evening.

'With what five people have you most enjoyed working?'

'None.'

Mrs Dyer took refuge in her chicken. The evening was taking on third degree burns. I glanced over at Sophia who looked delicious in a lace-topped dress with a tantalizing, see-through neckline. She was having her problems too. Not a word from Mr Doyle who looked at her through his spectacles as though merely checking to see if she was there, then turned back to his food. As an exclusive private dinner in the best suite at the Savoy, it was slowly resembling the after-prayer numbness in a house of mourning. I signalled Mr Doyle to ask his winning questions. He gave me a slow grin and said nothing. Sophia's eyes widened in disbelief. Here she was giving this character the full treatment, dressed by Schubert, perfumed by Givenchy, the lace-draped Scicolone bosoms being given a rare public outing, and he was virtually ignoring her—them. It was too much. 'Lissen Mr Dial,' she hissed, 'you won me, why don't you spik to me?'

Mr Doyle gave a nervous, falsetto giggle. 'Go on,' I said to him, trying to contrive encouragement out of paralysis. He got his first question in. 'You have wealth and success but you work ceaselessly. What drives you on and on?'

'Luffoffart' Sophia said, delighted that the ice had at last been broken.

I have heard remarks silence cocktail parties but Sophia's stopped the evening in its tracks. Holden stared at her in bewilderment. So too did Mrs Dyer, Mr Doyle and the wine waiter, caught between pours.

'Luffoffart,' Sophia repeated, looking to me for assistance.

'Say it slowly dear,' I said.

Moving into slow gear, she finally cleared up the mystery. 'LOVE . . . OF . . . ART' she said coolly and deliberately. 'Don't you spik English?'

Christmas in Switzerland for the Pontis that year, was a strange affair. Whatever they themselves thought, the world regarded them as fugitives. The powerful Roman Catholic Morality League had now moved to bring charges of 'bigamy and public adultery' against them. The cards from friends in Rome wishing them 'Happy Christmas' included the cautionary information that official hostility was approaching danger point. They were better off where they were. Sophia's sister Maria and their mother Romilda came to Switzerland bringing presents and moral support. The colony of film celebrities, resident in Burgenstock and elsewhere for the crisp, bracing tax advantages, issued invitations to parties and in turn were invited over to sample Sophia's home-cooked gnocchi al gorgonzola.

But the fashion-plate ski crowd with their interminable chatter about broken affairs and ankles, drove Sophia to quiet poker sessions with Romilda—quiet, that is, until both screamed Neapolitan style, accusing each other of cheating. Redeeming the general boredom were the occasional meetings with the late Sir Noël Coward, sometimes at his villa, or at theirs. Noël took a mildly derisory view of superstars. He thought few artistes deserved the title. 'After all, dear boy,' he once said, addressing me but smiling at himself in a mirror at Chaplin's home at Vevey, 'how many Noël Cowards are there?' He too was besotted, in his own suave way, by this magnificent specimen only an Alp away. 'She should have been sculpted in chocolate truffles so that the world could have devoured her,' he said from behind his familiar smoke-screen.

Those diversions apart, Sophia was glad to shake the snow off her ski-boots and get back to her favourite pastime—hard work. She flew direct to Hollywood in mid-January to film *Black Orchid* with Anthony Quinn. The picture, about Americans of Italian descent, had more than a hint of Tennessee Williams' *Rose Tattoo*. It featured Anthony Quinn as a shambling, lovable bull of a man who falls in love with a gangster's widow, Rose, played in a kind of lush low key by Sophia.

The director was Marty Ritt whose fine list of credits include *Hudd* for which Patricia Neal won her Oscar. A leathery, no-

nonsense movie maker, Ritt had some doubts about Sophia's suitability for the role. 'I thought she might be too young,' he said. 'But I certainly didn't resist her when I met her. Who could? But here was this all-powerful female playing a woman who was left with a child, supposedly mature, experienced and a widow, yet looking in the full bloom of her late twenties! But Sophia overcame it because she is resolute, but mostly because she has this perfect concentration. It was, I think, her first really serious role. She gave herself to me, and to the film, and was rewarded for it.'

In spite of the long list of celebrated actresses who have worked for him, Ritt rates them only as performers, not as sex-symbols, a breed he dislikes. 'I don't like those pictures which rely on them, and I'm always suspicious of both males and females who bank on it.'

If Sophia was an exception in his book it was because, 'though she was one hell of a female with what we might call a "high fuckability quotient" she was also a very superior lady. I was impressed by her on every level. I think she is a fine actress—often a great one.'

Having two stars, both highly charged physically, and conscious of it, posed a problem to the director. Both of them at maximum revs, sexually, in the love scene would have overbalanced it almost hilariously. But neither Quinn nor Sophia displayed any enthusiasm to put the brakes on. On the first rehearsal the pair turned so much steam on each other, Ritt called 'cut' to the surprise of the players and the annoyance of the absorbed onlookers. 'Very interesting,' Ritt grinned, 'but now let's do it at half the energy, at the rate you're both going you'll explode.' There were five re-takes on the scene before Ritt was satisfied he had reduced the pressure levels in both performers. 'Finally,' Quinn said, 'we were playing the scene so small it didn't seem to us to be like acting any more. But when we saw it on the screen it was as powerful as hell. Because the thing Sophia does, and obviously I do, is to over-charge instead of pulling back. Actors shouldn't push their masculinity,' Quinn expounded. 'It's like a director once said to me, "Don't try to talk with your balls in your mouth. Just put the balls where they belong, when you talk they'll be there." '

Quinn obviously took that sagacious advice, though critics disappointed in the film might have been glad if he hadn't. Any diversion, presumably, would have been welcomed to take the edge off the thick sentimentality in which the film often floundered. Yet in spite of the picture's flaws Sophia won, some months later, the Best Actress Award at the Venice Film Festival for her role in the film. It confirmed what Ponti always believed, in the face of dubious shrugs by the rest of the movie world, that Sophia had great resources of talent. That and a beaver-like determination would eventually prove its worth.

Black Orchid finished, Carlo and Sophia were thrown back into the limbo of the marriage, Mexican style. There was no returning to Italy where the controversy was constantly generating a new head of steam with envy and malice the side-orders of the day. But now the drama was acquiring a new sub-plot involving Sophia's jazz-singing sister, Maria. She had met and secretly become engaged to Romano Mussolini, son of Italy's Il Duce, who played some cool piano solos in the exclusive night-clubs and jazz sessions of Rome. They appeared at a Rome Jazz Festival and were photographed together. They announced that they planned to marry. The headline SOPHIA'S SISTER TO MARRY A MUSSOLINI was a gift to the newspapers at a time when Italy was still to recover fully from the ravages of the dictator's reckless ambitions. Romilda had mixed feelings. Romano had good looks and a powerful circle of élite as well as swinging associates. But the name had bitter connotations. Could the Scicolones take yet another scandal?

Sophia advised her mother to back away from the situation, though she expressed her own objections to Maria. 'I didn't want Maria to marry him, not because he was a Mussolini,' Sophia said, 'but because I never thought he was the right man for her.' But by the time Sophia had expressed her disapproval the two musicians were involved in close and torrid harmony. Rachele Mussolini, Benito's widow, living in self-imposed isolation in Northern Italy, shrugged indifferently at the romance. What indignation she could muster was turned ferociously on what she regarded as an ungrateful nation. They had sent her what was left of her husband after the lynch-mob of guerrillas had finished with him, part of his brain, a foot, little else. Maybe he had taken assorted mistresses, imposed a prolonged and vicious war on the Italian people. But when she speaks of him—as she did to Sophia at Maria's wedding—it was with a surprising degree of respect and admiration. She still refers to him as 'Il Duce' preferring to remember the posturing politician she married, not the monster he eventually became.

Her sister's love affair soon lost its novelty value, overshadowed as it was, by the Ponti 'scandal'. Only the English, according to Sophia, appeared to accept the situation with characteristic nonchalance. She was delighted when Carl Foreman phoned her in Hollywood to ask if she would fly over to re-shoot a small scene on the film and also attend its royal opening, by Princess Margaret, soon after.

Dressed by Yves St Laurent with a spare gown in reserve—movie stars do not do things by halves—she carried off this second royal occasion of her career in style. At the end of the film the audience rose to applaud her enthusiastically as they did Princess Margaret. She wished Domenico and Luisa had been there. With royalty and their distinguished aides to her left and right it might have convinced them that the profession wasn't, as they believed, dominated by white slavers and hookers.

Luisa had died three years earlier in Pozzuoli, but Domenico, then seventy-four, was strutting around the town, brandishing Sophia's cover pictures reminding everyone including those he'd been telling for years, that he was the Grandfather of The Star. Sophia says little about him now except that she worshipped him. But her Aunt Dora, in Pozzuoli, over a glass of white wine from the Ponti vineyard, insisted loudly on delineating the special Sophia–Domenico relationship. 'She was very close to both of them, but to Domenico she gave adoration. He had been more like a father to her and when he was ill she suffered every pain with him. When she was working in Italy she gave orders to the doctors to come at once whenever he needed them. She sent him special medicines from New York, from London, even from Hollywood. Whatever she thought might help him, she sent. And always there were the phone calls, long phone calls from other countries. When she moved into her villa in Rome she had a car specially constructed to take a bed in it. She came here of course. Many times. But,' Dora smiled, 'she wanted Domenico to enjoy her home. The chauffeur would come, we would carefully lie Domenico on the bed and he would be driven off to Rome.'

Even then, in the horizontal, old Domenico contrived a lordly wave to the inhabitants of the via Solfatara as the converted limousine purred slowly up the hill.

Sophia and Carlo returned to America for the last two films she had contracted to make there, *That Kind of Woman* which had Sidney Lumet as the director, and *Heller in Pink Tights* a spoof Western, placed in the distinguished hands of George Cukor. Ponti was still chasing the illusion that Hollywood would finally strike gold with his Sophia. Were they blind? Couldn't they see how great she was? Carl Foreman had said that one day she would be as big as Garbo, which was one of the rare occasions that the two producers agreed with each other. Yet Hollywood seemed incapable of harnessing the Loren talents to a successful movie.

Lumet was no exception, and Cukor only marginally so. *That Kind of Woman* which was shot in New York, was a lightweight idea which virtually disintegrated by the third reel. It involved a kept woman and her unconvincing dilemma trying to choose between the security offered by the rich George Sanders and the overcharged libido of Tab Hunter.

When Lumet, who had just directed *Twelve Angry Men*, received the script from Carlo he thought it was dreadful. But Ponti was persuasive. He was looking now for 'acting directors' by which he meant those who recognized the unlimited brilliance of his beautiful Sophia. Lumet had a dual motive for agreeing to make the picture. He was anxious to get New York recognized as a thriving production centre with facilities to match those in Hollywood. He banked on Sophia feeling happier, working in that city as opposed to the comatose environment of Hollywood. He was right, and Sophia was, he said, 'totally responsive from the word go. Rightaway,' he said, 'she knew what to do and was a total joy from beginning to end. And it was the usual Sophia story—everybody was in love with her, me included. You mind if I stay with the superlatives a bit? She literally takes your breath away when she walks into a room. She's got wit, she sings bloody well and linguistically she's extraordinary. What she doesn't understand in words, she understands in your eyes. It may have been the cliché of the day, but she really did want to move off the body level, stop being regarded as the big-breasted Italian with the steam coming out of her ears, and dammit, she's succeeded.'

He too discovered, like the celebrated pilgrims before him, that nothing less than total contact with the men in her movies is tolerable to Sophia. 'I learned that if she doesn't have that she can't function at all. My God! It's tactile. It goes to food. When she was happy she just had to pour out all her joy over a hot stove, cooking meals for the lot of us.'

There were moments of misery too as further accusations were picked up from the Italian papers and reprinted in New York. But Lumet admired the way she refused to let those periods of upset prejudice her work or delay shooting. 'When some bad news got out to the location she'd just sit in the back of the studio limousine, cry for twenty minutes, and then when you needed her, the assistant director would rap on the window and whack! out she'd come, a bit red-eyed but ready and smiling for work.'

Yet neither Sophia's eagerness to do a good job, nor Lumet's skill, could redeem the picture. 'The first forty-five minutes,' he claimed, 'are absolutely enchanting, and the rest is nonsense.' Most critics agreed with him, but again, excepted Sophia from the general theme, one saying, 'Sophia's seductive charm alone makes this film worth seeing.'

Cukor's *Heller in Pink Tights* failed for different reasons, although Carlo Ponti insists that it's a first class film and that Sophia was marvellous in it. Her co-star, Anthony Quinn on the other hand, considered it a disaster, largely because of the danger of satirizing a Western. (Lee Marvin's *Cat Ballou* had yet to arrive to disprove him.) 'You know what they say, "satire closes on Saturday". All I know is we both seemed terribly lost in the picture.' It was a fair summary of the plot which lost its way in a confusion of Red Indians, gunfighters, sheriffs and chorus girls. Sophia, the girl in the 'Tights', is an actress in a rundown stage company touring the mid-west of the 'eighties. Tony Quinn plays the manager. Cukor directs with style but the juxtaposition of parody and corny melodrama kisses the whole business goodbye.

Even before the film was shown Sophia and Carlo had that old sinking feeling that it was likely to end up in the boneyard where her previous adventures lay. Not that all the films had lost money. Indeed many of them recouped all their costs and more. But The Great American Dream, which was to transform Sophia into the new Garbo, had been a big, brave flop with a twenty-million dollar price-tag on it. But neither Carlo, who matched his convictions with his own money, nor Sophia, regret their short and happy life in Hollywood.

'I don't sneer at the adventure,' Sophia said. 'The films may not have been that marvellous but I learned something from all of them. I needed Hollywood to help me develop as an actress. It isn't their fault that they didn't know what to do with me. To them, Italians have always been mostly gangsters and waiters. And they never seemed able to accept a foreign actress for what she is. They feel they have to change her. Now maybe it is different. But then they looked at me and I could read it in their eyes. "We'll take a bit off here, put a bit on there, and soon we'll have her looking like everyone else." If I had stayed on that is what I would have become. So I came home.'

But home for the Pontis was anywhere on the safe side of the Italian border. Carlo took a house on the French Riviera close to the Aga Khan's villa. The Ponti Maxim, putting Sophia among the aces in her profession, applied equally to places and potentates. Soon Sophia and the Aga Khan were on first-name terms with mutual invitations to drop by at any time to slide into each other's pools—the former Scicolone privately pinching herself to see if it was all really happening.

But at dusk, Carlo and Sophia walked through their gardens

down to the deserted waterfront, talking over their problems for hours. 'It was a nightmare for us,' Sophia remembered, turning her head abruptly, irritated to find she was crying. 'We missed our country so much. Sometimes when we were in Switzerland I'd make Carlo drive me up to the St Gothard pass so that I could look at the sky over Italy. It was childish I suppose, but it meant something at the time.'

Had they gone back to Rome together, defiantly shared the same door key, then the law would almost certainly have pulled the roof down over them. The situation received a tantalizing twist in the form of an invitation to Sophia, to attend the Venice Film Festival's showing of *Black Orchid*, an American entry in the competition. The whisper was going around that her performance was so highly rated she stood a chance of winning the Best Actress Award.

There were other whispers too that snoopers were ready to home in on the airport or bob up from strategic positions on gondolas, in case Sophia, or Carlo, or the two of them, dared to show up in Italy.

Should they go together and to hell with the threat to their lives and her career? Would it be better as a hit-and-run operation with Sophia flitting in alone, hopefully picking up a prize, but with the risk of having her passport confiscated by the airport police? The questions posed a formidable challenge to Ponti's Milanese guile and to Sophia's Neapolitan couldn't-give-a-damn. 'In the end,' Sophia said, 'we decided it would be too much like slapping our own country in the mouth if we were to turn up there together. Finally, though I dreaded leaving Carlo, I decided to face it out alone.'

They parted on a warm September evening at St Raphael railway station.

'Don't lose your passport,' Carlo said as he kissed her goodbye.

'Tell that to the carabinieri in Venice,' Sophia laughed.

9

A Massage from Mr Sellers

While Sophia's train was rolling eastwards across northern Italy, Carlo Ponti made a few significant phone calls to selected friends in Rome and Venice. Sophia was not only the second Mrs Ponti, courtesy of Mexico, she was now earning upwards of a quarter of a million dollars a picture which was no bad stipend for a working wife. The notion that an over-zealous immigration official in Venice might put all that at risk and cause his queen even momentary embarrassment, had him barking orders and requests in all directions. He received powerful assistance from Venice where the faltering festival, a pale imitation of Cannes, badly needed a third act. The organizers didn't want the affair to flop because of a slight case of alleged bigamy.

Eventually, with a good deal of arm-squeezing all round, the word went out. It was going to be orchids, not recriminations for Sophia Loren. There would be no challenge either to her or her passport.

When her train pulled into Venice's Mestre station, Sophia found herself shaking. 'After everything that had been said and written about me I thought, "God knows what they will do to me." ' She stood for a few seconds in her carriage. Then walked down to the quay on to the canal.

What she saw was hardly a typical welcome for a 'public sinner'. The gondolas of Venice had formed up like a battle fleet, flags flying, whistles blowing and a chorus of 'Sophia, Sophia, Sophia . . . Benvenuto . . . Welcome home to Italy!'

It was a lump-in-the-throat sequence, early Mervyn LeRoy with a touch of Ziegfeld. Sophia surveyed the crowd and wept. They surged forward and mobbed her, some enthusiasts stealing a pinch or two, which made her feel even more at home. She stepped down into a speedboat and like a sexy Boadicea, sailed out to conquer the Lido. That night, facing an exploding galaxy of flashbulbs, she walked on to the stage and received the Volpi Award for the Best Actress of the Festival.

She expressed her thanks, kissed a few familiar cheeks and asked to be taken to the airport. Without Carlo beside her the occasion missed the one element that mattered. 'He was the one who had created me,' Sophia said, 'I couldn't face that night without him.'

She apologized to her hosts, ordered a private plane to be ready at the airport outside Venice. Carlo was waiting at Nice . . . with open arms, an antique necklace and a fierce hug of congratulation.

But the triumph at Venice, more a raiding operation, opened no doors to Rome. Theirs was still, despite the solemn charade in Juarez, an illicit union, evoking curiously assorted reactions. The Vatican condemned it and put the shutters up. The public either followed the Ecclesiastical line or relished every bulletin on the exiled couple, and the more prurient the innuendo the better. If it was a crime, then it was a crime of passion and the public loved a bleeding heart. Only Hollywood and the movie business failed to get the measure of it, to their intense irritation. There had to be an angle. Putting it crudely, as many did, the argument went: 'Either Ponti is a stallion in sheep's clothing, or this broad's father-fixation has taken her mind off the action.'

Most were unwilling to accept that the Ponti–Loren relationship in spite of the disparity of age and—who cared—height, was sublimely satisfactory to both parties.

'What nobody could understand then, and still can't,' Sophia said on an occasion when Ponti had wandered off into the garden, 'is the extraordinary power of the man. He generates a tremendous excitement for me. He is a sensitive lover, a cultured friend, the understanding father I never had.' She looked out towards the short stocky figure with his balding head reflecting the descending sun. 'Every woman's needs are wrapped up inside that man.' The measure of the claim embarrassed her. 'Well, all my needs anyway!'

The season in the South of France ended abruptly as Bardot took her latest love and jet-set hangers-on back with her to Paris. Anyway, Sophia's Château St Therese had upstaged Brigitte's more modest villa at La Madrague. Carlo took a large apartment overlooking the Arc de Triomphe in Paris and worked on his marital confusions while Sophia moved to Vienna to film *A Breath of Scandal*. Originally titled *Olympia* this Molnar comedy starred Sophia with John Gavin and Maurice Chevalier, in pursuance of the now dubious theory that star names meant star pictures.

It was a smoothly handled movie of Imperial Vienna, but the director Michael Curtiz got too much landscape and gold braid into the picture, not enough wit. Sophia's role of Olympia, a young widow banished by the Emperor for naughty behaviour, looked better than it played. At the end of it all, Ponti sat back, sighed deeply, and did some penetrating stock-taking. He'd invested a fortune of his and other people's money, buying the best available stories, hiring the world's top actors for Sophia. But something was wrong. Sophia was beautiful, talented, versatile and eager. Where were the big grosses? Why all the flops? Ponti went back to the drawing board, unwilling to admit, at least to Sophia, that the real problem had little to do with the subjects or their directors. Sophia was a Mediterranean animal rashly put down in an alien environment. Wrong taste, wrong touch, wrong language.

After gipsy-ing around the world for nearly three years of snap-crackle breakfasts and de-frosted telly-dinners she ached to get back home. It was now an obsession, and Carlo shared it. She was due immediately in Capri to begin *It Started in Naples* for Mel Shavelson. Her co-star this time was Clark Gable, maturely middle-aged but still the 'King' to millions. Maybe, Ponti decided, this superstar association would work better on her home ground.

But what was the legal position? Ponti's lawyers in Rome had tried the application for the annulment of his marriage to his former wife, and it had failed. The grounds—that he did not sincerely believe in the Sacrament at the time of that marriage—

were not accepted by the Church tribunal. He was cornered, but stubborn. 'I have to come back to Italy,' Ponti insisted to his legal advisers, 'and so must Sophia.'

The lawyers went into a huddle over the documents, the laws and the fine print on the Mexican proxy marriage. They phoned him in Vienna where he had joined Sophia. 'We might be able to get this marriage set aside which will get you off the hook, but it will mean Sophia won't be Mrs Ponti any more.'

Carlo shrugged. If the Mexican marriage stood, then in Italy he ran the risk of a bigamy trial, while Sophia would be exposed to the 'concubinage' allegation. They'd still be on the run. 'Do what you can,' he said finally, 'Sophia is coming back to Rome and I will follow.'

The decision to send Sophia on ahead was a legal imperative. They must not be seen together. Any hint of a man and wife relationship would be brazen and dangerous. 'I remember the lengths we had to go to, to pretend we weren't living together,' Sophia said, her long legs raised up on a priceless chunk of Roman masonry. 'We changed houses regularly. If we went to dinner parties we would often arrive and leave separately. Sometimes my mother would put us up at her home, or we'd stay with trusted friends. It was a weird existence but what could we do? We were still "public sinners" in some people's eyes. But at least we were in Italy. The Venice Film Festival had given me a taste of what it was like to be back. But it wasn't Rome. Going back there was one of the most moving experiences of my life. It was nearly fifteen years ago but the memory of it is as vivid as ever.'

She remembers Carlo's goodbye at the railway station at Vienna. He knew that the world's press and the swarming *paparazzi* would turn the Rome railway terminal into a circus. He arranged for her to be taken off at Chiusi, some distance north of Rome, and make the rest of the journey by car. But Sophia was too large and voluptuous a secret for the Italian railways to handle. The word had been passed from station to station. She remembers that when the train crossed the Italian frontier and at all the stops during the night, she heard porters whispering 'Sophia . . .

Sophia . . .' It was a moment which cried out for mandolins and extra tissues.

There was more to come. As the Orient Express shrieked into the Italian dawn, Sophia, her face pressed against the carriage window, caught a glimpse of the familiar names on the railway stations. Those words, the peasant women already in the fields, the sun putting a warm glow on the terra-cotta roof-tops, was more than she could bear. She wept. The gift-wrapping and the Cellophane had come off the package. A Loren had gone to Hollywood but a Scicolone had returned to Rome. Her tears took her all the way to Chiusi.

In spite of Ponti's secrecy network, a weak link in the chain resulted in a lone photographer being tipped off about her arrival there. He tailed her car, other newsmen tailed him, and by the time Sophia arrived at the apartment which she had taken for her mother—and to provide diplomatic immunity for Carlo—a flurry of photographers and reporters were on the doorstep.

But these were only the smart operators. The main press contingent had waited in vain at Rome railway station. All they met were the twenty-seven pieces of baggage which covered the basic essentials for Sophia's short stint in old Vienna. She told the reporters outside the apartment, 'I hope to settle this situation of my marriage. Then, if God grants it, I hope to have the greatest joy in my life—a baby.' A woman cheered. Some cried. The press, satisfied, called it a day.

Carlo Ponti arrived a day later and moved into a house loaned by a business colleague. Both he and Sophia were aware that observers, official or otherwise, were deploying into strategic positions, on the lookout for the slightest hint of blissful co-habitation. But both parties considered this posed no insurmountable challenge to their ingenuity. Love, and Signor Ponti, would find a way.

Sophia was eager to go to Capri and get the measure of the legendary Gable whose films she had seen as a child in Pozzuoli. She had originally turned the picture down but when she heard Gable was in it, she rapidly changed her mind. Oddly, though she'd lived for fifteen years within a twenty-pence boat ride of the island, she had never had the money to get there. Now she was going in style, being paid a fortune for her services, and there was Gable waiting on the quayside, grinning apprehensively, running a nervous finger across the philanderer's moustache. He liked what he saw. 'Jesus,' he said to a cameraman, 'is that all mine for the duration?'

Shavelson saw the exchange of smiles between them, the formal hand-shake, the introduction to Gable's wife, Kay, and was pleasantly reassured that he wouldn't have another Cary Grant-type situation on his hands. The film, originally titled *Americano Go Home* until Hollywood lost its nerve and changed it, was a Technicoloured soufflé about a Neapolitan woman's battle with an American lawyer over the fate of the nephew they discover they have in common. Vittorio de Sica was cast as an Italian lawyer, hamming the part magnificently, his broken English a fair imitation of Hollywood's stock Italian waiter. Gable's Italian wasn't much better, with 'A River Dirtchy' among his more benign contributions.

Sophia was, by general assent, excellent in this picture. She showed herself to be a comedienne, and her honky-tonk dance number, brown thighs swaying sinuously behind purple cats-tails plus a cunning bit of business with a falling shoulder-strap, drew from Gable at the completion of the shot, 'This girl makes you think—all the wrong thoughts!'

The production was not entirely devoid of friction, with the diplomatic Basilio, the favoured friend at Sophia's 'court' being called in to smooth ruffled egos. The one occasion when Sophia appeared riled was not so much a display of temperament but her well-disguised determination not to be over-shadowed by one of the world's most adored and powerful actors. During a break in the shooting one afternoon on Capri, she went to Shavelson. 'I know Gable is a very big star,' she said, 'but I don't think he's being very fair with me.'

'How do you make that out?'

'Well, somehow he manages to position himself so that my worst side is always turned towards the camera. He doesn't have to worry about his career but I have to worry about mine.'

Shavelson went over to Gable, who growled, 'What the hell's she talking about? She's lucky. Both sides of my face are lousy. And my backside isn't that good-looking either. You just tell me what side she wants to show and I'll get out of her way!'

When the three of them saw the 'rushes' later, all conceded Sophia had a case. 'She knows what is best for her—she always does. That's what's so devilish about her,' Shavelson said.

Sophia's style of working, both in Capri and Rome, puzzled Gable, as it has all the actors and directors she has worked with, with the exception of Mastroiani and de Sica who understood. Off the set, Sophia rarely fraternizes with the rest of the cast, preferring to stay in her dressing room and mostly in the company of women. Ines, her secretary and confidante, is rarely away from her. A slightly built young woman with jet black hair, a sharp-featured but attractive face, Ines orchestrates Sophia's working life with the amiable firmness of a fight-manager. She is chaperone, gofer, sparring partner, soft shoulder, baby watcher, appointments gauleiter and she knows all the working parts of the Loren machinery. When Carlo is away and Sophia feels lonely and vulnerable on some distant location, the star and Ines often share the same bedroom. And they'd be in it at 9.00 p.m. when the other stars were just gearing up for fun. 'I couldn't understand it,' Quinn said. 'On the *Pink Tights* location she'd just never go out. Always locked away with this girl Ines. I'd say to her, "What the hell do you do all day?" But it never made any difference. She was friendly on the set, but when the work was over, it was over. I could never get close to her. If she wants to know you, she sets the ground rules. Otherwise it's forbidden territory, behind a piece of beautiful crystal-clear unbreakable glass.'

Clark Gable solved Sophia's profile problem and the pair of them continued the film amicably. Only Carlo was having difficulties. The lawyers had spelt it out. Should he and Sophia be seen together in what was nicely termed 'meaningful situations' then the law which had been reluctant to act under pressure from the 'denouncers' might be forced to move in and arrest them. Though Signor Ponti is a most law-abiding citizen, when you have a wife like Sophia Loren pining for you, and in a blue towelling bikini on the Isle of Capri, legal impediments tend to dissolve in the heat of the sun and the moment.

Carlo took the risk and the plane to Naples. If Italy, which was secretly proud of its Sophia, couldn't understand what was luring him to Capri, then that country's love-worshipping image was a fraud. He drove to Sorrento where the Gables and Sophia met him with the hired boat to take him to the island. But news of the meeting filtered through to Rome where reluctant law officials smiled wanly at each other, and re-opened the file marked 'Carlo Ponti'. By luck, or a piece of astute timing, Sophia's return to Italy coincided with the public prosecutor's annual holiday. By the time he returned, the fusion of the Pontis with the Isle of Capri had been blissfully consummated. The filming was finished, the Gables gone.

Government lawyers studied the papers, dubious of the chances of making a bigamy charge stick. Absent from the denunciations was the one which would have impressed the courts most of all. A complaint from the wife of the only marriage Italy legally recognized, Giuliana Fiastri. No such complaint had been received. For her, the marriage was long over. Denouncing Carlo wouldn't put it together again.

The courts made no move, merely announced that 'the case was under study'. But leading Italian lawyers locked horns on the case, some arguing that even if a bigamy charge were brought, it would be nullified by a general amnesty, just granted to celebrate an Italian victory at Solferino a hundred years before. Others sneered at this, claiming that as bigamy was a 'recurrent crime', those charged with it were liable to proceedings until the allegedly bigamous marriage was annulled. The Italian newspapers polarized into opposing camps, preaching loving kindness or threatening damnation, with one fervent character writing in *Oggi*: 'They should be burned in public.'

Ponti went about his business. He would break them, they wouldn't break him. Sophia, red-eyed most of the time, pleaded, 'all I want is to marry Carlo, in church if they will let us, have his children and give them the things I never had as a child'. The response was a renewal of the campaign to ban Ponti's films and further snarling in the press.

With all this hate blowing up, England, *The Millionairess* and Peter Sellers seemed like a life-line to heaven. Sophia couldn't wait to get there. Peter Sellers could hardly wait to meet her.

Sophia Loren's casting as *The Millionairess* in the film version of the Shaw comedy, did not receive automatic endorsement from the Hollywood studio putting up the money. Her name had been put to Twentieth Century Fox by the British film-maker Dimitri de Grunwald who received the rasping comeback: 'What the hell do you want her for? She's been in nothing but disasters. Now if you get Ava Gardner you have a deal.'

De Grunwald insisted: 'Look, the whole beauty of this film is the chemistry. Sellers and Loren will set each other alight.' The argument was pursued right up to the signing of the contract. De Grunwald was relieved when Sophia arrived off the train at Victoria Station to clinch it.

Katherine Hepburn had always wanted to play the film part. According to Sophia, Katie was peeved when she heard that the Italian star had beaten her to it. But Sophia commented, not unkindly, 'I do think the part requires more sex appeal than, um, well . . . it would have been a different kind of picture, don't you think?'

Peter Sellers' first view of the said sex appeal, when Loren's Paris boat-train clanked into Victoria, left him marginally incoherent. 'She really threw me,' he said. 'I thought then, and still think, that she was the most beautiful creature I'd met in my life.' Mr Sellers' euphoria received an erotic boost when, on the first day's shooting he found that in his role of a browned-up Indian doctor he had to massage her naked back. She was ready for him, bra-less but face down, the smooth brown back exposed for his touch. The ordeal was too much for him.

'When we do the take,' he mumbled, 'do I really have to massage you?'

'Of course you will, darling,' she laughed.

'It's all right then, is it?' he asked urgently.

'Of course it's all right,' Sophia mocked. 'You're a doctor aren't you?'

Sellers hesitated, looking around to see if Carlo Ponti was within eye-shot. 'You see,' Sellers explained, recalling his dilemma at the time, 'I'd never played a part like this before. I always thought they faked this kind of stuff. But there she was with her bra down. I thought "Strewth if I touch her she'll give me one." '

But Sophia's insistence and Sellers' increasing interest in the idea overcame his qualms. Slowly he spread his hands over her back gently kneading it from the nape to the waistline. Sellers does not remember precisely how many re-takes there were, for in that simple opening shot he had fallen 'very much in love with her'. He had massaged his way into a tricky situation.

'I mean,' he said by way of mitigation, 'there was this magnificent, fantastic woman, a really very, very beautiful woman. All I can say is that I don't think I have ever been in love with anyone the way I was with Sophia.'

As the shooting progressed, so did Sellers' passion for his co-star. He took her to Chinese restaurants. She cooked spaghetti dinners for him at her luxurious English retreat in the country. Basilio Franchina observed it all with some concern. He was not worried about Sophia's capacity to handle the situation. But he was uneasy about the effect Sellers' emotional involvement might have on the picture.

As Sellers remembered it:

'He was a sort of watchdog and of course he became very incensed about it. He said to me (Sellers' Sicilian imitation):

' "When the husband he finds out about this there will be trouble!"

'I told him: "Well if he has to find out about it, it's just too bad." '

What took the heat out of the situation was the arrival of Carlo Ponti in London, and the theft of Sophia's jewellery—£185,000 worth—when she left her chalet in Hertfordshire to meet him.

The thief scrambled through a 3-foot-square window, crept upstairs only a few yards from the lounge where Sophia's friends were watching television, forced open a drawer, opened a leather case and got away with diamonds, rubies and emeralds fashioned into necklaces, earrings and brooches. Much of it was uninsured. Police phoned Sophia in London. She and Carlo drove to the chalet. Sophia stared at the empty jewel case, broke down and sobbed.

'It is so unjust, unjust, unjust,' she cried. 'It isn't just the value of the jewellery. I can earn to buy some more. It is what they symbolize in my life. I pulled myself up out of the slums of Naples where we were always so terribly poor. The jewellery was the proof that I would never be poor again.' This last thought may have entered the mind of the thief. £2,000 in notes were left untouched in one of the drawers.

For days, the shock of the robbery left Sophia numb, despite the presence of Carlo, the persistent passion of Mr Sellers, and the certain knowledge that Ponti would soon replace the lot as casually as people refill their ballpoints. It was left to Vittorio de Sica, playing a role in *The Millionairess*, to put the matter in perspective. A formidable gambler, that silver hair and dignified bearing much cherished in the casinos of Monte Carlo and Cannes, he gave her the 'easy come, easy go' routine which he himself knew only too well.

'Listen, my love,' he soothed her. 'We are both from Naples. The Good Lord has given us other things. It is only jewellery. What is a hundred thousand pounds . . .?'

'Nearly two hundred thousand,' Sophia sniffed.

'It is the same thing. You are a woman with beautiful gifts from Nature. Look at them!'

'You look at them,' Sophia smiled, regaining her spirits.

'Now you understand!' de Sica beamed. 'Maybe we go and finish the picture.'

The following day, the assessors issued a description of the missing jewellery. Those curious about the market value of being Sophia Loren or Mrs Carlo Ponti were given mind-boggling satisfaction. The former waif, named Sofia Scicolone in Pozzuoli had lost:

A ruby necklace; sapphire and diamond necklace and matching sapphire ring; antique diamond necklace and matching diamond earrings and ring; antique emerald necklace and matching emerald earrings; a pearl necklace with one white and one black string; three-string white pearl necklace; two diamond brooches; antique Russian brooch in three pieces; gold evening bag; a two-and-a-half-yard gold chain; antique gold snake with rubies and emeralds instead of eyes; heavy gold bracelet shaped as a belt and incorporating a watch.

Ponti, faced with lawsuits and worse, was more concerned about Sophia's safety than he was about the lost jewellery. He ordered round-the-clock police guards on her chalet with Alsatians to roam the grounds at night. While the dogs watched the property, Basilio was keeping a friendly eye on Peter Sellers.

There are two versions of the Sellers–Loren connection. The Sellers account, which he retailed to me in the wake of his short gale-force romance with Liza Minnelli, was not, it is fair to say, endorsed down to the last sigh, by Sophia Loren. A jury required to deliver a verdict on the conflicting evidence, would have quite a problem. Sellers simultaneously uncorked a bottle and his feelings:

'I adored her and I had the feeling all the time that it was mutual. Other than Carlo Ponti I'm certain there were only two men that she ever had any deep attachment for and that was Cary Grant and myself. I mean she adores my kind of humour. She loves my jokes and we got on famously. One day during the film I told her that I was in love with her. A day or two later she came on the set in a beautiful white dress, by Balmain I think it was. She was in a wistful mood. I said to her:

' "Anything wrong? Has anything upset you?"

' "No, no," she said, adding, "No, I'm fine."

'And then she said, "I love you that's all." I believe if Carlo went tomorrow, God forbid, she'd come to me. I tell you straight. As it is I'm happy that she is fulfilled. She has what she wants. Carlo and I are good friends. He's always pleased to welcome me in Rome. And in a way, he has accepted this special relationship the three of us have been through, taken me as one of their family. I think Sophia is a marvellous actress who still hasn't reached her true greatness. I love her and always will.'

Sophia Loren's construction of the episode was a shade less heart-expanding.

She was as coy as any rich, secure mother-of-two might be, talking about past wooers.

'Yes, I love Peter very much, in my way,' she replied. 'Not the way I love Carlo. That is the kind of love which leaves a scar on you. I understood Peter's problems. I knew he was in a very delicate situation. I was very close to him as much as I could be, but love is something else. He is really a great, great friend. With most of my films I rarely remain in touch with the actor afterwards. But with Peter it was different. I consider him a member of my family. There are people that I feel at a certain moment they need me or I need them. We have built up a fine relationship over the years and I think that is rare for a man and a woman, when the woman is married to someone else.'

With Cary Grant the relationship was different. 'If you ask me, "did you love him more than Peter?" it is impossible to answer. The situation was different. Maybe at one moment in your life you are more vulnerable. Maybe you think you are more in love than you really arc. You can only ever know when everything has passed and you can ask yourself: "Was I really in love with this man, or just fond of him?" '

Carlo Ponti viewed the amorous intent of both parties with a sympathetic grin. Like the beefeater guarding the Crown Jewels he had not the slightest objection to admirers pressing their noses up against the plate glass.

When *The Millionairess* was completed, Dimitri de Grunwald flew with the film to show it to the top brass at Twentieth Century Fox in Hollywood. The late and legendary Spyros Skouras sat, prayer beads in hand, surrounded by his cigar-smoking acolytes in the private viewing room. De Grunwald said the film was ready to run. Skouras nodded his giant head and all sat back to watch the film. Since it had Sellers, the priceless Alastair Sim and was scripted by the humorist Wolf Mankowitz, de Grunwald was reasonably confident that the assembled tycoons would laugh, if not fall about.

'There was not a movement, not a laugh—just a paralysed

silence,' he recalled. 'I remember thinking "this must be the single, unfunniest film ever made". When the lights went up, everybody took their cues from Skouras who was frowning and playing with his beads.'

The silence was finally broken by someone asking: 'What are you going to do about those accents?'

'What accents?' de Grunwald asked, mystified.

'That Alastair Sim feller, can't understand a word he says. And the cockney chap, and the Indian, and the . . .'

Dimitri de Grunwald said, 'goodbye gentlemen' and flew back for the London press show. It played to some loud, appreciative applause. The notices talked of a 'witty, sparkling, whimsical, brilliant, flamboyant picture' with 'scintillating performances by Sophia Loren and Peter Sellers'. Extravagant stuff but not all that exaggerated.

The same Fox chiefs who had given the film so funereal a reception in Hollywood saw the formidable British grosses and offered Sophia a contract for half a million dollars, double the figure she received for *The Millionairess*.

But Vittorio de Sica had called her from Rome. He wanted her to star in *La Ciociara* shown in England and America as *Two Women*. Some years earlier the plan had been to star Anna Magnani as the mother, Sophia playing her daughter. But de Sica wired her in England: 'I love you. Trust me. Play the mother.'

'There was not enough money in America or the world,' she said, 'to prevent me from making that picture.' The ardent reunion of Sophia and de Sica in Rome in the autumn of 1960 was like a duet for two penitents. Sophia had gone to Hollywood against de Sica's advice and despite the Venice award for *Black Orchid*, had little else of value to declare on her return. Nor could Vittorio claim he'd taken his own advice. He too had taken a nose-dive, acting in some trivial pictures and Italy was asking: 'Could this be the Master who made *Umberto D* and *Bicycle Thieves*? De Sica's offer of *Two Women* could not have come at a better time.

The story, based on the novel by Alberto Moravia, centres on the ordeal of a mother and daughter caught up in the pendulum of war; first by the retreating Germans on the rampage through the

Italian countryside; then by the advancing Moroccan troops tearing their way through the mountain villages.

Vittorio last saw Sophia (in *The Millionairess*) as an almost edible confection by Balmain, black-corseted, pink-bosomed, her eyes and teeth as dazzling as her lacquered hair. She would now have to go through a complete laundering to remove the gloss. She would have to revert to the kind of life she knew, smudged, dishevelled and destitute. After Hollywood's garish processing, Sophia could hardly wait. De Sica took her on one side, and his short sermon offers an intriguing clue to the genesis of an Oscar-winning performance.

'Sophia,' he said, 'you are twenty-seven years old. You must appear to be at least forty. And you have a young daughter. You had her maybe when you were eighteen. You are a peasant woman, with peasant tastes, peasant feelings, life and war has made you feel older and look older than you are. You must use no make-up, nothing at all. Have the courage to become this character, I guarantee that you will give a wonderful interpretation of it.'

Sophia reacted as though hypnotized. 'From that moment,' de Sica said, seated beside an affectionately inscribed portrait of the star, 'she became the woman of the film. Perhaps much rested upon my intelligence, but a lot rested on hers too. Though I taught her, directed every move, when the tears came and the anguish in the film, it was her heart, her soul, her own experiences that she was drawing on. And when I saw it I realized that she had come back to Italy. She had come back to me with this vital desire to re-express herself in her own language.'

Two events during the shooting of the film in Rome, might have combined to shatter her nerve on the set. Halfway through the shooting, she and Carlo were called to the law courts to answer questions by an investigating magistrate examining a request to proceed against them for bigamy. Both had anticipated the summons. They had been living together since Carlo's visit to the location on Capri. They could no longer endure the charade of clandestine meetings in other people's homes. But they had been well briefed by their lawyers.

Carlo sat in a waiting room of the court. Sophia was called in to face Judge Guilio Franco. Sophia in clinging chiffon, looked superb. The Judge looked at Sophia. While he formulated a sentence in his mind, the actress spoke first demanding to confront the woman who had denounced them. The Judge replied that this wouldn't be possible. Sophia was angry. When the denunciation was made two years or so earlier, Carlo's marriage to Giuliana Fiastri was virtually over. She would like to have told her accuser that.

The judge asked her: 'Are you married?'

'No,' Sophia said briskly.

The judge frowned. 'Are you married to Carlo Ponti?'

'No.'

'No?'

'No,' Sophia repeated. 'My passport is here. It says I am Sofia Scicolone, spinster.'

'Thank you.'

'It is a pleasure.'

Carlo was called in. He looked for a helpful hint in Sophia's eyes. She merely said, 'I love you,' and it was his turn.

'Are you married to Sophia Loren?' the judge asked.

'No.'

Further probing on the question produced the same answer. The strategy of Ponti's lawyers was becoming clear. Somehow they were going to have to prove the Mexican marriage invalid. This done, no bigamy charge could stick.

A day later, while working in a temperature of over a hundred degrees, Sophia fainted three times on the set. This, together with the cancellation of a planned trip to London for the opening of her film *Gold of Naples* led to rumours that she was expecting a baby. Her mother Romilda Villani, asked by the studio how soon Sophia would be available for work, exploded; 'What do you want to do? Kill her? You will, with the condition she is in!' This appeared to confirm the whispers.

But a week later, Sophia called me: 'It's not true about the baby. I wanted to have a child, Carlo's child, but I was not pregnant. I think I fainted because I was very tired. I've been working for five months now, sometimes seven days a week without a rest. But it's a shame. I'd make a good mother.' This forlorn interlude was rapidly sweetened by Carlo presenting Sophia with a gold and platinum tiara studded with diamonds and other gems which once belonged to Pauline Bonaparte, Napoleon's sister. A handsome consolation for a case of 'fatigue'.

The shooting of *Two Women* was drawing remorselessly to an end. So realistic was Sophia's involvement in the film, she broke down in tears on more than a dozen occasions.

At the end of it, Hollywood had been exorcized from her system. Just how successfully, could be judged by the notices. 'Sheer dynamite,' wrote the critic of the London *Mirror*. He went on:

'Sophia Loren, shedding much of her usual glamour, gives a memorable performance . . .'

Another in a London evening paper said:

'Sophia Loren reveals greater power, subtlety and feeling for mood than even Anna Magnani.' (Nectar to the girl who had been chosen over La Magnani's head.)

'The mother's agony,' wrote critic-turned-author Thomas Wiseman, 'as conveyed by Miss Loren as she realizes what is going to happen to her child whom she has so desperately sought to protect, is almost unbearably real.'

Stanley Kauffman wrote: 'Physically, Sophia Loren is not as suited for the part as Anna Magnani might have been. But her beauty does not prevent her from giving a full-blooded performance, earthy and female, brimming with laughter and sex. On her own ground, and especially with the help of de Sica she is splendid!'

The awards flowed in on an ocean of praise. She won the Silver Ribbon—the Italian Oscar. The Best Actress Award at Cannes. The New York Critics' Award as the Best Foreign Actress. She was to wait six months or more for the decision on the most prestigious bauble of them all, America's Academy Award.

Surprisingly Sophia considers the role as being 'one of the easiest things I've done. The character was so strong nothing could destroy it. Also I was working within the range of my own experience. I didn't need to imagine what kind of a woman the mother was. I had the picture of my own mother and her suffering always before me. I know what I saw in Naples. Rape was an everyday occurrence when the foreign troops came. I wasn't raped but I knew those who had been. I saw the tears and heard the screams. When de Sica said "action" I already had the whole scene in my mind.'

Carlo celebrated Sophia's success by presenting her with another necklace, it being his plan, not contested by Sophia, to replace every gem stolen from her in England. Peter Sellers flew in to join in the general festivities in which Maria and her jazz-playing fiancé Romano Mussolini, figured prominently. Their marriage date set, Romilda invited Romano to play the piano in her apartment at a party given in the young couple's honour. It was a conciliatory gesture to off-set Rachele Mussolini's coolness towards the match.

Romano sat down at the piano and began performing expertly in the style of Oscar Petersen. Sophia, Maria, Romilda, were enthralled by it, and so too was a young American jazz enthusiast brought along by one of the guests. Romano breezed into a stylish rendition of 'Chicago, Chicago . . .' which put the jazz buff almost into a trance. Finally the ecstasy of it all drew him unsteadily to his feet. He pushed his way through the guests, looked adoringly at the young Mussolini and gulped;

'Gee I'm really sorry about what they did to your dad!'

Sellers said he collapsed secretly into a corner.

The recital was over.

Mother and child. Edoardo born 1973. (*Tazio Secchiaroli*)

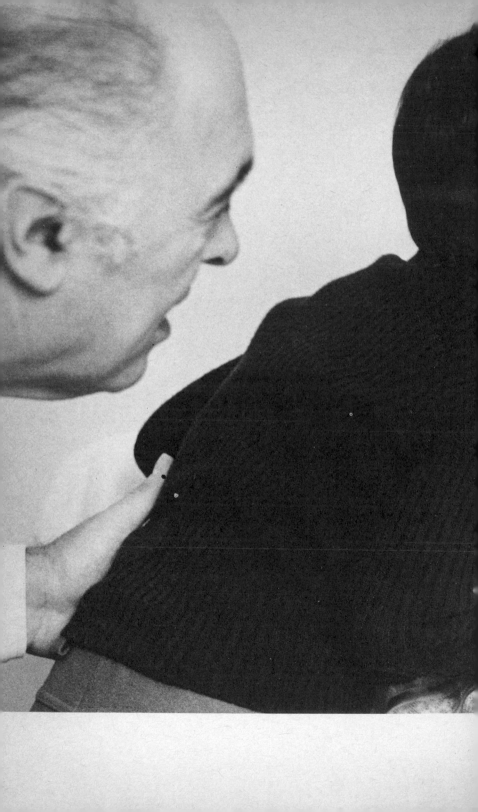

The ecstatic Pontis, Carlo, Cipi and Sophia, welcome the new arrival Edoardo. (*Tazio Secchiaroli*)

On location, Sophia between the late Sir Noël Coward (*left*) and Peter Ustinov. He directed *Lady L*. (*Camera Press*)

Sophia Loren and the late Vittorio De Sica, friend and confidant . . . an uncanny
understanding between a brilliant director and star.

Left Best Actress Award, *Black Orchid*, Venice 1959.
Right Sophia Loren turns cook – for President Tito of Yugoslavia at his villa on Brioni.

Delirium at dawn. Sophia wins the Best Actress Award (The Oscar) for
Two Women. Cary Grant 'phoned the news. (*Pierluigi*)

10

The Oscar

The great Loren–Ponti serial featuring scenes in the Vatican, Mexico and a courtroom in Rome, gave its world audience scant insight into the characters of the two principal performers. Sure, Carlo made the required gestures of defiance, while Sophia's green-tinted eyes glistened occasionally as she reiterated her longing for a settled marriage and a brood of bambini to go with it. It was good, heart-stirring stuff and neither party felt any obligation to release more intimate details. Like Nixon and the Watergate tapes they were determined to maintain 'the confidentiality' of their relationship.

But they were failing to halt the burning curiosity which spluttered like a bomb-fuse all along the Via Veneto, to Paris, London, New York and Hollywood. Despite the contortions of keeping one eye to a keyhole and an ear to the ground, the followers of the drama found their inquisitiveness infuriatingly unabated.

Though few admitted it, most thought that it was downright unfair that such a ripely beddable creature should be exclusively reserved for the ... well ... unprepossessingly short, portly and balding Mr Ponti, twenty years her senior. The public looked at him, then more lingeringly at her. What they saw in Sophia was an extraordinary physical affluence with more than a touch of sorcery to it. There was nothing flawless or classical about it. It was Nilotic, the delicate features, long neck and imperious carriage a fair imitation of an African water-carrier doing her stuff for a 'Come to Sunny Sudan' poster. The irate janitor in Pozzuoli who accused the cheeky young pilferer of having 'thief's eyes' should have seen the 1960 version of them. Almond-shaped and black-pencilled at the corners Cleopatra style, audiences and personal callers read all kinds of erotic messages in them, with no little assistance from their owner. But it was, still is, part of the act.

Sophia, as *Two Women* proved, was happier when she could break out of the mould. Moreover, as frequently happens with actresses who make their fortunes out of their looks, Sophia was never sure she was as lovely as others said she was. Now when she is short on reassurance, she looks at her priceless possessions, her bank balance, and her Rolls-Royce and reluctantly concedes that no old hag presides over the Villa Ponti.

Meanwhile Ponti makes no apologies for being the sole beneficiary in the bountiful treasures of Loren. While the gossip-writers flounder up to their tongues in dark innuendoes, Ponti chuckles all the way to Sophia's Louis XVI four-poster bed. Unlike that ill-fated Burton and Taylor relationship, the Pontis' is much more hidden and exclusive. They operate a kind of complicity which nothing, and no one, can penetrate. Like TV wrestlers, their moves are astute, instinctive, worked out with a perfection of mutual understanding. Thus when each was interrogated alone in the Rome courtroom, there was not the remotest danger of one saying anything different from the other.

They share the same driving ambition—Ponti's based on an irresistible urge to wheel and deal, Sophia's, the need for security, prestige, plus an unabashed craving to be famous.

And both have a highly developed compulsion to make money. Otherwise why, after the delirious success of *Two Women* did Sophia agree to perform in that frothed-up piece of Spanish history, *El Cid*? When she was working in her native Italian, with the perceptive de Sica holding the reins, she acted unconventionally, instinctively and was brilliant. Yet here she was again, plunging into some Iberian hokum with that archetypal hero of the sandals-and-toga Epic, Charlton Heston.

Sophia's defence of the money-urge has been the simple and understandable one in the rags-to-riches vein. Probing this delicate area, one phrase was frequently repeated. Sophia's Aunt Dora, in Pozzuoli said:

'Sophia is very generous but she doesn't believe in throwing money out of the window.'

At her seaside villa near Rome some weeks later, Sophia's sister Maria said:

'Sophia has been wonderful to the whole family, but she doesn't throw money out of the window.'

And at the Villa Ponti, where there are a hundred and one windows, Sophia herself said:

'Look, I worked very hard all my life for my money. I don't believe in throwing it out of the window.'

If the phrase sounds a shade close-fisted, the explanation is that the Ponti generosity, like their life behind the sixteenth-century walls of their villa, is nothing they care to discuss with friends or strangers. It was some months after the event before the world learned that Sophia had paid for an Italian baby to be flown to South Africa to have a heart operation by Dr Christiaan Barnard. Not long after, watching a television programme, Sophia saw the anguished face of a Madame Claire Lestienne, who too was suffering from a critical heart complaint. 'There is only one surgeon who can save me, if I can go to his hospital in Houston, Texas,' the woman said.

Sophia turned to Ines: 'Phone them up and say I'll give the money to send this woman if they guarantee not to mention my name.'

Both operations were successful. It was therefore asking too much of Madame Lestienne and of the mother of the baby, to conceal the identity of their life-giving benefactor. Sophia's irritation at being named was due not merely to modesty, but the fear of the construction cynics would put on it.

She gave a vintage Rolls-Royce to film-maker Joe Levine's son, who collects them. Generously gifted all the co-stars in her films. Romilda and the family in Pozzuoli speak almost with reverence of her massive handouts over the years.

So now I can raise the matter of the typewriter screw. It was half an inch in diameter and a generous estimate would put a figure of fifteen pennies on its value. Its precise function is to hold the ribbon wheel of an Olivetti typewriter in place. Each machine has two screws. I lost one during one of my visits from London to the Ponti villa at Marino.

'Do you have an Olivetti portable?' I asked the millionairess who sat beside a marble table with a gilt Louis XIV base.

'It's possible. Why do you want to know?'

'I'm missing a screw off mine.'

'So?'

I felt strangely as though I'd been caught with my hand in the till.

'Could you . . .' (I swiftly discarded the word 'give') '. . . lend me a screw and I will return it to you when next I come to Rome.'

'Ines,' Sophia commanded, 'Mr Zec wishes to borrow a screw. Take one off the typewriter, and, lend it to him.'

A year passed in which countries were invaded, governments deposed, astronauts roamed the cosmos, and the Pontis' fortunes went from affluence to opulence.

I received a phone call from Sophia in Rome who wished to know whether I was arriving the following weekend as planned. I said I was.

'Good,' she said. 'And don't forget the screw.'

'What screw?'

'What do you mean, "what screw"?' demanded an irritated voice from the Villa Ponti. 'The one I lent you, remember?'

No, Miss Sophia Loren does not throw money out of the window.

El Cid began promisingly for Sophia. She was mobbed at the Madrid airport and had to be rescued by her two co-stars, Charlton Heston and Raf Vallone. Windows were broken, people trampled on, police thrown to the ground. Sophia was delighted. A normal arrival.

But the Loren–Heston chemistry, despite the volatility of the two principal ingredients, failed to ignite. For a moment, during their long love scene, prone on the floor of a stable, the director Tony Mann thought he had them reasonably aglow. I watched them with him and we noticed that minutes after he called 'Cut!' Sophia continued to snuggle into Heston.

But not with passion. A freezing wind was sweeping in off the Guadaramas. Heston in wool and chain-mail was reasonably protected. Sophia in a light dress shivered. 'This is the only time I've been warm in Madrid,' she said as she finally rolled off 'El Cid'.

The film was sufficient of a soap-opera to make money but it threw Sophia back into the rut again. While she prepared to leave, Ponti busied himself collecting antiques for their villa at Marino. They had to get something out of the movie even if the notices weren't good. He bought a thirteenth-century baptismal font made out of granite, and a 14-foot marble table-top which he shipped to Italy. From Naples (on *Two Women*) he had bought a sixteenth-century marble fountain from a derelict villa and transported it to Marino. A trip to Russia produced a shipment of magnificent birch trees. A visit to a Hamburg production brought hundreds of azaleas. Location shooting at Fort Knox might present him with a problem.

Sophia returned to Rome to find a storm blowing up over her sister Maria's love affair with Romano Mussolini, son of the Fascist dictator. Determined to marry Maria, he went to see Donna Rachele the then 75-year-old widow of Il Duce who indicated coolly that he could have aimed a little higher than the sister of a movie queen.

She altered her view when she and Sophia met at her villa Carpena at Forli, near Bologna. Sophia went by car with her mother Romilda. As they drove north through the mountains the two women giggled at the scenario:

Famous movie star, born illegitimate, now facing bigamy charges and possible excommunication, going with her unmarried mother ('Garbo's Double') to call on the widow of a discredited dictator whose jazz-playing son was marrying a singing Scicolone.

Basilio Franchina, busy writing scripts on the Riviera could have worked miracles with that material. More so when Sophia and Rachele sat down together to a glass of Frescati wine. In the small private chapel converted from one of the rooms in the villa, Rachele Mussolini keeps some of the remains of her husband.

According to Sophia these include an eye and a piece of brain. The rest is in the local cemetery.

'When she talks about it,' Sophia said, 'it is macabre. And yet she doesn't cry. She is an old woman but still handsome. Her hair is absolutely white. And she is very small, and so thin, with piercing blue eyes. When she spoke about Mussolini she still called him "Il Duce". But it was as if she were speaking of another man. Sometimes she was bitter. She said he was surrounded by bad people. But she never tried to defend him. And you can't discuss it really. She loved him very much and is still in love with him in spite of his mistresses and the way he treated her. For her, at any rate, it was a love story and she doesn't care what the world thinks.'

Rachele Mussolini warmed towards the movie star. She invited Sophia into her farmhouse kitchen and cooked pasta and veal for the two of them. 'Once she told me terrible things,' Sophia said. 'She had been given a driver who was at her disposal every day. On the night she learned that Mussolini had been killed, she asked the driver to take her to the Americans because she believed that they were the only people who could prevent her from being killed the way her husband was.

'She was afraid of the Germans more than anybody else. She was trying to escape, afraid that they would have taken the children. But that night when they were driving alone through the mountains, the driver stopped the car and tried to rape her. She was sick with the humiliation of it, the knowledge of her husband's death still burning in her mind.'

They met again, Sophia and Mussolini's widow, on the day of Maria's wedding to Romano Mussolini, held at his mother's villa. The ceremony took place in St Anthony's Church at Predappio, where the Duce was born. He built the church in 1934 as a gift to his fellow townspeople.

A crowd of 5,000 packed into the square and church when Sophia arrived in her chauffeur-driven Rolls. In the wild crush, the bride fainted on her way to the church hall. Romano fainted too and had to be given an injection by a doctor. After the ceremony the family went to Mussolini's tomb where Rachele three times gave what onlookers took to be the Fascist salute. Then she bent down and placed flowers on the grave. She also put a few on the grave of Adone Zoli, the ex-President of the Council who had allowed her to give Benito a proper burial.

Romano drove Maria away on their honeymoon. As Sophia's car pulled out of the town it was involved in a collision with a motor-scooter. The rider, Antonio Angelini, 24, was killed. Police questioned Sophia and her chauffeur for two hours in a grocer's shop. They were finally allowed to leave. The whole episode in Predappio had been an ordeal. Sophia was glad to get back to Rome.

The Mussolini marriage had some welcome spin-offs before it finally ended with mutual and rueful agreement in 1970. Maria bore Romano two children both, in their babyhood at least, astonishingly like Il Duce. When the first, Alessandra was two years old, Peter Ustinov was on a visit to Rome. He found Sophia and Maria playing some music in the living room. The baby had crawled out on to the balcony.

'For God's sake!' Ustinov exclaimed, 'don't let her go there!'

'It's quite safe,' Sophia said.

'It's not that,' Ustinov said, 'but that's just how her grandfather started, crawling out on to balconies, and look what happened to him!'

The sisters ran out and brought Mussolini the Third back off the balcony.

El Cid won critical points for spectacle, sword play, sound and fury. But Sophia couldn't match the impact of 6,000 extras, the hailstorm of arrows, bloody axes and the galloping pageantry. She was disappointed with the picture. It had not been a happy production. Halfway through it she fell and fractured her collar bone. When the film opened in New York, she sued the producers for not giving her name equal size and type with that of Charlton Heston's on the posters. Judge Samuel Hofstadter, in charge of the preliminary hearing, observed tartly, 'It's a question whether Miss Loren is really in danger of suffering loss of prestige because she doesn't have her name emblazoned on Broadway in the same type, the same size and on the same line as Mr Heston's.'

But despite this judicial clip over the ear, he sent the case for trial. It was eventually settled out of court, both parties sweet-talking each other into a fair compromise.

After the marzipan of *El Cid* Sophia was relieved to be returned to de Sica. Ponti was producing *Boccaccio 70*, a frolic in three parts, directed by an extravagance of directors, Federico Fellini, Luchino Visconti and Vittorio de Sica. Fellini's piece involved Anita Ekberg in a great bosomy sex parody, but the idea was swamped in a confusion of tricks, sermonizing and fantasy.

Visconti didn't do much better with his tale of a rich, sexy wife's (Romy Schneider) arrangement with her husband, an impoverished nobleman, in which she could only get him into bed with her by charging the same price as his favourite call girls. This segment sags into oblivion.

De Sica's heroine is Zoe (Sophia) proprietress of a shooting gallery who supports her sister and brother-in-law by offering herself every Saturday night in a raffle among the local lechers. The critics, no doubt expecting masterpieces from this summit of Italy's most distinguished directors, felt let down, badly. But Ponti, though glum at their reaction, was pleased that they gave the acting honours to Sophia ahead of Ekberg and Schneider. De Sica was not displeased either when his contribution was unanimously voted the best of the three.

The release of *Madame Sans-Gêne* the film Sophia made with Robert Hossein who played Napoleon, contributed to her winning the award for the Best Foreign Actress in the annual Cinemonde poll. But professionally and internationally she was in limbo, badly in need of a boost. A confused thriller she made with Anthony Perkins in Paris, *Five Miles to Midnight* directed by Anatole Litvak hardly blew the dust off her dilemma. The film had been costly, and though Loren looked stunning in it, it opened, closed and was forgotten.

The great deliverance came in a 7.00 a.m. phone call to her in Rome from Cary Grant in Hollywood. The date, 10 April, 1962.

'Who is this speaking?' Sophia asked drowsily.

'It's me, darling. Cary. Cary Grant. You've won!'

'Won what?'

'The Oscar. It's yours. The Best Actress of the Year. Congratulations!'

Sophia put the phone down, buried her head on Carlo's shoulder and wept. Signor Ponti gulped too, and pondered what new trinket might be equal to the occasion. Romilda shrieked and phoned Pozzuoli. Vittorio de Sica heard the news over the radio and drove over to Sophia's apartment. Maria Mussolini and her husband, roared in his sports car across town to share in the heady celebrations. Champagne was poured into quivering glasses as Sophia sat like a queen taking the hugs, obeisances and kisses from a procession of friends and relatives. The phone rang throughout the day with Ines taking messages from Sinatra, William Holden, Carl Foreman and dozens of film-makers around the world. There was nothing from Anna Magnani who was originally set to play the Loren role in *Two Women*. And no word from Gina Lollobrigida.

Sophia's feelings raced through a variety of sensations. Ecstasy, humility, delayed shock, palpitation—a Geiger-counter passed over her would have bleeped to a standstill.

She wanted to thank the world. But not merely with some charitable offering. It had to be tactile. Actually part of her.

That morning while the telegrams were still pouring in, she went to a blood bank and gave a pint of blood. 'Good Neapolitan blood' she said to the nurse with a smile, though a voice inside her chortled, 'and Oscar-winning blood too. You don't get much of that!'

When I phoned to add my good wishes she said, 'I can tell you one thing. I'd give this and a hundred other Oscars if a doctor had told me this morning that I was having a baby.'

Sophia's craving for a child, Ponti's, had become obsessional. She thought about it, dreamed about it, prayed for it, dressed the child in her mind scores of times, wrote a whole permutation of names on the backs of scripts, menus and used envelopes.

'I was made to have children,' she said, 'the yearning I felt was like a constant ache. Whatever I did, no matter how successful it was, all the praise, all the money—I still felt only half a woman. Carlo wanted the baby just as passionately as I did, but with the bigamy charge hanging over us, and all that talk of being public sinners, we thought it would have been selfish to bring a child into that kind of world. One illegitimate child in the family is enough. But my body kept signalling me, telling me it was ready to give life, yet my brain warned me against it. I had all this love bottled up inside me, it was fierce, almost like an animal's. I just had to force it out of my mind. Women will understand.'

Sophia's euphoria over the Oscar did not last long. The bigamy fear had substantial foundations. Carlo's lawyers were informed that a Rome magistrate who had been deliberating over their depositions on the previous hearing had decided to proceed with the bigamy charges against them. Ponti was leaving on a flight to New York when the news was given to him. He smiled grimly. 'I have full confidence in Italian justice,' he said, picking his words from his internal file labelled 'inscrutable phrases'.

Sophia was told of the new threat while she was on location near Leghorn, filming *The Condemned of Altona* under de Sica's direction. 'One minute you get an Oscar. The next minute they want to send you to prison.' De Sica took her hand. 'If they put you in prison, we'll shoot the rest of the film there,' he smiled.

But the projected court proceedings were ominous enough for Sophia to cancel her role in *The Victors* for Carl Foreman, due to start immediately after the de Sica film was finished. All work again. Like an Olympic marathon runner, Sophia programmed herself to go on until she dropped.

She told Foreman of her problems, of the real danger that with the charge hanging over her she might not be allowed to leave the country. He understood and put Rosanna Schiaffino in the role.

As he drove to his New York hotel from the airport, Carlo brooded over his situation. He phoned Sophia in Italy:

'Don't worry. When I come back I fix everything. You won't go to jail. If necessary we'll change our nationality.' (This may have been shrewd prescience, or his lawyers may have clued him in on what was to be their ultimate strategy.)

'If we have to become Russians to stay together, that's what we'll do!' Ponti boomed confidently over the trans-Atlantic cable.

Carlo had this miraculous capacity for taking the heat out of a situation.

'I love you madly,' she said to him.

'I know,' he grunted good humouredly. 'Ciao.'

Two days later, Sophia was taken to a hospital at Tirrenia near Pisa, suffering from a throat infection. At first she appeared to recover but then relapsed with a soaring temperature. Her personal physician flew up from Rome. A throat specialist was called in from Pisa University. It was while she lay feverishly ill, that she heard the announcement of Marilyn Monroe's death.

The news reduced her to an hour of weeping. She was clearly identifying herself with Marilyn.

'I knew her position only too well,' she said. 'People dig into your past, refuse to leave you alone. Every bit of scandal that can be found out about you is dragged into the open. It eats into your family life. They destroy you if they can.'

The tangled skein of legalities which Carlo was aggressively trying to unravel, now hung around their proxy wedding in Mexico five years earlier. It was essential to get that annulled. If it could be shown that they were not legally married there, the charge of bigamy could not stand.

By luck, or some astute legal footwork, Ponti's advocates were able to convince a Mexican judge that the marriage was invalid due to 'certain errors in documentation'. The annulment was granted. But that sentence is an almost laughable summary of the cloak-and-dagger operations. These involved a hundredweight of documents and a whole frown of legal experts around the world. Those working on the script, many in a language that they did not understand, complained that they were seeing writs before the eyes.

First there was Ponti's Mexican divorce from his wife Giuliana Fiastri. Not recognized in Italy. So in Rome, at least, she was still Mrs Carlo Ponti.

Then there was Carlo's proxy marriage to Sophia. Not recognized in Italy. So in Rome, at least, she was still Sofia Scicolone.

Now there was the annulment of the proxy marriage. But on what was it based? The crucial document supposedly signed by Carlo and Sophia before a notary public in Rome requesting the proxy marriage, had vanished from the archives of the civil authorities in Juarez, Mexico.

No signed document, no proper marriage, the proxy marriage was therefore invalid. That was the good news.

The bad, was the court's frosty response; true, the marriage was invalid because Ponti was already married, but going through the ceremony was itself illegal, and therefore bigamous.

But how can it be proved, the defence lawyers asked, that Carlo and Sophia contracted to marry in Mexico if the vital document *which would have to be signed in Italy to be valid*, can no longer be found?

With that firecracker tossed into the arena, normal chaos was resumed. Both sides retired exhausted. Carlo and Sophia occupied separate domains, continued a clandestine marriage while Ponti burrowed away for a more satisfactory solution.

'The annulment meant little to me,' Sophia said, 'I was still a concubine. I was back to living in sin, and neither Carlo nor I knew whether at any moment, the law might take our passports away.'

It was irritating but Carlo and Sophia shrugged it off as a small price to pay for sharing the same rapture if not the same roof. But then, unexpectedly, Sophia was caught two stinging blows, one by a Milan newspaper, the other from one of the highest authorities in the Catholic Church.

Sophia had gone to church to act as godmother to her sister Maria's 12-day-old daughter Alessandra. As she emerged into the wintry sunlight, she held the baby in her arms, delighted that photographers were recording the event. She hugged the baby as if it were her own.

The following day a professor of theology at Milan's Catholic University criticized her in a Milan daily paper saying that as a 'public sinner' she should not take part in church ceremonies. 'She should,' he said, 'have stayed in the shadows.'

This was followed by a stern rebuke from the Vicariate of

Rome, which, without mentioning Sophia by name, said she was violating canon law.

But the Jesuit priest who conducted the christening, Father Virgilio Rotondi, remained remarkably calm in the storm. He declared with great ecclesiastical finesse:

'I thought of the serious danger of a public scandal that would have been caused by driving Miss Loren out of the temple.

'Roman Catholic canon law is not compelling when a grave disturbance may derive from its enforcement. The law regulating God-parentage follows this principle too.'

In case this explanation did not completely disarm his Vatican critics, the good priest pointed out that he had, before the event, explained to Sophia's mother that the star could not, in strict canon law, be the godmother.

'Unfortunately when I arrived for the ceremony I discovered that no one had told Miss Loren about it. Her relatives just hadn't the courage. What could I do?'

By then Father Rotondi had had the advantage of getting to know Sophia. Nothing short of an earthquake or a lightning arrest by a posse of carabinieri would have kept this godmother away from Alessandra Mussolini's christening.

De Sica's *Condemned of Altona*, based on Sartre's penetrating, claustrophobic stage play, *Altona* opened to modestly admiring notices. Abby Mann's screen treatment of the torment of a Nazi war criminal driven almost insane with guilt, was too sombre for public consumption.

Sophia gave an intelligent performance but Sartre on Celluloid appeared too daunting for all concerned.

There was no respite for Miss Loren. Even before the last scene had been shot she was preparing to leave for Madrid for her role as Sir Alec Guinness's daughter in *The Fall of the Roman Empire*.

She spent the mandatory three days in bed after *Altona*, then it was off to the scorching heat of Madrid. It was three days of convalescence.

She was more machine than movie star. She was fuelled, raced to maximum revs, switched off for basic maintenance, then turned on to full power again. By choice. To friends who begged her to slacken off and enjoy some of the goodies she had so relentlessly acquired, Sophia shrugged and said, 'I work. What else can I do?'

The Roman Empire as built by Sam Bronston dutifully fell and the critics went wild over it. They hailed Guinness's Marcus Aurelius as a masterpiece and James Mason's role as the Greek philosopher who tries to convert the Barbarians to the Roman life-style, as superb. They further added that any movie star—they meant Sophia—who could hold her own against all that, the chariot races, the lunging javelins and the rest, was clearly an actress to be reckoned with. She was required to look beautiful, make love, and soften the blood-soaked brutalities raging around her. She did it well. In the bar one evening, the actors dispensed compliments the way Cockneys drop their aitches. Alec Guinness confessed to me he adored her, and then went off to dance the Twist with her. He had never done it before. He has never done it since. Stephen Boyd claimed he idolized her. Omar Sharif declared he loved her. Anthony Quayle was 'enchanted' by her. Mr Samuel Bronston 'worshipped' her. She took the laudatory gift-wrapping in her stride. 'I like to be loved,' she giggled as we sat beneath the Emperor's rostrum, 'preferably by the best people.'

Bronston's Roman Empire was dismantled and put into store to await the next epic. Sophia flew back to Rome, and then on to Naples for the first location shots of *Yesterday, Today and Tomorrow*. This de Sica three-episode comedy was more her style. She played by turn, a Neapolitan slum wife who sells contraband cigarettes and keeps out of jail by the legal amnesty for chronic pregnancy; a two-timing mistress of a Milanese writer; and a good-hearted tart of Rome.

It brought her together with Marcello Mastroianni, resulting in, at last, the erotic combustion Ponti had striven for, and invested millions in, for years. The highest-paid hero of Italian movies, Mastroianni's appeal is based on a faintly amused bone idleness, warm brown eyes, plus the breast-seeking vulnerability of the devout coward. He yawns a lot. He allows himself the complement of three wrinkles in his forehead, a calculated frown, and even if he could cure the hoarseness in his low, bedroomy voice, he would resist it on the sound principle that his countless female admirers would chuck stones at his windows.

These two, Sophia and Marcello, had been in separate orbits for years. It took Ponti to recognize that, like nitro-glycerine, the two chemicals apart were as harmless as baby powder, together they could blast off a roof.

Sophia started working with him in Naples and from the first day their mutual appreciation had the sound track of the pre-mating love calls of the African baboon. Sophia came right out and said that he was more sexy off-screen than on. Mr Mastroi-anni's moustache twitched like Chaplin's and he said it was a photo-finish whether Sophia would make a better wife than a mistress.

It was in the first week of this languidly pleasant location that Sophia discovered she was pregnant. She told Romilda and mother and daughter exchanged troubled looks for a second or two, then fell into each other's arms.

That night she told Carlo. He kissed her and smiled. She read his thoughts. What kind of identity will the child have—born of union between an alleged bigamist and his concubine living (in sin) under the threat of excommunication by the Vatican?

It was a fleeting cloud and it disappeared as Carlo made plans to hire the finest specialists, nurses, midwives, doctors, medicines, vitamins, helpers and the other basic requirements of the im-mensely rich and devoted.

Two days before the unit was due to leave Naples for further location work in Milan, Sophia felt a slight pain but dismissed it. She travelled by train to Milan and again felt pain. She remembers it now as sharply as on the day it happened. Her second child, Edoardo sat in her lap, her arms protectively cross-wise like a parachute harness. She hugged him until he winced. The gesture was part thanksgiving, part pride of ownership.

'At that first moment in Naples,' she said, 'when I knew I was pregnant, I was the complete woman. Here was the first child of my life, the complete expression of my love with Carlo. I cried with happiness. I thought that everything else I had was nothing compared to this gift that God had given to me. I prayed for that baby. I promised that after motherhood I wouldn't ask anything more of life. Then suddenly I felt as though hands were reaching out to take the baby from me.

'Then I felt this stabbing pain again. They took me into a clinic. Perhaps a woman who craves for a baby shouldn't give way to her feelings. At least that's what I thought at the time. I know differently now. All I know is I became very scared. That night in the clinic I found myself crying, "Oh God, don't let me lose my baby."

'But I did. I felt terribly crushed. I had been three-and-a-half months pregnant, and suddenly, the life had gone.

'I now had a new kind of problem,' she said. 'It didn't look as if I could make babies.'

11

The French Solution

Sophia's performance in *Yesterday, Today and Tomorrow* which featured her in one of the most delicious stripteases on film, brought rave reactions from the critics. They compared her with Monroe, Carole Lombard and other heroines who play their sexuality for comedy. Showman Joe Levine was as keen to get his hands on that picture for American distribution as he had been for *Two Women* and *Boccaccio 70* which he had bought even before Sophia's Oscar nomination. Joe is always ahead of the field.

'I'd had some sort of argument with Ponti long ago and I didn't want to get involved in any more deals with him,' Joe said.

'But you know that old adage—"Never call anybody a son-of-a-bitch unless you mean it!"—once I saw that picture I just had to have it. (Money being a great pacifier for competing promoters.)

'We went back to the Excelsior Hotel and I made the contract in their room on the hotel notepaper, giving them my cheque on the spot.

'What was so great about Sophia was the way she pushed the picture even though it was so good she could have stayed in Rome and boiled spaghetti, it was still going to make a fortune. When we got to San Francisco, a press agent there who had a genius for screwing things up said:

' "Better not go through the main airport lobby, Miss Loren, there're a thousand press photographers waiting. You'll get mobbed." And he started wheeling her through a side door.

'I gripped his arm and asked: "Where the hell do you think you're taking her?"

'The press agent pushed on. "Leave it to me. We've got to avoid that crowd."

'Sophia stopped, prodding him Neapolitan-style with her finger. "Listen. That's what I'm here for. To get mobbed. If they don't mob me then I'm no good to the picture, Mr Levine, or you!" '

She went on later to put her hands in the wet cement outside Grauman's Chinese theatre alongside the other famous imprints of the stars. She was modelled life-size for the Hollywood Wax Museum using enough wax for two Debbie Reynolds or three Shirley Temples.

Sophia had not been able to claim the Oscar in person on Academy night. Joe Levine collected it for her and later delivered it to her in Rome. She poured a bottle of champagne over it.

'Then I took it,' Levine said, 'and told her I had to take it back to America with me to have her name inscribed on it. Hell if she didn't break down and weep. She'd worked her ass off to get it. She just didn't want to let it go.'

All three films, *Two Women*, *Boccaccio 70* and *Yesterday, Today and Tomorrow* were immediate and high lucrative successes in America as they had been in Italy. The last one produced a fascinating argument between Ponti's company and a resourceful female called 'Black Market Connie' of Naples.

Concetta Muccardo, 'Connie' to the characters among whom she peddled her black market cigarettes, had been sentenced to seventy days in jail. But she didn't go. She had a baby—her fourth—instead. Italian law which is as enthusiastic about pregnancy as Arab sheiks are over new oil strikes, permits expectant mothers sentenced to prison, to stay free until they've had their babies. It seems that while Connie was enjoying this pre-natal reprieve she carried on with her black market activities and was promptly given more sentences.

But each time officers came to take her to jail she was pregnant again. Doubting carabinieri were invited to rest a hand on Connie's belly for a confirmatory kick by the inmate. And it was Connie's story, of course, which Sophia played in *Yesterday, Today and Tomorrow*.

When news of the production reached Concetta's alert ears she stormed in with a request for suitable compensation. She had gone through a lot, and a fair number of contractions, to reach her exclusive situation. She was entitled to a share in the proceeds.

'Give her the money,' Sophia said enviously, 'I should have her luck!'

Concetta Muccardo settled for £2,000. Since then another Italian woman has used the same dodge—with a score of eleven children delivered while under sentence, an all-time record. Her husband said it was a pleasure to help her.

If the Italian courts were content, endlessly, to open then adjourn the hearings on the bigamy charges, the Pontis after nearly five years of it, had had enough. They felt like paroled fugitives and were beginning to wonder whether their love of Italy wasn't requiring too high a premium.

Salvation appeared to lie in what the Romans neatly called 'La Soluzione Francese'. France, though a Catholic country, permits divorce, forbidden in Italy until 1970. If Carlo became a French citizen, the argument went, he could (his Mexican proxy wedding having been annulled) divorce Giuliana Fiastri, then marry Sophia.

While Sophia made films, Carlo made plans. As an opening move to establish their French connection, he bought at a cost of more than half a million pounds, a magnificent block of apartments opposite the George V Hotel in Paris, keeping the three-tiered penthouse as their Parisian pad. It was a pretty expensive foothold though it was not legally obligatory. The French Government bestows citizenship on whomsoever it pleases—and it pleases them most heartily when the applicant is Croesus-rich in a variety of hard currencies.

Ponti admitted having had slight misgivings about pitching his tent on the French side of the border. 'After all I've been an Italian for fifty years,' he said to me at the time. 'But the French, in their tolerance have recognized that my wife of seven years, really is my wife.'

Meanwhile Sophia, now the highest paid star in Italy, ploughed into a ferocious programme of pictures as though Judgment Day were just around the corner. De Sica's *Marriage—Italian Style*, based on Eduardo de Fillippo's perceptive and witty stage play, had all the ingredients for a successful movie; Sophia Loren, Marcello Mastroianni again and what began as a bright screenplay. Sophia plays a warm-hearted hooker (she was beginning to corner the market in this role) who tricks her reluctant lover, Mastroianni, into a phoney marriage. But despite the early funny business, the joke blows like forced rhubarb. Neither Sophia's sick-bed emotions at the end nor Mastroianni's skilled sheepishness can relieve the film's sudden jolt from humour to pathos.

For all that, Sophia went with it to Moscow and won their Best Actress Award for the picture. Crowds streamed away from Lenin's Tomb to catch a glimpse of the Curvaceous One doing her proletarian wiggle-about in Red Square.

She also picked up, for the fourth time, West Germany's 'Bambi', their equivalent of the Oscar. Pausing just long enough to change currency, she flew to Israel to make *Judith*. Her role as an illegal immigrant seeking vengeance against an ex-Nazi general who betrays her into a concentration camp brothel, looks great, but plays unconvincingly.

The only tangible result from that excursion to the Holy Land, was to get her films banned in Arab countries. She is in good company. Elizabeth Taylor's films have also been declared off-limits in Arabia because of her known sympathies for the Israeli cause. *Operation Crossbow* brought Sophia back to work in England, this time without her jewellery. Scotland Yard's relief was shared by Ponti. He had replaced in full the £185,000 worth stolen on her last trip. He preferred it not to become a habit.

Operation Crossbow was a wartime piece built around Hitler's last-ditch attempt to destroy London with rockets. Sophia is the wife of a Dutch collaborator; George Peppard, an American secret agent. It was a laborious picture and on the last day's shooting at Elstree, Sophia spoke for the first time about feeling 'utterly exhausted' revealing something of the almost masochistic compulsion to work without respite. Like a tired steeplechaser galloping obediently towards a fence it doubted it could clear, Sophia was flagging but couldn't stop.

'I am feeling so very tired,' she said to me at the time, 'I've been working non-stop for so long. I badly need a rest.'

Yet she went immediately from *Operation Crossbow* (hers was a smallish part in an unmemorable picture) into *Lady L*, an expensive soufflé expertly whipped up by Peter Ustinov. She's the girl who delivers the laundry at a Paris brothel and ends up marrying into the British aristocracy.

Sophia was well prepared for the part having dovetailed herself smoothly into English high society. With a little help from Sir Alec Guinness, the BBC and the recommended works of P. G. Wodehouse, this Neapolitan primitive was beginning to sound like Oscar Wilde's Lady Bracknell. I heard her call chaps 'old boy' and their wives 'my dear'. At the Savoy Hotel where seventy-two orders of the chef's speciality 'Chicken-Breast Sophia' went at one lunch sitting, the gentry behind the reception desk marvelled at Sophia's finishing-school English.

Like that old joke of the American millionaire who put on his first custom-made Savile Row suit and cried because 'we lost India', Sophia trilled deliriously over tea at the Ritz and knew the tune of Rule Britannia.

The late Robin Douglas-Home (educated at Eton, nephew of a former British Prime Minister), overheard Sophia speaking like milady in the Savoy Grill. It so offended his high-born susceptibilities he left me in the bar to dash off a column in the *Daily Express*:

'Her imitation is sprinkled with lots of "old boys" and all those patronizing expressions of the much-caricatured, stiff-upper-lip type of Englishman. Someone should tell Miss Loren that the accent and the type she is mimicking are as dead as the dodo.'

Sophia, who could have swallowed this pint-sized old Etonian for breakfast, reacted with: 'Anybody whose name is "Home" but pronounces it "Hume" is in no position to criticize my accent.'

She shopped at Fortnum's and allowed the Duchess of Bedford to pour her China tea at Woburn Abbey thanking Her Grace in the tones of a visiting Queen Mother.

The practice was more than helpful since she was to play an

eighty-year-old woman who bore a striking similarity—in Ustinov's script—to the late Queen Mary.

Ustinov was not the first director to get his hands on *Lady L.* George Cukor had started it some years earlier with Gina Lollobrigida in the lead. Metro spent more than a million dollars in preparing the costumes and sets, before finally shelving the project because of difficulties over the script.

Now with Sophia Loren, Ustinov directing, the other leading roles handled by David Niven and Paul Newman, the studio was convinced it had found a gilt-edged formula. But when the costs began to mount, the front office characters who count paper-clips, lost their nerve.

'I began to feel like a Cabinet Minister in a country that really couldn't afford one,' Ustinov said to me, now able to laugh at the whole affair.

'We made the picture in the days of censorship so one had to suggest all sorts of things instead of being able to come right out and show it. There were some brothel scenes with Sophia that we could do marvellously today but Metro which had declined but not fallen, insisted we create the kind of brothel where you could take the whole family. I rather regretted that,' he said whimsically. 'Nobody can play a prostitute in an Italian brothel as superbly as Sophia, especially when she turns into a nun at the end.'

Ustinov found, as Stanley Kramer had done on *The Pride and the Passion* that having Sophia around was a welcome antidote against some of the idiot caprices of film-making. And what success there was with the picture—limited though it was—he attributes mainly to her. Altering her brothel scenes to appease the front-office prudes made the sequence false.

'But Sophia's character maintained its integrity,' Ustinov said. 'Her great strength is that powerful animal quality and an enormous sense of humour which she turns to a sense of outrage. She is at her best when she's buoyant and indignant against great odds.'

Peter Ustinov, similarly outraged, was required to show the same buoyancy when the pressure was on.

'First they wanted a huge film, a road show, lasting three hours. Then somebody came a cropper and road shows were out, so they came back to me and said, "Can you cut the film to one hour and fifty minutes", which isn't easy when you're well into a picture you've designed for three hours.

'Sophia was playing a young woman and then has to play an eighty-year-old which nobody minded because she is seen very sexy and very beautiful at the beginning. But then Paul Newman wanted to wear a moustache and beard, and that really produced a problem.'

Sophia's reaction to the circus over Paul Newman's moustache was a long, private belly-laugh in her dressing room.

When the bosses in New York heard that the beautiful Newman features were to disappear under a face-full of whiskers, one of them put in a Transatlantic call to Ustinov:

'Christ we're not going to pay him all that amount of money so he can put things on his face. If he wants to wear a moustache he's got to take it off occasionally.'

A few days later, a still apprehensive mogul in Hollywood phoned Ustinov again, this time in the middle of the night:

'Has Newman still got that frigging moustache on?'

Ustinov replied drowsily: 'Look we've trimmed it a bit.'

'I want that thing off his face—period!' roared the demon barber of Culver City.

Behind the studio's insistence, it seemed, was a marginal failure of a film in which Newman had worn a moustache. They were scared it might happen again in *Lady L.*

Ustinov also remembers that the head of Metro at the time wanted to change the dangerous anarchists in the original story.

'Can't you make them a bit more like Robin Hood—you know, robbing the rich to give to the poor?'

Ustinov chuckled deeply. 'They always had to have this moral side to it. A Watergate with no baddies!'

Ustinov contrasted the two work-styles, Sophia's and Paul Newman's. 'Sophia,' he said, 'is almost too good to work with, too obedient. But at the same time, since nearly everything written for the films is written by men, it is absolutely essential to listen to what the female star has to say. And her feminine instinct has an unerring wisdom to it. She is enormously astute. Like Elizabeth Taylor, she's capable of moving any way a director requires her to, but she'll stop it if she feels the director doesn't know what he's doing.'

Paul Newman, amiable though he was to all concerned, played a different game. Sophia was functional, Ustinov hardly discussed scenes with her, just mimed a couple of gestures and let her instinct take over.

'But Paul Newman likes discussing everything, sometimes for a couple of hours. He needs it,' Ustinov said, 'the way a car needs to go to a filling station. You had to steel yourself to be worn out by two hours of Method conversation, about interpretation, which had you groggy at the end. Sophia just waited there as patiently as I did, saying, "When's he going to stop?"'

Despite all this the notices were kind. Leonard Mosley in the London *Daily Express* praised Newman, Niven and Ustinov but added: 'None of it, of course, measures up to Sophia Loren's effortless performance. Whether dressed in widow's weeds or boldly displaying her strapping thighs, she is a delight to the eye. What a superb and energetic animal she is.' Other critics were equally lyrical. Her Ladyship cooed with delight over tea and buttered scones at the Savoy.

The euphoria continued when *Yesterday, Today and Tomorrow* opened at a small cinema in the ancient town of Tiverton, in Devon. Thirty young gents from the famous public school, Blundells, near by, broke bounds to see the film on hearing about Sophia's striptease scenes. They slipped out in small groups but were recognized by the classics master Mr George Thomas as they came out.

Sophia was touched to hear that when the headmaster demanded the culprits to own up, twenty-one of the thirty bravely stepped forward. All had their backsides lashed six times by their housemasters that night. Then the housemasters went to see the movie.

Carlo Ponti became a French citizen in January 1965. His former wife took the same route and also became French, in June of the same year. The notice was published in France's Journal Officiel on 4 July. The decree making Ponti a Frenchman was signed by the Prime Minister of France, the late Georges Pompidou.

This top-level interest in the Pontis was based on Ponti's status, and the potential wealth he could bring into the country. And having Sophia Loren on the premises was no small capture either. The way was open for a simple French divorce, and then at last, finally, and without legal booby-traps laid all the way to the altar, Carlo and Sophia could be man and wife.

Sophia sobbed when Carlo showed her the official citizenship document.

She had been in love with him for thirteen years, 'bigamously' married to him for eight of them. They celebrated with a bottle of champagne. Among the telegrams and bouquets was a bunch of carnations with the unsigned note: 'France's finance minister welcomes a new taxpayer.'

Sourly, legal authorities in Italy declared: 'Bigamy charges against Ponti have not yet been withdrawn. Until we hear to the contrary, justice must take its course.' The long-delayed charge was fixed for a July hearing six months later. Sophia sighed, 'Here we go again,' and flew to England, renting a Georgian stately home near Ascot, Berks, to prepare for *Arabesque* with Gregory Peck.

This improbable comedy-thriller, directed by Stanley Donen, has Sophia playing an Arab woman to Peck's role of an American professor hired to decipher a secret message. There's much chasing around, and a dual shower bath (she nude, he clothed) before we establish that Sophia is not the harlot she appears to be. Gregory Peck's deft, light-comedy touch, is attributed by critics to the effect Sophia had on him. 'She has never looked more beautiful,' one critic wrote. 'It is no condemnation of the film to say that so long as she is around, which is most of the time, you really don't care about the rest.'

While she was filming it, the Rome court, unmoved by Ponti's newly acquired French citizenship, opened the hearing on the

bigamy charge against him. The trial began without the two leading characters. The Italian public which had been fed for years on
the Ponti scandal, took little interest in the proceedings. The
court was almost empty when lawyers began to read the angry
letters of denunciation from women in Milan and Pozzuoli. The
latter group asked for steps to be taken 'according to the law,
against two bigamists and especially against Sophia Scicolone of
Pozzuoli'. The use of her birth name, and not Loren, was insult
by omission. The taunt was not lost on Sophia and particularly
on her Aunt Dora in Pozzuoli. 'Many of these women were just
jealous of Sophia,' she said bitterly. 'They want to destroy what
they cannot have.'

Carlo Ponti's statement, read out for him in court, was candid
and to anyone who knows America, obviously the truth. He
said:

'I married Miss Loren after obtaining a Mexican divorce from
my first wife in order to make my relationship with her legal
outside Italy which does not recognize divorce.

'The legality (of the marriage) was necessary above all in
Hollywood where we had to go regularly for reasons of work—
and where an irregular union would have been badly received.'

The statement made no other point or asked for favours. The
hearing lasted twenty-three minutes. Case adjourned for three
months.

Sophia dismissed the legal cliff-hanger from her mind. She had
two important dates on hand—her visit to the Moscow Film
Festival, and a dinner with Charlie Chaplin. She had read an item
somewhere that he was considering her for his picture *A Countess
from Hong Kong*. The notion that the great little man should pick
her out from the massive talents available, thrilled her into several
sleepless nights.

The Soviets who idolized Chaplin to the point of searching his
ancestry for traces of good red Russian blood, had an extra reason
to fall at Sophia's feet when she stepped off the plane at Moscow
airport.

When this tall, sexual proclamation of a woman, swayed gracefully down on to the tarmac, all restraints and inhibitions about

the 'bourgeois cult of personality' vanished. The crowds cheered. Many asked for autographs: ('Please to say "to Sacha from Sophia"') said one, and women mobbed her, touching her clothes and examining her make-up.

The crowds followed her to the Tsar's Palace, the graves of Chekhov and the 'Method' man, Stanislavsky where Marlon Brando and other afficionados might have been grateful had she whispered a prayer on their behalf.

At the presentation ceremony where she won her Best Actress Award for *Marriage—Italian Style*, Sergo Zakhariadze, the eminent Russian actor kissed her warmly. It was more Cannes Film Festival than Communism, but Sophia—as she was to prove cooking spaghetti for Marshal Tito later—could sweep Iron Curtains aside with her eyelashes, or whatever.

She flew back to London with caviar, telescoping Russian dolls, and a couple of unsigned letters which declared hot passion in bad English.

She'd had a couple of days off. She was ready for work.

Charles Chaplin's return to motion pictures at the age of seventy-six after a gap of nine years, was unquestionably the film event of the year and the reception he gave at the Savoy announcing the fact, was as crowded as a Presidential press conference. Hounded out of America in the wake of the McCarthy hysteria, he moved to Vevey, Switzerland, where he dreamed, planned and sometimes made, films.

A Countess from Hong Kong had been gathering dust in his script drawer for twenty-five years. He took it out, updated it and told us that 'it was a romantic comedy'—a deadly label to pin on a movie in the swinging sixties.

Chaplin wrote the scenario, the music, hired Sophia Loren and Marlon Brando and directed the picture. His choice of Sophia was made after he saw her in *Yesterday, Today and Tomorrow*. Brando was picked 'because' Chaplin explained, 'a woman as powerful as Sophia needs an actor of equal strength and calibre'. Both stars preened and cooed like mating pigeons at the notion of being directed by the Great Creator in the art of the cinema.

Typically, Chaplin went in person to Sophia's rented house in Berkshire, carrying a bunch of flowers and the script.

'I don't have to read the script,' Sophia said to the portly little genius who sat in front of her with his hands clasped. 'I make the film for you even if you just want me to read the telephone directory.' Chaplin was touched but he gave a performance just the same.

He read every line in the script, playing Brando's part as the idealistic American diplomat (the irony of that was lost on Chaplin as it was missing from the picture) and he gave a masterly impersonation of the coquettish, sometime prostitute who was really a refugee Russian countess, who stows away on Brando's home-going liner at Hong Kong.

The Chaplin magic which had enticed two superstars into his picture, had them genuflecting all the way to Pinewood studios, persisted for a while on the set. Brando told the writer David Nathan that when he was asked to do the film, he thought Chaplin 'had gotten the wrong number. To me it seemed I was the most unlikely choice. I continued to be bewildered until two weeks after shooting started. Then it began to dawn on me what it was all about. Charlie had read the script to me, demonstrated and explained the scenes. Even then I didn't understand what the film was going to be about. I read the script, then read it again, then tried reading it upside down.'

Came the revelation, 'like a slow flow of coffee up the sugar cube,' Brando said. 'He is the most articulate, delicately attuned director I have ever worked with.'

Sophia was equally lyrical. Driving away from the set with her towards the end of the shooting, she said to me: 'I put all the love I could into that film. He is an incredible man. I love him and respect him immensely.'

She was a little less glowing about her brooding co-star. One afternoon as she brushed past wearing a clinging silk ensemble, Brando playfully slapped her on the backside. Sophia recoiled with the scorn of a Scicolone plus a hint of *Lady L.* She grabbed his arm. 'Don't ever do that again,' she said tersely. 'I am not the sort of woman who is flattered by it.'

The film opened to pallid, and in some cases, disastrous notices. 'Somewhere along the road we've lost the man in the baggy pants,' said the critic of the *Morning Star*, a left-wing paper that would be expected to root for Chaplin. 'What a shame, what a disappointment, what a bore,' said the *Daily Express*. 'The direction is dull and unimaginative, and Marlon Brando is sadly miscast.'

Chaplin's reaction, as he read the early editions at the supper party after the film, was bitter. He was shocked and disgusted. How could England of all places, do this to him?

Brando had in fact, given one of the worst performances of his career. He was stolid and unconvincing, suggesting that his remark about reading the script upside down may not have been a joke. Sophia, following the pattern of all her English-speaking roles, was excepted from any general condemnation.

Hurt most of all was the creator of the film. We talked about the film, and Sophia, when he invited me to Switzerland for the marriage of one of his daughters. 'Sophia Loren,' he said, 'has a touch of Eleanora Duse. I loved her in the part, and I loved my picture.'

He sat for a moment in silence drawing an age-mottled hand across his lips. I had reminded him of an episode which had cut him deeply. Noël Coward, James Mason and a score of distinguished painters and writers came to pay their respects, but he hardly listened to them. 'The British critics were grossly unfair,' he said to me. 'My story held up well. It had beauty and good human qualities. What do people want these days? I saw a film recently full of nudity and obscenity and it disgusted me. A man brazenly kissing a woman on her exposed breast. Is there no meaning any more to love, the purity of feeling that comes when two young people just simply hold hands? Doesn't the world want that any more?'

The short, unhappy answer was that the world didn't want films like *A Countess from Hong Kong*.

It was sad for Chaplin. A write-off for Brando.

But Sophia looked beyond the tepid press notices. She had worked for Chaplin. History would include his achievements among the Wonders of the World. 'I was thinking that when he took me in his arms on the set to show Brando how he wanted a scene played,' Sophia smiled, 'I was thrown right back to Pozzuoli, asking myself, "What's this Scicolone doing, dancing with Charlie Chaplin?"'

The film flopped at the box office, but that same year Sophia won the Alexander Korda Star, a special award, newly created by the prestigious British Film Institute. The twenty-pointed gold medallion named her as 'The International Star of the Year'. Bad films, apparently, don't necessarily destroy good actresses. Her trophy cabinet at the Villa Ponti was beginning to run out of space.

The Korda Star, the Oscar, the Bambis, the Moscow, Cannes and Venice Awards—Sophia Loren, actress, had not done badly. But as she walked the lawns in late evening at the rented house near Ascot, Mrs Carlo Ponti-elect, nurtured feelings a cartload of prizes and tiaras couldn't stifle. At night when mothers and babies appeared on television she turned her head away in case Carlo saw she was crying. Other film stars with infants of their own also noticed the tears when Sophia held the tots in her arms.

Originally her urge to have Carlo's baby was not the conventional yearning for motherhood. She admitted candidly early on in their relationship: 'For many years I was afraid he would leave me to go back to his wife. I knew he loved family life and that he suffered through staying away from his children. So, in order to keep him, it was absolutely necessary for us to have a baby. But the months sped past, then the years and nothing happened.'

Her fears of losing Carlo diminished rapidly as he demonstrated, with a little help from Van Cleef, Bulgari, Dior and a palace full of masterpieces, that no infant was essential to lock him to Sophia.

She spoke freely about this yearning to bear a child in almost every interview she gave. She was going to have Carlo's baby whether they were married or not. Better if they were. To hell with it if they weren't. After a while the words and their meaning became ossified through constant repetition. But the obsession never left her. Once, on a balcony overlooking the Bay of Naples she said to me:

'You ask me always why do I work so hard, always work, work, work. I do it because of a feeling of deep unsatisfaction. It is hard for me to explain. When I lost my baby a little while ago it was a bigger shock than people realized. Losing that baby was like having a part cut out of my own body. I felt I had failed myself, and, worse, I felt I had failed Carlo. So I work,' she said, her voice trembling. 'That way I do not think too much.'

Ponti understood the torment. He spoke to French ministers and legal experts pressing them to speed the processes by which he and Sophia could marry. He made frequent flights to Paris, called lawyers in Rome, New York and Mexico. The Great Unravelling was completed on 21 December, 1965. A French judge granted Giuliana Fiastri, the first Mrs Ponti a divorce on adultery grounds. This was made possible only by Ponti becoming a French citizen, Giuliana automatically becoming the same. (So too, did their son Alex, 15 at the time, and their daughter Guendalina, 17.) France was acquiring a boat-load of new citizens to legalize the connubial bliss of Carlo and the second Mrs Ponti.

Carlo was—in all eyes except the judicial ones in Rome—a bachelor. Sophia Scicolone, according to her passport, was a spinster known as Loren. She felt confident enough a week after Carlo's French divorce to slip into a Rome store and look at some possible wedding outfits. A Loren shopping spree in Rome was itself an event. When the whisper got round that she was being measured for 'going away' clothes, wedding rumours swept through the town and were promptly denied by both parties.

But in fact a marriage had been arranged—with the precision of a military campaign. All that was missing was the zeroing of watches and a pre-nuptial barrage of diversionary fire. Some of that came a little later.

Why Carlo and Sophia should have been so coy about letting the world in to see their marriage, is baffling. They had had a pretty big audience as 'public sinners', Ponti as an alleged 'bigamist', Sophia as his willing 'concubine'. But the marathon was over. It was all settled bar the signing, and the mandatory kiss over the town-hall inkpot.

Both Sophia, 31, and Carlo, 53, were determined that this one event, the last act in one of the most bizarre courtships in the world of love and law, should take place behind a smokescreen laid across Paris. The publication of banns was waived as a concession to Ponti's desire for secrecy.

At their apartment on the Avenue George V, Ponti, the Supremo, set out the campaign. The ceremony would take place at Sèvres, outside Paris on 9 April, 1966. Sophia and her sister Maria would spend the night together at a friend's house in Paris. 'The name and address must be given to no one,' Ponti commanded.

Sophia phoned Basilio in Cannes. 'Be in Paris tomorrow. Come straight to our building on the Avenue George V. Tell nobody what you are doing or where you are going. Ciao.'

Ponti moved into a vast suite at the Hotel Lancaster on the Rue de Berri in Paris. Nobody questioned why one man, and not a very large one at that, should require so spacious a lay-out in the hotel. Mr Ponti was a millionaire producer. He was entitled to the odd toy or two.

On the morning of the wedding Basilio received an early phone call at his hotel. A Ponti lieutenant instructed him: 'Come to the office (in the apartment building on the Avenue George V) but don't come direct in case you are followed.' Romilda, the bride's mother stayed away, looking after Maria's daughter Alessandra, in Rome. Sophia said that Romilda agreed to this because her sudden arrival in Paris would have given substance to the wedding rumours. She was also spared the realization of what she herself had missed.

At the Mairie in Sèvres, Monsieur Charles Odic, the Mayor, told Mlle. Lucie Cheval, clerk in the drab register office at the town hall, to be prepared for a special wedding.

'Who is it?' she asked.

'You will see!' the Mayor said, soprano with excitement.

Sophia and Carlo took separate cars and different routes from Paris. It was more avoiding action than a betrothal. They seemed

With Marcello Mastroianni – the ultimate chemistry, *Marriage Italian Style* (1964). (*Tazio Secchiaroli*)

Sophia Loren as seen in *A Breath of Scandal* (1960).

On *Judith* in Israel (1965). (*Pierluigi*)

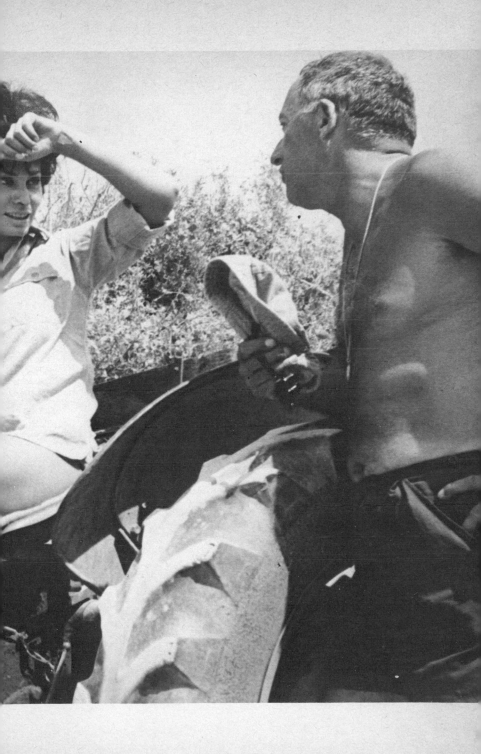

A scene from *Arabesque* with Gregory Peck (1966).

A Countess From Hong Kong, with Marlon Brando (1966).

With Marcello Mastroianni in *Sunflower* (1970).

Right The elderly *Lady L* (1965).

Below Playing Aldonza to Peter O'Toole's Don Quixote and James Coco's Sancho Panza in *Man of La Mancha* (1973). (*Associated Press*)

delighted to find that both had actually made it to Maître Charles Odic's large oak desk.

The ceremony was in French and commenced at precisely 10.00 a.m. and the amiable Monsieur Odic who sensed he was never going to play a scene with Sophia Loren again, gave it the full treatment. Once or twice, when his voice faltered, Basilio, the film-maker, felt an urge to shout 'Cut—let's take it again!'

Sophia held Carlo's hand. Maria and Ines, Sophia's secretary, wept. Monsieur Odic reminded the couple of the vows they were taking and asked them to remember they were marrying for life. If Sophia was tempted to reply that they had both already occupied the territory for some years, she concealed it behind a wide smile. She signed the register as: 'Sofia Scicolone, artiste.'

Carlo added his under the flourishing title: 'Docteur Carlo Fortunato Pietro Ponti.'

Monsieur Odic beamed and pumped Ponti's hand. Basilio kissed Sophia. He had loved her for a long time. Her embrace carried an additional squeeze of consolation.

'Despite all the formalities,' Basilio recalled, 'it was very moving. Sophia had given everything in her life, all her feelings, so much of herself for this moment. When it came, she must have felt a tremendous release of tension.'

In fact Sophia felt almost a sense of anti-climax. 'I cried of course,' she said, 'but Carlo had been part of me for so long, I felt as though I'd been married to him almost from the day I was born. We now had a piece of paper with a rubber stamp on it. Okay it was official. But it was rather like reading a theatre programme long after you'd seen the play.'

After the ceremony Sophia phoned her mother in Rome.

'Darling—finally you made it!' Romilda said, 'I'm very happy for you.'

The couple and their friends went for the wedding breakfast of asparagus, salmon and steak at the Coqhardi, a chic restaurant a few miles outside Paris. Sophia wore a Dior dress of white silk. Ponti, a smile bursting with pride of ownership. Toasts were drunk to the 'bride and groom' with much sisterly giggling from Sophia and Maria who saw the funny side of it all.

The Ponti wedding night was spent at the Hotel Lancaster. The morning after, Paris newspapers repeated the wedding rumours. Ponti promptly denied them.

It was eleven days before the Mayor of Sèvres, almost ready to explode with excitement, finally released the news.

It may have been coincidence that on the same day French film journalists awarded Sophia Loren the Lemon Prize, given annually to the performer most lacking in courtesy to the press. They no doubt resented not being invited to the wedding, given bedside seats at the Hotel Lancaster.

She dismissed the Gallic backhander with a Neapolitan word appropriate to the occasion. She should worry. While the disgruntled Frenchmen were offering her a lemon, the Publicity Photographers' Guild of America had just voted her 'The Most Beautiful Actress in the World'. And the powerful American Theatre Owners' Association had named her 'Actress of the Year'.

These were delicious goodies to take with her to Matera, in Southern Italy to film *Happily Ever After* with Omar Sharif.

The movie had a lively beginning. She broke a finger in a fight sequence with the Egyptian actor which so distressed Lloyds of London they flew a top executive out to examine the damage. (With Sophia being insured for double the cost of the picture, a damaged digit could be as bad as a disaster at sea.)

The Lloyds man inspected the injury and was so delighted to find that it was minimal, he broke a leg slipping in his hotel.

Both fractures, Sophia's and the insurance man's, added to the fun in the hotel bar at night.

Sophia seemed more exhilarated than most.

Mrs Carlo Ponti was pregnant again.

12

Inside Sophia Loren

ANNOUNCEMENT: (13 December, 1966.) Sophia Loren, 32, expects a baby in May, Mr David Wolper, a film producer, said in Los Angeles tonight. He added that as a result she has postponed the TV film she was due to make in Rome.

ANNOUNCEMENT: (31 December, 1966.) Mother-to-be-Sophia Loren is ill. She was ordered to bed for two weeks by her doctors in Rome yesterday.

ANNOUNCEMENT: (7 January, 1967.) The Italian news agency Ansa reported tonight that Sophia Loren had been taken to a Rome clinic and there were fears she might lose the baby she is expecting.

ANNOUNCEMENT: (9 January, 1967.) Sophia Loren who was taken to a Rome clinic on Friday was said last night to be in no immediate danger of losing the baby she is expecting in May.

REPORT in *Paese Sera* Rome: (12 January, 1967.) SOPHIA LOREN HAS LOST HER BABY. There were rumours that she had been in danger of losing her life during the course of an operation. Carlo Ponti who had stayed in the clinic all night, wept. After Sophia Loren suffered acute pain and haemorrhage, the decision was taken, in consultation between the doctors, Ponti and the patient herself, to operate. The surgery was performed by Professor Pietro Marziale assisted by Professor Atlante and a team of emergency personnel. Blood and urine samples were taken while Sophia Loren was still in a drugged condition after the anaesthetic but no results of the tests have been issued. Telegrams of sympathy have arrived from all over the world, including messages from Princess Grace of Monaco, Marlon Brando, Jean

Paul Belmondo, Juliette Greco, Peter Sellers, Audrey Hepburn, the film director Gillo Pontecorvo and Charles Chaplin who has telephoned several times for news of the actress's health.

No actress in the world has had the failures and successes of her reproductive innards chronicled so avidly as has Sophia Loren. Ploughing through the available bulletins, hospital statements and blow-by-blow accounts by the lady herself is a gynaecological field-day. When she was pregnant, the world rejoiced across acres of print in every language from Mandarin to old Samoan. When, unhappily, she miscarried, the sympathy surged like an ocean of tears around the entire coastline of Italy.

Adding piquancy to it all, of course, was the fact that her aberrant birth pangs and the army of specialists called in to orchestrate them, occurred during what was regarded by some as an illicit relationship.

A pregnant married movie star is news. A pregnant, un-married movie star is bigger news. A pregnant, unmarried movie star accused of sinful 'concubinage' is the Page One splash. A beautiful, pregnant, unmarried superstar who loses her child, is high drama.

Yet, though Sophia Loren's ecstasy and anguish were given global coverage by the news media, the reports failed to indicate causes. An important omission.

Her second miscarriage had occurred during the shooting of a film, called ironically, *Happily Ever After* (later *More than a Miracle* in the U.S., *Cinderella—Italian Style* elsewhere, and not much of a picture by the critics). But when we talked about it, sufficient time had elapsed for Sophia to discuss with candour the traumas of frustrated motherhood. The setting, at the villa, was appropriate to the subject. Behind her was an immense Renais-sance masterpiece of 'Mother and Child'. She looked out towards the vast pool where fat little stone cherubs shimmered white in the noonday heat. And speaking, as she did, in a bantam-sized bikini, the breasts more saucered than cupped, the clinical details were most helpfully illustrated. I asked her:

'What was wrong with the internal machinery?'

'Nothing,' she said sharply. 'Nothing at all. Look, what happened is personal, but you ask me so I tell you. It is better that I do anyway. All the stories about my miscarriages suggest I wasn't built like other women.

'First you must understand something of the misery I felt. I can't speak for all women in this situation but I guess they wouldn't feel very different from the way I did. When I had my second miscarriage I really despaired. I had seen some of the best specialists but they couldn't explain why I was losing my babies. Somehow I couldn't carry a child in the womb for the full nine months.

'Of course that is tragic for any woman. But for a Neapolitan woman it is almost a disgrace. I felt abnormal, ashamed. And as it finally turned out it was all for nothing.

'I had two terrible experiences with one doctor who treated me in Italy. Two miscarriages, both agony for me, and I need never have suffered them.' Her voice trembled. 'I hate that man, I really do. Why? Because after two miscarriages a doctor is afraid to risk a mother having the usual birth. He wants the baby to be good and alive without complications. And so he gives you a Caesarian. But after you've had one Caesarian you have to have a second and maybe a third. Then—finish. No more babies.

'I hate that doctor—I will not name him but he knows the suffering he caused me—because I wanted to have many children. I'm made for it, and I love them. But all that has gone, through that one man.'

The maternal malfunction, it turned out, was caused by a simple imbalance of hormones. 'All I needed to keep my baby in the womb for the full nine months was a course of Oestrogen, and I had to go to Switzerland to discover it,' she said. 'I had heard of a brilliant Swiss specialist, Professor Hubert de Watteville. Two months after I lost my second child I went to see him in Geneva.

'He gave me an injection of Pentothal, I fell asleep and he gave me a complete internal examination. When I awoke he looked very embarrassed. "I'm sorry," he said, "I don't know

SOPHIA

why you lose your children. The only explanation that occurs
to me is that maybe when you are three months pregnant the
uterus doesn't close enough. But that is no problem. We can tie
it up. Frankly there's no reason why you shouldn't have a normal
pregnancy. You're perfect."

'I was perfect!' she said grimly, 'but losing my babies one
after the other. A year later, when I became pregnant again I
called the professor in Geneva. I told him that I was having
danger signals again that I might lose the baby for the third time.

' "Come to Geneva at once," he said, "and you will go back to
Rome with a baby."

'Carlo was in London when I found I was pregnant. I telephoned him there and he said, "What is it?"

' "I am waiting a baby," I told him.

'He said: "Oh no! Not again!"

'He was scared for me, afraid I would have another miscarriage.
But I took the plane to Geneva, with Ines. Professor de Watteville
did an analysis of my urine for twenty-four hours. Would you
like a glass of Frascati?'

'Thank you.'

'Is cold enough?'

'Fine.'

'Good. Anyhow, after he took my urine for twenty-four hours
he discovered that the level of Oestrogen was so very low he gave
me an injection. Every week I did the same thing right through
the pregnancy. Twenty-four hours urine test, then the injections
and I was okay. He put me in a hotel near his clinic, I locked the
doors and waited for Cipi.'

Sophia Loren's seven months' incarceration in Switzerland,
most of the time at the Intercontinental Hotel Geneva,
pampered, patrolled and guarded, gave a new meaning to the
phrase 'solitary confinement'.

She moved into the £100 a day suite, with Ines, and two
members of the staff from the Villa Ponti at Marino, and didn't
emerge into the sunlight and civilization until ready for delivery.
Food was cooked in a kitchen specially created for her. Every
move and sound around the *enceinte* Sophia was controlled with

198

the sure-footed caution of a bomb disposal unit. Those with a sudden urge to cough, sneeze or worse, were ordered with a steely glance, to take their germs and themselves to the nearest exit or open window.

As an extra precaution against one knows not what, Ines slept in the bed next to Sophia's. They played poker most of the day with guaranteed disinfected, germ-free, serve chilled, playing cards. Doctors came daily, under Professor de Watteville's instruction, to check the Ponti pulse rate, heart-beat and urological proceedings of the day. Letters (expertly checked for normal pollution, pestilence or plague) arrived from all over the world. U.S. soldiers serving in Vietnam wrote saying: 'We're praying for you!'

Priests of all denominations sent blessings and invited their congregations to include Sophia in their Thought for the Day. Astrologers offered their services in case the distinguished Professor de Watteville needed a little help from the planets.

But the most astonishing response was from the public—the wives and mothers of Italy, France, the United States and particularly Britain. Somehow, the besieged courtship and anguished miscarriages of Sophia Loren had strummed their heart-strings. They grabbed knitting needles and crochet hooks and set to with the frenzy of the mitten-knitters of World War I.

Baby-bonnets, bootees, gloves, vests, dresses, jackets and a whole clatter of rattles arrived in Geneva and Rome, together with heart-expanding wishes for a successful delivery. There were flowers pressed in bibles, toys, gold crucifixes and scores of letters from mothers with intimate advice on What To Do When The Pains Start and tracts like, 'Don't Work for the Womb—Let The Womb Work For You.'

'Sometimes I felt I wasn't having the baby for Carlo, I was having it for the world,' Sophia smiled. 'When a soldier fighting in Vietnam writes to say he is praying for me, it's really shattering.'

Meanwhile the unborn celebrity inside Sophia remained snugly oblivious to it all (or if he wasn't, he issued no pre-natal statements at the time).

As D-Day approached, Carlo Ponti cancelled all his engagements and homed in on Geneva. Romilda and Maria checked into the hotel. Bulletins were relayed from door to door on the Via Solfatara in Pozzuoli.

When the infant began nudging Sophia, urgently demanding to be born, Sophia was moved to the nearby clinic. She rang a bell and Professor de Watteville arrived.

'I think I'm ready,' she told him.

'I'll give you an injection to make you sleep,' he said.

During the anaesthetic Sophia had a nightmare. 'I dreamed that the baby had died,' she recalled.

'I kept hearing a voice saying, "He's dead, he's dead, your baby is dead."

'In my dream I began screaming. "Don't let him die. I beg you. . . ." '

'You have a boy,' the Professor said. Ponti came into the room. She threw her arms around him. 'At last . . . at last, I am a complete wife to you.' Then later Romilda and Maria arrived. There were many wet cheeks at the Intercontinental Hotel, Geneva, that day.

Meanwhile the world's media, experiencing labour pains on a global scale, were hammering on the door. Hubert (after the Professor) Leoni (after Ponti's father) Carlo (after papa) Ponti Junior, was news.

The press assembled into an improvised briefing room. A correspondent compared it to Eisenhower's conference on the eve of the Normandy landings. Facing them were Professor de Watteville, Doctor Hans Bramatter, a leading pediatrician, and Doctor Annalise Weiss, the chief anaesthetist at the hospital. It was a solemn moment. As though God were being interviewed on the Creation.

'The operation (Caesarian) was carried out quite normally,' the Professor announced, 'and I repeat that the mother's condition does not arouse any disquiet. Signora Ponti showed exemplary courage both before and after the operation.'

The Professor was clearly relieved and delighted by Sophia's successful delivery. He told the eager questioners:

'There is no secret. I believe in the attention to all details. The role of the diet is important—I would say vital. I prescribed for the mother the correct balance of hormones, vitamins and minerals and we had to eliminate all the unfavourable bacteriological influences that we could.'

He turned to Doctor Bramatter who had assisted at the operation (time one hour, baby emerging feet first).

'Would you care to add something, Doctor?'

Doctor Bramatter gave a bashful nod.

'I don't say this just because of the circumstances,' he began, 'but this is really a fine baby, normal and healthy from every point of view. His little heart beats at a rate of 120 pulsations. There is no difficulty in the nervous system and his reactions are more than good. The weight is three and a half kilos and the length fifty-two centimetres.'

The journalists were grateful for the good doctor's helpful information. But after a fair amount of whispering a spokesman was elected to ask the sixty-four dollar question:

'Would Sophia Loren breast-feed the baby herself or would a wet-nurse (from a well-attested short list on offer) be called in to do so on her behalf?'

Dr Bramatter fielded that question. 'Signora Ponti wishes to do so herself and we too will do our best to give her the possibility of feeding her son personally.'

Precisely what assistance Sophia might require in the operation was not made clear. Breast-feeding is second nature to Neapolitans. In her suite at the hospital, the mother indicated her impatience to get the supply going.

It was Carlo Ponti's turn to get into the act. According to *Il Messaggero* he surprised everyone by his display of emotion—presumably because revealing it was uncharacteristic of the Milanese in general, and film producer Carlo Ponti in particular.

'We are extremely happy,' he began, 'and at this moment . . .' he was unable to finish the sentence. His voice choked and a sob broke out. After a few moments, Ponti started speaking again in a clearer voice only his glistening eyes betraying his feelings.

'I thank the professors who attended Sophia with extreme

patience and with almost paternal care. I thank them for having given to my wife and me the joy of this magnificent day.'

The briefing was over. Carlo Junior was subsequently coupled to the most majestic bosom of the day. Geneva, and the world, returned to normal business.

The arrival of Sophia's infant exposed the continuing absurdities of the bigamy charges brought interminably against Ponti. His former wife had given him a divorce—French style, and remained friendly. All parties were now French citizens. The two leading characters in the case, Carlo and Sophia, were, whether Italy recognized it or not, man and wife, and now parents. The protracted legal manoeuvre trying to pin bigamy on him, concubinage on her, was becoming the longest running comedy in Rome. A bit of a bore too.

Even the 'denouncers' who started it all were beginning to wish they hadn't. The wires between Mexico and Rome hummed with the frenzied activity of lawyers trying to help each other off the hook.

They finally unearthed a judicial nugget. A faulty document. On 27 April, 1967, an appeal court in Rome ruled that the 1957 proxy marriage in Mexico was invalid because the signatures of two witnesses did not appear on the documents. Just how this happened was not made clear, and nobody wanted to ask. The judges said, with evident relief:

'If Mexico does not recognize this proxy marriage then neither can Italy.' So—no marriage in Mexico, no bigamy in Italy. It was as simple as that. To get there, though, Mr and Mrs Ponti had been forced to take a somewhat circuitous route via a short residential status in Switzerland, three years exile around the globe, then a house on the Avenue George V in Paris as a first step towards becoming citizens of France. It was a long haul to sustain a love-match—and stave off the threat of jail.

Yet when that threat disappeared, it was replaced by another one, this time aimed exclusively at Sophia. It came from the man who had remained in the shadows of her mind for years, her father, Riccardo Scicolone. He had become increasingly peeved by articles attributed to Sophia, in which, he alleged, she blamed him for the tough early years of herself and her mother. He considered he had been unfairly maligned and brought an action for libel. But in the preliminary hearing, the court ruled that the charge of libellous intent was debatable, adding:

'The statements (in the allegations) do not appear to be of a clearly aggressive significance to the reputation of the complainant . . .'

A few days later Riccardo Scicolone withdrew his case. Reflecting on it, Sophia said: 'Of course I felt resentment in the early years, more for my mother than for myself. But time heals. Sometimes people make a mistake, they recognize it, then they correct it. My father did that and it is finished. I understand him now. He also had his problems. I wish him well.'

A prosperous building contractor, Signor Scicolone, whose marriage to Nella Rivolta, a Milanese woman, broke down years ago, now leads a quiet life. Occasionally he goes to see films starring Sophia Loren. As he sits in the darkness, watching the superstar he sired, he is entitled to a little self-congratulation. Part of him was up there on the screen. He could also wonder, 'Suppose that splendid animal, Romilda Villani had not been passing at the time . . .?'

Sophia Loren, the richest actress in the world, presiding over a treasure-stacked palace near Rome, is relieved that the question doesn't arise. Ponti, Paramount and Pozzuoli have no complaints either.

The arrival of Hubert Leoni Carlo Ponti Junior—named 'Cipi' after the initials, phonetically, of his father, pushed movies into the background for a year or so. It was just as well. The dazzling momentum of *Two Women*, *Yesterday*, *Today and Tomorrow* and *Marriage—Italian Style* dawdled into some dreary pictures. It was not enough that Sophia's performances were applauded despite the adverse criticism of the films. Vittorio de Sica, due to bad luck or bad choice of subjects, was no longer sustaining the brilliance and the buoyancy which had made his alliance with Sophia the most fertile partnership in motion pictures. It was sad to see the withering reviews of *Sunflower* which starred Sophia and Mastroianni, notably the London *Times* which spoke nostalgically of *Bicycle Thieves, Shoeshine* and *Umberto D* and wondered what had happened to the master's touch. A contrived melodrama by Cesare Zavattini, *Sunflower* involves a wife's search for a husband supposedly missing believed dead on the Russian Front in World War II. The film loses its way and its credibility early on in the proceedings and fails to recover.

De Sica took a short sabbatical from the partnership. Another director took Sophia in hand to make *Questi Fantasmi*—(called *Ghosts—Italian Style* in America) which was all but incinerated by the critics. The film made a few embarrassed appearances in the U.S. but mercifully Ponti steered it clear of Britain's shores.

A dramatic vote in the Italian Parliament of the day, permitting divorce (on somewhat laborious conditions) encouraged Ponti to star Sophia in *The Priest's Wife*. The film poked a little sly fun at priestly celibacy, Mastroianni playing the cleric whose spirit was willing but whose flesh was weakened—by Sophia Loren. Predictably the film was officially blasted by the Vatican, and, curiously, by Egypt's semi-official newspaper, *Al-Ahram*, which resented the film's mocking attitude. 'In doing so,' the paper said, 'Egypt was showing the spirit which protects the respectability of all religions.'

It was not a bad comedy. The script was smart, but maybe priestly celibacy isn't much of a joke to those who may be tormented by it. Part of the film was shot at the Italian spa at Abano, where Bavarians slide in and out of the steaming mud baths like playful hippos.

To test-run Sophia's attitudes to the theme of the film, I invited a Catholic priest, Father Sampers of the Convent of St Alphonso in Rome, to join in on a discussion. A tall, gentle Dutchman, he sat on a couch beside Sophia and they talked about celibacy, chastity and the pill. Father Sampers wanted to know:

'Why should this film be made at all, except to provoke a controversy?'

'Forgive me,' Sophia declared, 'the controversy is here in life whether we provoke it or not. It really happens. A priest falls in love, lives secretly with a woman and has children who are told to call him "uncle". It is the hypocrisy of it that I cannot stand— the feeling that as long as nobody knows about it, and there is no scandal, it does not matter.'

Father Sampers smiled the sad smile of a man who had heard it all before.

'If a priest cannot stand the discipline it is always open for him to resign. Anyway, a love between a man and a woman is not necessarily bound by physical love or marriage. I can tell you of my own personal experience,' he said.

'Years ago I knew a person very well. We were in love. Finally it was the woman who said: "It is better you go with the church than with me." '

'Why can't a priest have both?'

'It is a conflict of devotions, of rules,' Father Sampers explained. 'Maybe they are required to make the choice too young, when they cannot truly know what a woman is. . . .'

'Or can give!' Sophia flashed, her direct gaze bringing a slight colour to the priest's cheeks. 'What I cannot understand is why the Catholic Church insists on celibacy when most other religions do not?'

Father Sampers shrugged. 'Well England drives on the left-hand side of the road, Italy and many other countries drive on the right.'

Sophia laughed. 'But at least everybody is allowed to drive.'

'A remarkable woman,' Father Sampers said as we shared a car to the airport. 'As beautiful as a statue. Wonderful eyes of course,' he conceded, 'but the mouth . . .' he looked solemnly over the top of his spectacles, 'a little wide don't you think?'

Sophia had not shaken the good priest's loyalty to his calling, but she had clearly made an impact on the man inside the garb. This 'presence', the subtle self-parodying by a woman who knew her own strength, was charming its way into the world's upper echelons, captivating presidents, disarming dictators.

Marshal Tito of Yugoslavia preceded Golda Meir in giving Sophia the warm presidential handshake. He invited her (together with Carlo, Cipi, the nurse and secretary) to move into a luxury villa as his guest on the Yugoslav island of Brioni. They stayed there for a month, commuting frequently between the villa and Tito's home on the island, for dinners with their host. Formalities dissolved into good bantering stuff, the moment the soldier-statesman got the measure of his guest. It was clear, from her description of him that Sophia too had treated him to her own all-purpose appraisal, the opening stanza of which, began:

'He's a little robust, with a nice skin and good complexion. He has a very tanned face with light eyes, an open honest expression, and he looks into your eyes all the time. He is so charming, it envelops you. Such a warm earthy man—a real man of the people. And he adored my cooking. One day he came into my kitchen to see what I was doing. He asked me if I would cook dinner for that evening. I knew he liked spaghetti and spicy things so I cooked him three kinds of sauce for the pasta so that he could have a taste of every flavour.'

The sauces completed, the President's cook-for-the-day produced a second course of egg-plant parmesan which had Tito wondering seriously why, with this talent, she bothered to make movies. (He spoke to her through an interpreter, though with Cipi he used German which the infant was fast acquiring from his Swiss nurse, Ruth Bapst.)

Tito showed the Pontis round his vineyard. 'You know what I do when it is time to make the wine? I invite my ministers here when it is ready to pick the fruit off the vines. In the afternoon when we have eaten, I say to them: "Listen, we've nothing to do, why don't we have some fun? Let's go and pick the grapes." '

And like the good Communists they undoubtedly are, the ministers roll up their sleeves and do their bit for the presidential vino.

Sophia still corresponds with President Tito and his wife Jovanka. He says the actress is welcome to return any time she pleases—with or without the parmesan.

With the status went the symbols—the acquisition of which, on the Ponti scale, required their home at Marino to be fortified against everything except a direct hit by a nuclear missile. But in spite of the iron grilles, the guards, and the 'ATTENTE AL CANE' behind which salivated some of the most baleful Alsatians in the country, the Pontis were robbed twice. Thieves got away with all the cups and trophies Sophia had won over the years including the Oscar. (She bought a replacement for sixty dollars.) They ransacked Ponti's wardrobe and a cabinet, getting away with three hundred gold and silver antique trinket boxes the Pontis had collected on their travels around the world.

The arrival of the precious first-born made the security arrangements existing at the time seem like 'open house' in Marino. Guards with walkie-talkie sets patrolled the entire estate. Engineers were called in to install highly sophisticated anti-burglar devices around the place and were no doubt induced to swallow the plans on completion of their work. In spite of all that, I still rate the formidably built Clothilde who (if she will forgive me) manned the main gate, as the most persuasive deterrent since boiling oil. Nothing and no one gets beyond her until they have been checked against the visiting list, all but finger-printed and saliva-tested.

But if Sophia felt safe in Rome, she was apprehensive about New York where muggings and break-ins had made hotels vulnerable and the streets of Manhattan no place to walk at night. She flew there in October 1970 for the premiere of *Sunflower* and for the film-plugging interview on the David Frost programme which preceded it. As a public relations exercise, gratefully indulged by film stars, Van Cleef, the famous jewellers, loaned Sophia the largest diamond ring out of Elizabeth Taylor's reach. Close-ups of this scintillating golf ball were flashed frequently on the TV screen as Sophia responded engagingly to David's oleaginous good cheer. Amongst the peak audience watching the show were hoodlums not particularly hooked on Sophia's early struggle in Pozzuoli. They looked at the ring, and slipped out to case her hotel, the exclusive Hampshire House, where Carlo, Sophia, Ines, the nurse and baby occupied a private apartment on the twenty-second floor.

The following evening, Carlo Ponti received a phone call to say that his father had died in Milan. The news hit him hard. He ordered a car to take him immediately to the airport, and a seat on the first available flight to Italy. Sophia drove with him to the airport, then returned to her apartment. It was 9.00 p.m. She felt sad for Carlo. He had been deeply distressed and was in tears when he left her to board a plane to Milan. Tired and upset, she told Ines who slept in her room whenever Carlo was away, she was turning in early. Cipi was asleep. Ines and the nurse were watching television in the living room. Sophia went to her bedroom then came running back.

'I've seen a shadow in my room. There must be someone there!'

'Impossible,' Ines reassured her, 'there's no way anyone can come in.'

Sophia was still nervous. 'Come back with me,' she insisted, 'I'm sure I saw the shadow of a man.'

They went back together, Ines convincing Sophia that the shadow was sheer fantasy. Sophia went to sleep.

In the early hours, five men broke into the hotel, took over the switchboard, held up the night staff, one of them ordering the porter to take them to Sophia's flat, holding a revolver to his ear.

At 7.00 a.m. Ines got up to make some coffee. Sophia Loren was still asleep in the adjoining bed. She remembers being jolted awake by incessant screaming.

'I thought I was having a nightmare at first. The screaming seemed so very distant. I awoke and realized that it wasn't a dream. But I still didn't realize what was happening. I thought it must be a young girl in an adjoining apartment.

'There was a knock on the door and a man came in carrying a bunch of keys on a large ring. I was still in a stupor. For a moment I thought he was a doctor carrying a stethoscope. I felt my heart jump and I was sick with fright. The sound of screaming and this stranger who for a moment I mistook for a doctor, meant only one thing to me. My son. He was ill.

'I screamed, "It's Cipi isn't it—what is wrong with my baby?"

'The man said, "Don't panic and everything will be all right."'

Then I realized that it was Ines screaming in the next room. It was a terrible sound.' (One of the gang had clubbed her secretary with a pistol butt.)

'The room was in darkness. The man said "get up" pointing the gun at me. "Where's the light?" he shouted. I reached for the bedside light and switched it on. It was then I saw the man properly for the first time. He wore dark glasses. I remembered thinking, terrified though I was, how much he looked like Belmondo. He pointed his gun at me. "This is a hold-up," he said. It was like a second-rate gangster film. He started throwing my jewellery round on the dressing table.

' "This is junk, junk," he said. "I want the real stuff. And if I don't get it . . ." he began waving his gun at me. Another man had come in with the concierge and the manager, holding a gun to their faces. The manager, poor man, was so weak with shock they let him sit down on a chair. While all this was happening Ines was still screaming and moaning in the other room. I gave the man a ruby ring which was on the table. He grabbed it, but he wasn't satisfied. There were some other jewels loaned to me by Van Cleef for the big Rockefeller Ball that night. We would have been safely back in Rome but for that occasion. The man took those jewels too but he said: "These are junk too. I want the big ring." That was the one the jewellers had given me to wear on the Frost programme. It was the most beautiful diamond I had ever seen in my life. What a fool I was to place so much importance on it. Here I was being threatened by a gunman, my secretary was being attacked and God knows what was happening to my baby. I shouted at the man. "It is not my ring. I borrowed it from Van Cleef. But I gave it back the same night. I implore you to believe me." He came towards me. "Where is that ring?" he said. "You better get it."

'I begged him to take my word. He was a young man, maybe about thirty-five. I stared at him closely. I didn't realize it was dangerous to look a thief in the face. They are always scared you might identify them. He became furious. He grabbed me by the hair and pulled my head down until I was lying on the floor. Then he emptied my wallet of a few hundred dollars, took the ring and the Van Cleef jewellery. Another man came in and shouted: "Hurry up, let's go." But the man who was holding me had a sudden thought. Before he left the room he turned and said: "Okay, where's your kid. Just tell me where the kid is."

'When I heard that and thought they were threatening to kidnap Cipi I began to shake. It was a mixture of an agony of fear for my son, and fury at myself for having such a stupid fascination for jewellery. I had some more diamonds and things on a table in the corridor. I ran past the gunmen. One of them, thinking that I may be going to call the police, grabbed me. "Take this," I said to him, handing him a bag of jewellery. He took it and they ran off. I swear to you from that moment, when I held Cipi in my arms again and saw that he was safe, I was taught the biggest lesson of my life. Believe me, I have deleted the word "jewellery" from my vocabulary. To own something which could make other people resort to murder and kidnapping, is a threat not a possession. If I must wear jewellery at all it will be fake. Perhaps I needed diamonds to prove something to myself. Maybe they were the symbols of success in my career. But it is stupid.'

Cipi ran in from the pool. He stopped, the water dripping from his sturdy brown body on the lush carpet. He smiled and Sophia ran and swept him up in her arms.

'They don't make them like this at Van Cleef,' she said.

The Pontis flew back home from New York after reluctant sessions with the FBI. They hardly cared about the stolen jewellery, still less about the gunmen. It had been a nightmare. It was a relief to get back to the peace of the villa, the six acres of vineyards, the arched paths winding between the birches and cypresses, and good, solid Clothilde on the main gate.

Sophia had a film to make in Italy, but the important assignment, preceded by a United Artists fanfare in the style of Barnum and Bailey, was *Man of La Mancha* with Peter O'Toole as Don Quixote.

When the deal was signed, Sophia, in accordance with the vows she took in New York, asked Carlo to discontinue his practice of presenting her with a chunk of expensive jewellery at the end of every film she made.

'Better you give me another baby,' she laughed.

'It's a deal,' the producer replied.

And Carlo Ponti never reneged on a contract.

13

O'Toole, and the Burton Disconnection

Sophia Loren's leading men may be dissimilar in size, shape or ego-rating, but they have this in common—an unshakable adoration for the lady. As we know, Cary Grant and Peter Sellers were in a separate category, prepared, at the drop of a Ponti, to zoom round to the front door with a posy and a ring. The fact that their chances in that area were slimmer than a newt's eyelash in no way took the edge off their appetite.

Aside of this pair, Sophia's relationship with her co-stars has been on the same back-scratching level of a queen with her bowing, hand-kissing knights. The admiration has been as unstinted as it has been largely uncritical, with some significant exceptions. Her long-standing friendship with Marcello Mastroianni has been a subtle one with both parties content to let the curious read what they like into the association. But behind the smoke screen—his lustful moustache-twitching, her unzipped sexuality—the couple take their favours and garlic-fumes elsewhere. What they share is a stubborn perfectionism and a touching, unswerving, totally dedicated respect for the art of making money. That said, they fight and argue in the way only Italians know how. It takes someone with the stature and Solomon-like wisdom of de Sica to arbitrate between the two competing profiles.

And then there is Peter O'Toole.

Sophia's notion of the actor when she signed to film *Man of La Mancha* with him, was of a cheerful, talented movie star, raised on Shakespeare and David Lean, who would fit nicely into her collection of top-rated leading men. She was totally unprepared for the barn-storming bhoyo from Connemara who spoke like a character created jointly by Sean O'Casey and S. J. Perelman.

She had seen him as *Lawrence of Arabia* and with Richard Burton in *Becket*, heard about his considerable stage successes, and was thrilled to have a man of that class as her *Don Quixote*. If others had some doubt about their 'chemistry'—that deadly criterion—nobody expressed it. With ten million dollars, a rape sequence, O'Toole as the Don and Sophia leading a fanfare of strumpets, it would be all right on the night.

But how did they blend, the soft-centred Sophia and the actor whose ferocious goodwill once had to be cooled down in jail, with plaster and plastic surgery for the cracked ribs and broken nose?

'Magnificently,' roared Mr O'Toole, 'I love that cow!' To those familiar with the actor's cautious bestowal of compliments, it was the ultimate accolade. The O'Toole technique with superstars, to prevent his own ego from being left out in the cold, is to feed them a mixture of honey and prussic acid. If the needling strikes a nerve, the lean face with the almost lidless eyes under streaky yellow hair, smiles penitently in search of a forgiving bosom.

He called her 'Scicolone' from the start, throwing it at her in the middle of the first rehearsal. It was a calculated risk. But Sophia read the message, and in the words of O'Toole, 'just cracked and fell around the room'. Sophia soon knew she had no Charlton Heston (or his bland equivalent) on her hands. The work-style was controlled hysteria. The language, O'Toole monopolizing the choicer phrases, was rough. They gambled with the rest of the cast and cheated outrageously. They got up to mad escapades and practical jokes, and in between they made the picture.

Sophia played Aldonza, the bed-happy scullerymaid who Don Quixote sees in his imaginings, as the virginal Lady Dulcinea. 'They tried to de-glamorize her for the role,' O'Toole said, grinning at the very idea. 'Failure. The less glossy she is, the more attractive she becomes, especially in the legs-apart, blouse-ripped, eyes-flashing, posture.

'I also discovered she has a favourite profile and she arranged things accordingly. To make sure of it her contortions were magnificent. Her lightning leg-work, ducking and weaving would shame Mohammed Ali. And she was absolutely open and unblushing about the whole thing. I just trotted along on my high heels, poking my head into the lens when I could, mouthing those miserable lyrics and hoping for the best.'

Mr O'Toole was at home in Hampstead, and in great form. His reminiscences gurgled as lavishly as the first bottle of wine of the day. He does not speak in the language of Olivier.

'I honestly thought I was the best at being full of shit,' he said. 'But this angel has the edge. All I could do was watch and learn. She worked the left-profile flanker with sheer mastery. Instead of turning and walking out of a shot up the stairs, thus giving the paying public a glimpse of the dreaded right profile, she glided upwards and backwards. My look of boggling admiration was not lost on her. She went into her dressing room for a quick squirt of hilarity, and came out with some sixteenth-century mascara running down her cheeks. We became quite hysterical. At one point she said:

' "You are more full of sheet than I am!" '

O'Toole blushed at the compliment. It augured well for the production. Sophia's discipline staggered O'Toole, who thought he'd learned a thing or two at Stratford-upon-Avon.

'She has this absolutely unstoppable clockwork professional mechanism put together over the years that tick-tocks, ticktocks, on and on,' he said. 'You remember the line, "A genuine half-hunter gentleman, with dead-beat escapement." '

Nor could he fault her for effort. The famous rape sequence in which she has to fight off ten groping pairs of hands, drew this rueful comment from one of the 'victims':

'She punched and kicked everybody at least once, and I can tell you she kneed me in the orchestras!' (Rhyming slang; orchestra stalls, balls.)

As Arthur Hiller, the director, completed each scene, the leading players leapt to the nearest card table, to resume the poker game which the filming had annoyingly interrupted. Sophia, Peter O'Toole and James Coco (Sancho Panza in the picture) swore, threatened and shouted over the cards in the style of an average board meeting in the Cosa Nostra. 'We assumed totally different personae,' O'Toole grinned. 'Scicolone swung from cool reserve to a scratching, gesticulating, cursing Neapolitan.'

'And you?' I asked him.

He put his hand on his heart, the pale eyes taking on the expression of a mystic. 'Nothing, I swear, except a little simple bullying and cheating. True, we ganged up on Coco by concealing deuces and aces in my boots and her tits, but I will say this for him, and her—they have genuine mirth. So bloody rare.' (For those uninitiated in the pranks of superstars on a multimillion dollar movie O'Toole is clearly your guide.)

'As for Sophia as a woman, the more I was with her the more edible she looked. I mean, Jesus!—the creature is delicious. I'm never bowled over by these ladies with their special hair and their attitudes and public faces. I met her first in Taormina when we were both receiving Donatello Awards. We've won three each,' he added, with a shrewd concern for the figures. 'My first impression was of a well turned out, extremely skilful piece of machinery. It was much later, when we began to work together, that I could see her for what she was. No crap, no artifice—just an extraordinary, sexually attractive lady.

'Listen, there's so much of it there, who could ignore it. But it was not that bloody cliché of my falling in love with her. Just a straightforward, enormous sexual attraction. But what would you expect? I'm not made of effing tin-tacks!'

It was just as well that the two stars did get along. The film had had an abortive start. Director Peter Glenville and another writer had begun it, but for various reasons, didn't stay with it. Arthur Hiller took over with other writers and the original script, not to mention Cervantes, took a hammering.

The musical numbers required both stars to sing. 'Sophia's number *Aldonza* was true tripe,' O'Toole laughed, 'but I remember thinking, "a remarkable achievement for a non-singing Wop, but if only she'd look at me when she's singing."

'I decided to amuse myself by making the lovely bitch look at me. She really tore into the number. She looked at me and was marvellous. So I was careful to see,' he said generously, 'that her left profile was featured.'

The filming continued with millions of dollars rolling on the budget and United Artists wondering privately whether La Mancha's 'impossible dream' would be their unendurable nightmare. Sophia was not happy on the picture. Peter O'Toole, behind his circus act, saw it and marvelled at her control. There were hold-ups, last-minute changes and a fair display of tantrums by sundry personnel.

'But that woman's professionalism was fantastic,' O'Toole declared. 'The emphasis is on the work, and screw everything else.'

His death scene—a three-piece tableau with Sophia and James Coco—illustrated what he meant.

'I was lying there on the floor, apparently dead, and holding my breath as long as I could. But it isn't easy mate. And holding your breath after loudly singing a ditty isn't any easier.

'Anyway the good Sophia saw my predicament and was superb. She bunched my nightie so I could catch a breath. She slyly covered a visibly thudding vein in my neck with her hand. She hid the folds in my false forehead with the hem of·her dress. She made me look what I was—dead!'

Sophia displayed a similar concern, for herself, when the scene was re-staged for the stills cameraman. As they composed themselves for the shot, a Bardot-looking blonde sauntered uninvited into the group, dangerously up-staging Sophia. Actresses—at least those with ambitions to get on the Ponti payroll—do this at their peril. Sophia's reaction in the words of her Don Quixote was:

'A one-tenth of a second glance, sheer razor-blades, from those incomparable eyes, followed by a short sharp elbow in the left tit. Pop! the intruder went in off the bedpost, landing in a distressed pile well out of the shot. Miss Loren,' he added with some reverence, 'knows what she wants.'

Hollywood scarcely understood the burden Sophia carried in the picture. The script stuck pretty closely to the Broadway original which had been built around the solos of the three principals.

Sophia was virtually on her own, singing in a foreign language, working in a foreign language, the lines weightier than those of an average musical. She may have panicked internally, but it was important for the picture and for Ponti, not to show it.

While O'Toole went out on his nightly carousals around the bars, Sophia returned to her hotel and was in bed asleep before he'd emptied his first glass. Now and again when the depression hit her, she sent for Cipi.

O'Toole had noticed towards the end of the shooting that Sophia looked pale. 'At one time she went positively green. I thought nothing more about it, until she phoned me from her villa late at night. I think Carlo Ponti was away and she couldn't contact her mother or her sister. Basilio was in Nice.' O'Toole asked her:

'What is it, Sophia?'

'I want to talk,' she said.

'What about?'

'I'm pregnant,' Sophia said. 'I had to tell someone.'

The film ended with the ritual exchange of presents. Sophia gave O'Toole a bronze replica of a Sicilian warrior complete with drawn sword which he took to imply a strong hint of the Mafia. He countered the gesture by giving her a pile of shark's teeth—'it was the best predatory touch I could think of,' he said.

They parted, O'Toole to work on another picture in Britain, Sophia to make *The Journey* with Peter's friend and boozing companion, Richard Burton. The casting demanded some comment. O'Toole wrote to her in mock-fury, accusing her of fundamental treachery:

'The news is all over Ireland that I am spitting blood at the moon, aghast because you have abandoned me for a bandy-legged pock-marked little Welshman . . .!'

If the public had taken to the film the way Aldonza and the Don had taken to each other, *La Mancha* would have matched the grosses of that other transplant from the stage, *Fiddler on the Roof*. But it was not a commercial success, though both O'Toole and

Sophia received fine notices. Fortunately, Sophia had a more exciting 'production' in prospect.

Sophia Loren, the mother, is a fascinating animal. Superstars have tended to keep their offspring out of the way, fitting them in between dinner dates and divorces. Sophia goes to the other extreme, hovering soft-footed outside the nursery door at night, rising at dawn to kiss the infant eyelids awake. She could, of course, buy Hamley's in London and F.A.O. Schwartz in New York just to make sure she doesn't run out of toys. But apart from the life-sized giraffe gazing permanently at the Rome skyline, Cipi's could be the nursery next door.

The first maternal hug of the morning plus the booster shots given throughout the day are so tender and tactile, even the most steely-hearted producers grin like imbeciles making the sort of baby noises they'd rather die than have observed by their subordinates.

When I visited the villa eleven weeks after the First Birth, it was clear that all clinical precautions were being taken prior to the child receiving his first inoculations. Visitors were not required to deliver sworn affidavits of robust health, but they were certainly expected to reel back from the crib and whistle behind their face masks, declaring the child to be the most beautiful, intelligent and talented eleven-week-old of all time.

Carlo Ponti was content to keep his distance, pacing around like a thoroughbred stallion, happy to have sired the baby which Sophia—and well-wishers around the world—had prayed for.

After two miscarriages and a Caesarian delivery, a mother's urge to protect the child she yearned for is fierce, animal-like. An intruder breaking through the security system and slipping his arm through the nursery window, would have the Loren teeth through it, to the bone.

When Sophia discovered she was pregnant for the second time, she phoned Professor de Watteville in Geneva, who prepared the routine as before.

She left the villa earlier than planned when a lunatic axed his way through the wire fence telling the police who took him away, that he had come to kidnap Cipi.

In her suite at a Geneva hotel, Sophia again took on the self-denying ordinance of total immobility. But Cipi having been safely delivered and now developing sturdily, she was more serene. Occasionally Carlo sat at the bedside and read some of the sensitive poetry of Giacomo Leopardi, which was a shade more tranquil than stud poker with Peter O'Toole.

Edoardo Ponti was born on 6 January, 1973. The world was delighted, but the arrival, being a repeat performance, could hardly expect—and did not receive—the same global coverage. The mother, of course, made no distinction. 'The only difference was that I was a little less worried,' she said. 'Having proved that I could do it, I felt that much safer. But just the same, you're never sure until the baby is actually lying there beside you.'

Once again Sophia was grateful to God, Carlo and Professor Hubert de Watteville.

There was a brief hiatus to see Edoardo over his first sturdy burps, and allow the Loren shape to regain its pre-natal symmetry. He received all the benefits of breast-feeding which his brother, then five, had enjoyed, and was flourishing. Pronounced in mint condition, Edoardo was un-hooked from the main supply, put on solids and his mother returned to the business of making pictures. *The Journey* based on a story by Pirandello, to be directed by Vittorio de Sica—his thirtieth film—this time co-starred her with Richard Burton.

But as the world discovered, in the most tearful real-life serial since those maudlin epics of Mary Pickford, the film was the least of Sophia's preoccupations.

The marriage of Mr and Mrs Richard Burton was about to explode.

It is my personal, and admittedly crudely expressed view, that Sophia and Carlo Ponti needed that invasion of their villa by the Burtons, like a hole in the head. They had refashioned this sixteenth-century haven of a Prince of the Church escaping the pollution of Rome, into the most lavish yet tranquil hideaway

SOPHIA

this side of Hearst's San Simeon. Their own marriage had battled successfully through a cross-fire of malice, insult, bigotry and legal confusion. They were now legally wed, rich, had two kids and in no mood, I fancy, to play Marriage Guidance Counsellors to the bickering Richard and Liz.

But Ponti and Sophia had a film to make with Burton, and if they were required to do a little sympathetic hand-squeezing and tutting on the side, so be it. There were fifty rooms at the villa; space enough for the Pontis to enjoy business as usual during altercations.

Burton arrived from New York a month before the production was due to start, looking battered and bleary-eyed, wearing the penitent smile of the ruefully hung-over. He was glad to get to the Ponti villa which had the best wine of the region and the softest shoulder in Italy. He needed it. The shoulder at least. The wine (but no hard stuff) was on offer if he required it, though on his own admission, booze had been no small factor in the verbal mayhem which swept his marriage on to a reef.

The final explosion had taken place one black night in a friend's house on Long Island. As he confessed with some remorse to Sophia, and later to me:

'We both burst apart virtually at the same moment. To tell you frankly I blew my top in New York and slung Elizabeth out—telling her to leave within twenty minutes as I recall. But then I'd got to the stage when I was running around like a lunatic, behaving a bit madly, boozing of course.'

While Burton found some solace in the cloistered calm of Sophia's villa, Elizabeth was receiving her healing balm in the company of a Mr Henry Wynberg. Given the choice between the two havens for bleeding hearts, I rate Sophia Loren well ahead of Mr Wynberg.

They sat together in the shade of the magnolias, Burton moist-eyed and brutally self-reproaching, Sophia softly commiserating, a fair imitation of a Jewish mother taking a confessional.

A one point in his agonized soliloquy, Burton said miserably:

'You know, Sophia, the trouble with me is women don't like me any more.'

220

'Don't be silly,' Sophia reassured him, 'you are a most brilliant and fascinating man.'

Burton told me he felt better after that. He could not, he said, speak too highly of the woman who opened her heart and doors to him when he had fallen to the lowest point, emotionally, in his life.

'Sophia would be an outstanding woman in any age. She is sharp and witty in both languages, and as sane as bootlaces. A combination of Mamma Mia and what we call in Wales a "cwtcher"—a "comforter". I was very lucky to have her around. She held my hand, larded my ego. It was no small bounty to have such a fabulous woman looking after me, telling me what to do instead of my telling everybody else what to do. She kept me for nearly two months. A feast of a woman and as beautiful as an erotic dream,' he lilted.

All this though, was in the afterglow of that spectacular reunion in Rome which, for one palpitating moment, suggested that the Burtons were happily back together again. Long before that, had come the terse announcement of their plans for a divorce, with some acerbic comments in the wings from the two contenders.

Carlo Ponti, who needed a fit and emotionally stable Burton for the picture, gave a resigned Milanese shrug. But across Rome, another producer, Franco Rossellini, nephew of the eminent Italian director, chewed on his knuckles. He had completed all arrangements for an Elizabeth Taylor picture scheduled to be shot in Rome at the same time Burton and Sophia were due to start theirs.

To have these two haranguing extroverts in the Eternal City at the best of times—and as the best of friends—could be ecstatic if he were lucky, murderous if he were not. But having them there as an estranged pair, glowering at each other over the legal briefs. . . . It was going to be a long hot summer.

He, and no doubt Ponti, were apprehensive of its effect upon the two productions, with the possible danger of a barrage of recriminations hurtling between the opposing camps.

Rossellini drove to see Sophia, ostensibly for lunch, but in fact to see whether she could play peacemaker in the drama. Basilio

SOPHIA

was there too. He was not unfamiliar with the marital gear-crashing of superstars.

Rossellini arrived to find other film men there on a different mission. He urgently needed to talk to Sophia, and so did they. It was then the interlude occurred which featured their valuable quarry standing outside a lavatory door, quizzing Carlo Junior about the success or otherwise, of his bowel action of the day.

That accomplished, delivering the Italian equivalent of 'Eureka!' on hearing Cipi's tidings, she returned to the lesser business of the day.

Other events intervened which, though painful for Elizabeth Taylor, threw a rosier light on the movie problem. A sudden abdominal attack brought her to a Los Angeles hospital for urgent surgery. Despite Mr Wynberg's tender support, it was Richard Elizabeth asked for in the feverish hours of the night.

Burton asked Carlo Ponti and de Sica if they could spare him for the weekend. No minor request, in a production already hit by de Sica's serious illness immediately prior to the start of the picture. Ponti agreed, on Burton's assurance that he would be back to work on the Monday morning.

'The chips were down for me,' Burton said. 'Elizabeth called for me. I flew twelve hours over the Pole, spent one night with her. It meant flying twice over the Pole in less than three days. But I wanted Elizabeth, and she wanted me. I felt like death, and looked it, but I took the Polar flight back on the Sunday as promised.'

The arrival of Elizabeth Taylor in Rome on the afternoon of Friday 20 July, 1973—the event just naturally cries out for the time, the place and the hour—was vintage Hollywood. Even the participants must have seen the faintly grotesque side of it.

Shoals of police, armed and watchful on the tarmac. The world's photographers there in force, with the piratic *paparazzi* around them, a frieze of furtive eyeballs. Burton arrives in his Rolls with its smoked windows, fur seats, TV and drinks cabinet. He is tense and tired behind dark glasses. Elizabeth emerges from the plane to screams, shouts and a rush by the mob. The photographers punch and kick each other to get The Great Embrace. (Meanwhile, back at the ranch, The Landlady is checking on the final arrangements for bedding and boarding the ill-starred lovers.)

In seconds, Elizabeth and Richard are in the Rolls, the door opened long enough for the crowds to see what they had come for—a contrite head buried in a forgiving shoulder. His in hers.

The Rolls leads a motorcade of reporters and cameramen all the way to the Villa Ponti. But guards stop them at the gate. Like Commandos the *paparazzi* lead an assault on the Helio Cabala Hotel above the villa and dig in on the rooftop and the upper windows, their telephoto lenses aimed like machine guns at the villa.

That night, the Burtons are left alone, even by their hosts. They have plenty to talk about including Mr Wynberg. The Pontis and Mr Franco Rossellini keep their fingers crossed. The Burtons rise late the following morning.

For a while the harmony of Richard and Elizabeth, with Sophia acting the placatory third party, looked as though it might last. Elizabeth started work on her picture (*The Driver's Seat*) while Sophia and Burton continued their *Journey*.

Burton relished the piquancy of going to bed with Sophia on the set during the day, for the film, and climbing between the sheets with Elizabeth at night, 'for real'.

'Not bad going,' he laughed, 'for a chap who has come from the bowels of the earth . . . and I get paid for it too, mark you.'

He brimmed over with conjugal contentment. When Sophia walked over to join us he swung her round, ran a finger between her bare shoulders, and tasted it.

'Vanilla, I think,' he mused. 'You want to kiss me for luck?' he said offering his lips.

'Certainly,' Sophia replied, regally offering her cheek.

The reticence was not lost on Burton. 'We are in the presence of a lady,' he said gravely.

We returned to the dressing room to wait for Elizabeth. She breezed in all violet-eyed and voluptuous. She said Sophia had been absolutely fantastic. 'Just an Earth Mother—that's all.' The familiar banter then began.

'You're a fat belly,' Burton said, trying the insult on for size.

Elizabeth had meant to hit back with, 'You're a burden Burton,' but the words came out, 'You're a Burton burden,' which put her slightly at a disadvantage with her eloquent husband.

She grabbed him round the waist. 'I'm going to bite you,' she said—and did.

It was love in the style of Mr and Mrs Burton. Richard decided to respond in kind. He tweaked her on each breast like a performing seal.

'Honk Honk!' Burton hooted.

Elizabeth glowered at him.

Burton squeezed again, this time a shade more gently.

'Honk . . . Honk . . . ?' he inquired hesitantly.

Carlo Ponti, Sophia Loren and Vittorio de Sica went home contented. They had a happy leading man on their hands.

But a divorce followed inevitably. Sophia was sad. 'Richard had become one of the family. I loved working with him, and wanted his marriage to succeed. I was glad to have them both in my home.'

It was clearly a diplomatic communiqué designed to conceal what must have been a taxing, knife-edged ordeal. Her, 'I think now I would like to have a holiday,' was heavily understated, and nearer the truth.

Yet holidays for Sophia Loren are like pit-stops for racing drivers. A quick check on the chassis and internal mechanism and she's zooming back in the race. The children bring her sublime contentment; Carlo is the husband, the lover and the father figure—the stack of film awards her badge of success; their palace in Marino makes it easy to play the queen.

But the real adrenal charges come from work—the lights, the cameras, the tension in the pit of the stomach, the compliments of directors, the bulging-eyed admiration of her leading men. It was what she had dreamed about in Pozzuoli. Sofia Scicolone, born in a ward for unmarried mothers, raised on a shoestring and sour bread in wartime Naples. She'd made it. The Star.

As she drove to the studio to prepare for her next picture, *The Verdict* with Jean Gabin, she snuggled into the soft leather of her Rolls. She was approaching her fortieth birthday. That week an emissary from Madame Tussauds had come to measure her for the figure which will stand among the world's All-Time Stars. Her face, in the character of the goddess Ceres, had been sculpted on to a medallion commemorating the twentieth anniversary of the U.N. Food and Health Organization with the words 'Food For All' on the reverse side. (The fact that Ceres was the Goddess of Corn was merely a coincidence.)

She had worked with the great Chaplin, sung duets with Noël Coward, dined with the Queen and cooked for Tito. She had filmed with virtually every leading actor in motion pictures, and if some of the films were bad, the Oscar looked good.

Her mother, Romilda, may not have been wed by the man she met long ago near the Trevi Fountain in Rome. And being 'Garbo's Double' led nowhere either. But at least she was living in luxury, adored by the daughters who call her 'Bella Oppo' (beautiful eyes), the Mother of the Star.

Pozzuoli too has had its share of the cake. It had been little more than a acrid off-shoot of Naples, notable only for a mini-volcano too ashamed to sneeze in the presence of Vesuvius.

But Sophia Loren had nuzzled it into the guide books. The tour buses now stop at Number Five Via Solfatara. And when they do, Aunt Dora stands at the door, moist-eyed and proud.

Wife, mother, a star for more than fifteen years; a global impact achieved without stunts or lurid love affairs on the side; Sophia Loren was not displeased with herself. She had accomplished it all on her own terms. Nobody had been hurt, many helped.

But above all there had been no self-delusion. 'In the end,' she said to me as we walked along the ancient flagstone at the villa, 'the way people judge me as a woman is more important than the value they put on my work. I've always been suspicious of success. Sometimes the work is good, sometimes it is bad. But what has that to do with life? When I was young I had all the normal insecurities. I painted my eyes, wore tight sexy skirts, I talked too loudly and I drove fast sports cars. It was part of the act and I got over it. De Sica taught me you can't paint your way into a believable performance. I've been lucky, of course. Meeting Carlo was like having someone breathe life into me. But I worked hard too. No one can ever really know how determined I have been.

'When I wanted things really desperately, I developed an enormous strength which pushed every hostile or negative force aside. It was like that when I fought for Carlo; it was the same when I wanted children; and it is the way I work. Even now, with all this,' she said looking up at the villa, 'I never feel totally secure.

'Everything one has, one can lose. Can I be absolutely sure that Carlo might not one day be unfaithful? Can any woman ever be that certain? All I can do is to try to be the wife he wants and the best kind of mother to the children. I have the normal jealousies and I suppose Carlo has too. Maybe actors have been in love with me,' she said, her smile reaching back into the past, 'but there was never any danger. It is impossible to have a collision when the traffic is all one-way.'

Carlo, in a cap and open-necked shirt arrived for his mandatory cuddle-up of the day. I once saw Arthur Miller do the same thing to Marilyn Monroe, and for the identical reason. Miller said he needed the booster to fortify him for the rest of the day. Ponti was similarly invigorated.

They kissed and he left. 'Another happy day,' she said, 'I'm lucky. That's three in a row.' She said she had no regrets. 'I think I have lived my life openly without pretence. I wouldn't have wanted to be alive at any other time, or with any other man. I believe in God, like all my family. I was brought up as a Catholic but I could never take Communion because I was living with Carlo and since I loved him I could never make a vow to give him up.

'So . . . when I die, if I go to Heaven, fine. If it is the other place . . .' she giggled, 'I just hope they play poker there.'

14
Last Take

Sophia Loren arrived in London last July to film *Brief Encounter*. She installed herself, and Ines, in the Savoy Hotel's riverside suite normally reserved for solvent royalty. With a backdrop of flowers and telegrams of goodwill, she submitted to the ritual interviews with the polished virtuosity of the Eternal Movie Star.

She was Gloria Swanson in *Sunset Boulevard*, Bette Davis in *All About Eve* and there was more than a touch of Harlow and Monroe as one long slim leg slid provocatively over another. But in the beautiful, bodily essentials she was Sophia Loren. The Last of the Breed.

For the phenomenon of the screen goddess worshipped by the millions is fading fast. Sustaining the legend required an almost indecently rich Hollywood and a vast insatiable audience hooked on dreams. The treasure chest is down to petty cash; the crowds have moved over to television; the star system has faded like a plunging meteorite.

That bleached-white monolith at Culver City—Metro-Goldwyn-Mayer—which hired Sophia for millions in the fat years, now has frayed cuffs, counts its pennies and looks with envy at the thriving business of the morticians on the corner near the main gates. Not long after Sophia left the scene, the place was crudely dismembered by accountants, its props sold, triumphs forgotten. It stands now as the headstone of what was once the richest working village in the world.

Time was on Sophia's side. In an age that craved escapism and glossed-up sexuality on the screen, she, like Bardot and Elizabeth Taylor, could reign like a queen and live like one.

But few, if any, movie budgets today, could accommodate her million-dollar salary. Even Carlo Ponti, at his most expansive, would find it impossible to parlay Sophia through the same extravagances which marked what might ruefully be called, her Hollywood period. Yet the slave-girl of *Quo Vadis* can have no complaints. Her achievements stand. It would be foolish to exaggerate them, churlish to sell them short. She hitched up her skirt, stepped over the debris of wartime Naples and in twenty-five not uneventful years, has made quite a woman of herself.

The world knows her—with a fair display of admiration—simply as 'Sophia'. The general esteem perhaps, is because in the long haul from Pozzuoli to the Villa Ponti, success has not distorted the female who craved it. The wife, the mother, the woman who runs the Ponti household, tolerates no snooty intrusions from The Superstar.

At forty, she is still on the treadmill, but working, she claims, because of the need for self-expression, not self-delusion.

'The world makes stars,' Sophia said. 'I make films . . . and the best Spaghetti Vongole in Italy.'

Acknowledgments

I am grateful to the many people on both sides of the Atlantic who agreed, with varying degrees of enthusiasm, to be cross-examined about Sophia Loren. I think especially of Sophia's mother, Romilda Villani, her sister Maria Mussolini, and also of Aunt Dora and Rosetta d'Isanto in Pozzuoli. I owe particular thanks to Vittorio de Sica who, though a major surgical operation was imminent, invited me to his apartment in Rome to add valuable highlights to the general picture. Sophia's lifelong friend, Basilio Franchina, helpfully exploded a myth, while several noted actors, directors and producers sat with me at assorted waterholes to assist in the exploration. I herewith list, and thank them alphabetically; Richard Burton, Dimitri de Grunwald, Charlton Heston, William Holden, Stanley Kramer, Joseph E. Levine, Sidney Lumet, Anthony Quinn, Marty Ritt, Peter Sellers, Mel Shavelson, Peter O'Toole and Peter Ustinov.

And then, of course, there is Carlo Ponti—and Sophia herself. Their co-operation was both unstinted and unconditional. To them I add my affection.

Appendix I

THE FILMS

The early Italian work was mainly in small parts under the name of SOFIA LAZZARO. These included (1950–52)—

Cuori Sul Mare; Il Voto; Le Sei Mogli Di Barbablu; Era Lui, Si! Si!; Milano Miliardaria; Io Sono Il Capataz; Il Mago Per Forza; Il Sogno Di Zorro; E Arrivato L'Accordatore.

The more important films (still in Italy) as SOPHIA LOREN:

Year of release	Title	Director
1952	LA FAVORITA	Cesare Barlacchi
1952	LA TRATTA DELLE BIANCHE	Luigi Comencini
1953	AFRICA UNDER THE SEA (Africa Sotto Il Mare)	Giovanni Roccardi
1953	AIDA	Clemente Fracassi
1953	CI TRAVIAMO IN GALLERIA	Mauro Bolognini
1953	LA DOMENICA DELLA BUONA GENTE	Anton Giulio Majano
1954	CAROSELLO NAPOLETANO	Etore Giannini
1954	IL PAESE DEI CAMPANELLI	Jean Boyer
1954	UN GIORNO IN PRETURA	Stefano Vanzina Steno
1954	TEMPI NOSTRI	Alessandro Blasetti
1954	DUE NOTTE CON CLEOPATRA	Mario Mattoli
1954	PELLIGRINI D'AMORE	Andrea Forzano
1954	MISERIA E NOBILITÀ	Mario Mattoli
1954	ATTILA	Pietro Francisci
1954	THE GOLD OF NAPLES (L'Oro De Napoli)	Vittorio de Sica
1955	THE WOMAN OF THE RIVER (La Donna del Fiume)	Mario Soldati
1955	TOO BAD SHE'S BAD	Alessandro Blasetti
1955	IL SEGNO DI VENERE	Dino Risi
1955	THE MILLER'S BEAUTIFUL WIFE	Mario Camerini

APPENDIX I

| 1955 | SCANDAL IN SORRENTO
(or *Bread, Love and . . .*) | Dino Risi |
| 1955 | LA FORTUNA DI ESSERE DONNA | Alessandro Blasetti |

INTERNATIONAL FILMS

Year of release	Title	Director	Co-stars
1957	THE PRIDE AND THE PASSION	Stanley Kramer	Cary Grant Frank Sinatra
1957	BOY ON A DOLPHIN	Jean Negulesco	Alan Ladd Clifton Webb
1957	LEGEND OF THE LOST	Henry Hathaway	John Wayne Rossano Brazzi
1958	DESIRE UNDER THE ELMS	Delbert Mann	Anthony Perkins Burl Ives
1958	HOUSEBOAT	Melville Shavelson	Cary Grant Martha Hyer
1958	THE KEY	Carol Reed	William Holden Trevor Howard
1958	BLACK ORCHID	Martin Ritt	Anthony Quinn Ernest Borgnine
1959	THAT KIND OF WOMAN	Sidney Lumet	Tab Hunter George Sanders
1960	HELLER IN PINK TIGHTS	George Cukor	Anthony Quinn Steve Forrest
1960	IT STARTED IN NAPLES	Melville Shavelson	Clark Gable Vittorio de Sica
1960	A BREATH OF SCANDAL	Michael Curtiz	John Gavin Maurice Chevalier
1960	THE MILLIONAIRESS	Anthony Asquith	Peter Sellers Alastair Sim Vittorio de Sica
1961	TWO WOMEN	Vittorio de Sica	Raf Vallone Jean-Paul Belmondo
1961	EL CID	Anthony Mann	Charlton Heston Raf Vallone
1962	BOCCACCIO 70	Visconti, Fellini, de Sica	Luigi Giulianni
1962	MADAME SANS-GÊNE	Christian Jacque	Robert Hossein
1962	FIVE MILES TO MIDNIGHT	Anatole Litvak	Tony Perkins Jean-Pierre Aumont Gig Young
1963	THE CONDEMNED OF ALTONA	Vittorio de Sica	Frederic March Maximillian Schell Anouk Aimée
1964	THE FALL OF THE ROMAN EMPIRE	Anthony Mann	Alec Guinness James Mason
1964	YESTERDAY, TODAY AND TOMORROW	de Sica	Marcello Mastroianni
1964	MARRIAGE—ITALIAN STYLE	de Sica	Marcello Mastroianni
1965	JUDITH	Daniel Mann	Peter Finch

1965	OPERATION CROSSBOW	Michael Anderson	George Peppard
			Lili Palmer
1965	LADY L	Peter Ustinov	Paul Newman
			David Niven
			Peter Ustinov
1966	ARABESQUE	Stanley Donen	Gregory Peck
1967	COUNTESS FROM HONG KONG	Charles Chaplin	Marlon Brando
			Patrick Cargill
1967	HAPPILY EVER AFTER	Francesco Rosi	Omar Sharif
	(*More than a Miracle* in U.S.)		
1968	GHOSTS, ITALIAN STYLE	Renato Castellani	Vittorio Gassmann
1970	SUNFLOWER	Vittorio de Sica	Marcello Mastroianni
1971	THE PRIEST'S WIFE	Dino Risi	Marcello Mastroianni
1972	THE SIN	Alberto Lattuada	Adrianno Celentano
	(*The White Sister* in U.S.)		Fernando Rey
1973	MAN OF LA MANCHA	Arthur Hiller	Peter O'Toole
			James Coco
1974	THE JOURNEY	Vittorio de Sica	Richard Burton
1974	THE VERDICT	André Cayatte	Jean Gabin
*	BRIEF ENCOUNTER	Alan Bridges	Richard Burton

* In production July 1974

Appendix II

THE AWARDS

1956	Buenos Aires Film Festival	*Too Bad She's Bad*
1958	Japanese Oscar	*The Key*
1959	Best Actress of the Year Venice Film Festival Donatello Award Victoire Française	*Black Orchid*

1960/61	U.S. Film Academy (Oscar)
	Donatello Award
	Silver Ribbon—Italian Press Award
	The Golden Palm
	    Cannes Film Festival
	New York Critics' Award
	Belgian Oscar
	Japanese Oscar
	Best Actress of the Year
	    Cork Festival
	Victoire Française
	Show Business Illustrated Award
	Golden Globe—most popular actress in
	    the U.S.A.
	Film Industry Award (Cinelandia Trophy)
	Ohio, Cleveland Critics' Award
	Belgium's 'Prix Uilenspigoel'
	    Best Actress of the Year
	The Bambi Award (Germany)
	    Most popular actress of the year
	A.P.P.C.B. European Grand Prix
	British Film Academy
	    Best Actress of the Year
	Santiago Film Festival
	    Best Actress of the Year
		Two Women
		(*La Ciociara*)

1961	12th Film Festival—Rapallo	*Heller in Pink Tights*

1962   Belgium's 'Prix Uilenspigoel'
        Best Actress of the Year
        The Bambi Award (Germany)
        Bravo
        Best Actress of the Year (Spain)
        Best Actress of the Year—Critics'
        Association, Calcutta.
        Victoire Française
        Most Popular Actress of the Year (The
        Snosiki Award), Finland
        Belgian Oscar

1962   Voted Most Elegant Woman of the Year
        in nationwide magazine poll

1963   The Bambi Award (Germany)
        Bravo
        Most Popular Actress of the Year (The
        Snosiki Award), Finland

1964   The Donatello Award   *Yesterday, Today and*
        The Bambi Award (Germany)   *Tomorrow*
        Bravo
        The Golden Globe (U.S.A.)
        The Snosiki Award (Finland)

1965   The Donatello Award   *Marriage—Italian*
        Best Foreign Actress of the Year   *Style*
        (Moscow)
        The Golden Globe (U.S.A.)
        The Bambi (Germany)
        Bravo
        The Snosiki Award (Finland)
        The Golden Laurel
        Most Popular Foreign Actress of the
        Year
        Belgium's 'Prix Uilenspigoel'
        Best Actress of the Year
        Voted the Most Popular Actress of the
        Year by leading Milan newspaper
        Corriere della Sera
        The Alexander Korda Award   *Lady L*

1966   The Silver Mirror—Helen Curtis' Award
        for Elegance
        The Snosiki (Finland)

234

The Bambi Award (Germany)
Voted Star of the Year by the Film
    Exhibitors of America
Bravo

1967 ·   The Silver Mirror—Helen Curtis' Award
        Bravo
        The Bambi Award (Germany)
        Film Critics' Association of Bengal Award

1968   The Golden Laurel   *Happily Ever After*
        The Bambi (Germany)
        Bravo

1970/71 The Donatello Award   *Sunflower*
        The Critics' Association of Bengal Award

1972   The De Curtis Award for the Best Actress
        of the Year

1973   The Campidoglio Award

Index

INDEX